UNDERCOVER BILLIONAIRE

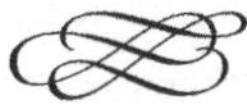

ERIN SWANN

WWW.ERINSWANN.COM - BECAUSE YOU DON'T ALWAYS HAVE TO BE A LADY.

This book is a work of fiction. The names, characters, businesses, and events portrayed in this book are fictitious. Any similarity to real persons, living or dead, businesses, or events is coincidental and not intended by the author.

Cover images licensed from Shutterstock.com, depositphotos.com

Cover design by Swann Publications

Edited by Jessica Royer Ocken

Proofreaders: Donna Hokanson, Tamara Mataya, Rosa Sharon

Typo Hunter Extraordinaire: Renee Williams

ISBN13: 978-1674755014

The following story is intended for mature readers. It contains mature themes, strong language, and sexual situations. All characters are 18+ years of age, and all sexual acts are consensual.

❀ Created with Vellum

ALSO BY ERIN SWANN

The Billionaire's Trust - Available on Amazon, also in AUDIOBOOK

(Bill and Lauren's story) He needed to save the company. He needed her. He couldn't have both. The wedding proposal in front of hundreds was like a fairy tale come true—Until she uncovered his darkest secret.

The Youngest Billionaire - Available on Amazon

(Steven and Emma's story) The youngest of the Covington clan, he avoided the family business to become a rarity, an honest lawyer. He didn't suspect that pursuing her could destroy his career. She didn't know what trusting him could cost her.

The Secret Billionaire – Available on Amazon, also in AUDIOBOOK

(Patrick and Elizabeth's story) Women naturally circled the flame of wealth and power, and his is brighter than most. Does she love him? Does she not? There's no way to know. When he stopped to help her, Liz mistook him for a carpenter. Maybe this time he'd know. Everything was perfect. Until the day she left.

The Billionaire's Hope - Available on Amazon, also in AUDIOBOOK

(Nick and Katie's story) They came from different worlds. She hadn't seen him since the day he broke her brother's nose. Her family retaliated by destroying his life. She never suspected where accepting a ride from him today would take her. They said they could do casual. They lied.

Previously titled: Protecting the Billionaire

Picked by the Billionaire – Available on Amazon, also in AUDIOBOOK

(Liam and Amy's story) A night she wouldn't forget. An offer she couldn't refuse. He alone could save her, and she held the key to his survival. If only they could pass the test together.

Saved by the Billionaire – Available on Amazon

(Ryan and Natalie's story) The FBI and the cartel were both after her for the same thing: information she didn't have. First, the FBI took everything, and then the cartel came for her. She trusted Ryan with her safety, but could she trust him with her heart?

Caught by the Billionaire – Available on Amazon

(Vincent and Ashley's story) Her undercover assignment was simple enough: nail the crooked billionaire. The surprise came when she opened the folder, and the target was her one-time high school sweetheart. What will happen when an unknown foe makes a move to checkmate?

The Driven Billionaire – Available on Amazon

(Zachary and Brittney's story) Rule number one: hands off your best friend's sister. With nowhere to turn when she returns from upstate, she accepts his offer of a room. Mutual attraction quickly blurs the rules. When she comes under attack, pulling her closer is the only way to keep her safe. But, the truth of why she left town in the first place will threaten to destroy them both.

Nailing the Billionaire – Available on Amazon

(Dennis and Jennifer's story) She knew he destroyed her family. Now she is close to finding the records that will bring him down. When a corporate shakeup forces her to work with him, anger and desire collide. Vengeance was supposed to be simple, swift, and sweet. It was none of those things.

Undercover Billionaire – Available on Amazon

(Adam and Kelly's story) Their wealthy families have been at war forever. When Kelly receives a chilling note, the FBI assigns Adam to protect her. Family histories and desire soon collide, causing old truths to be questioned. Keeping ahead of the threat won't be their only challenge.

Trapped with the Billionaire – Available on Amazon

(Josh and Nicole's story) When Nicole returns from vacation to find her company has been sold, and she has been assigned to work for the new CEO. Competing visions of how to run things and mutual passion collide in a volatile mix. When an old family secret is unearthed, it threatens everything.

CHAPTER 1

Kelly

I locked the deadbolt to my house on my way to work Monday morning. The scuff on my shoes reminded me of my umpteenth useless date last night. I'd walked away so fast from Harold—if that was even his real name—that I'd tripped on the curb. He clearly wasn't an accountant, as his profile had claimed. With the tattoo that had peeked out from the end of his sleeve, he probably rode a motorcycle or something.

"Hop on back, baby, and let me take you for a ride," might have been his next line if I hadn't escaped when I did.

No thank you. Not in a million years. Meeting a guy at a well-lit, crowded restaurant was scary enough. I'd leave the motorcycle dudes to my sister, Serena.

As I turned toward the street, the man in the dark suit looked away. Right on time, he walked down my street as I came out of my house, two safely predictable peas in a pod.

That was my life, all right: predictable and safe, though Serena described it as boring.

What the hell did she know? Her seat at work wasn't two desks down from a girl who'd been abducted and killed.

I focused my attention on the man continuing down the street. I'd never spoken to Mr. Dark Suit, and he always looked away when I came out. He looked married, but maybe that was just the attire. Hell, lots of people in Washington DC worked for the government and wore suits. They couldn't all be married.

I forced myself to ignore the hopelessness of my dating life and unzipped the pocket of my purse to retrieve my car key as I walked. After buckling up, I started the engine.

Why aren't there any decent guys in this town? All I wanted was an accountant who wasn't an ax murderer. Well, not quite *all*—I also wanted one who didn't still live with his mother.

I put the car in reverse.

Or maybe an actuary—anybody in finance, or even insurance, would be okay. A guy who liked math. He'd keep his toothbrush clean.

Fucking shit.

The low fuel light was on. Like an idiot, I'd forgotten to fill up yesterday. The gas station was in the opposite direction and now there wasn't enough time to fill up before I was due at work.

Cursing my awful luck, I got out and started after Mr. Dark Suit, staying on the opposite side of the street. Dupont Circle station was several blocks away. The DC Metro was swift, comfortable, and clean by American subway standards, but it was slower than driving, and Monday was not a good day to be late to work at the Smithsonian. Helmut Krause held his weekly status meetings bright and early every Monday, and attendance was mandatory.

I'd been late to the first one he'd scheduled after his arrival, and just my luck, he'd made a public example of me. He'd called me up to the front to explain why I was late, which had made me bad employee of the month. Talk about embarrassing, he'd even made me repeat my name to the group. I didn't know everybody in the building, but they certainly knew me after that. The under-the-breath murmurs and sideways glances had taken months to die down.

Shame, thy name be Kelly Benson.

Reaching the tracks, I chose a different Metro car than Mr. Dark Suit, and I changed to the blue line at Metro Center. The LED screen inside the car showing the next stop couldn't change fast enough. Finally we reached L'Enfant Plaza, and I made a dash for the escalator.

Arriving at our building, I passed through the metal detector.

Hal was the security guy at the x-ray station today, as he was almost every Monday and Wednesday. He checked his watch as my handbag ran through his machine. "A little late this morning?"

He and I had a running joke that my arrival was predictable enough that he could set his watch by it, but not today.

"A little."

During the quick elevator ride up to my desk to lock away my purse, I realized I actually had a few minutes to spare.

When I arrived at my workspace, a light tan interdepartmental envelope with my name on it sat on my desk. OPS was written in the *From* column. The guys in the Office of Protective Services all thought using OPS made them sound more important than just writing Security.

It wasn't heavy enough to be a copy of the access logs I'd requested.

I unwound the red string holding it shut and pulled out the single sheet of paper.

The printed words made my knees go weak.

> On Tuesday night reset the key code of the southeast door by
> the loading dock to 1-1-1-1
> Or end up like Brooks
> Do not contact anyone or end up like Brooks
> We see everything

I collapsed into my chair. I couldn't breathe. My throat constricted, preventing the scream of terror lodged there from escaping.

I willed myself to restart my breathing and closed my eyes.

When they reopened, the deadly threat on the page only looked worse.

"Ready?" my coworker Kirby Stackhouse asked from behind me.

Somehow I hadn't heard her approach. I quickly folded the note closed and turned.

She tapped the cubicle wall. "Come on, Kell. We don't want to be late."

I opened a drawer and hid the ghastly paper inside.

"You can tell me about Harold on the way," she added.

I rose on unsteady legs. "Nothing to tell."

"That bad, huh?"

I glanced down at the scuff on my new shoes. "Worse."

Kirby pushed open the door to the stairs—never miss a chance to exercise was her motto. She went quiet while we descended, and my mind returned to the note. Six months ago, Melinda Brooks—who'd worked two cubicles down from me—had left work on a Monday night like any other. She was kidnapped and found dead four days later in Rock Creek Park. The details had been sickening.

In the weeks and months that passed, life here in the Smithsonian had slowly returned to normal as the incident was forgotten. *She* had been forgotten, but not by me.

Following the crowd to the cafeteria, Kirby and I made it in time for the start of the meeting. We took up residence near the back. I slid in next to Evelyn Gossen, another senior auditor in our department. She had never been the talkative type, and my greeting merited only a nod this morning. She looked as bad as I felt.

Here in the back, Krause wouldn't notice if we snickered at something ridiculous he said, which was pretty much a guarantee. The meeting was supposed to get us all off to a very efficient, German start to the day. *Bullshit.* It had most of us needing a second cup of caffeinated beverage to stay awake while he prattled on.

Mark Porter smiled at me as he took the seat on the other side of Kirby. "Morning, ladies."

Having him find a seat nearby had become a weekly occurrence, but at least he'd stopped asking me out. I'd learned to nod back to him, rather than encourage him with words.

With the note burned into my memory, the only words that came to mind anyway were *Why me*? What had I done to be targeted? Who could I or should I bring the note to?

Looking over the sea of people, I realized the note could have come from any of them. It had come in interoffice mail, so I couldn't trust anybody in the building.

Just then, Helmut Krause started his talk.

Krause had brought this meeting system over from his last job at the Deutsches Museum in Munich, Germany. It was, after all, the world's *largest* museum of science and technology, he liked to remind us. Never mind that *we* had the Apollo 11 command module that had ferried Americans to the moon and back. That was my definition of technology.

Wendy had been the first on our floor to make the mistake of mispronouncing where Krause was from. *Munich,* he told us, was an English bastardization of the real spelling, München, and the word was to be pronounced *Moon-chen*.

I could never get the U sound quite right and avoided the word entirely.

Krause's speech this morning went right by me. Every time I blinked, I saw Melinda's face staring back at me. She'd been the second tragedy we'd experienced in the past year. The first had been the kidnapping and murder of Daya Patel, another Smithsonian employee, just six months before Melinda.

The only thing I heard while Krause talked was the sound in my head of the newscaster from the night they found Melinda. *"Tonight we have the tragic story of a young woman found strangled in the woods..."*

Her face had been the first thing on the evening broadcast. For a week or so, the story had dominated the headlines. But no more details became available, so the news people shifted to something about North Korea, then to a budget impasse the following week, and life went on.

But Melinda was always with me. She'd provided the recommendation that got me my job here. I would never forget her, or what had happened.

She'd left a letter for me in her apartment, sealed and addressed but unstamped. Her family had located it while clearing out her things three months later and given it to me.

I could still remember my shock when I'd opened it. It had contained a note almost identical to the one in my drawer today. *Look what I got for Halloween* she'd written on it. Instead of Brooks, hers had said she would "end up like Patel."

I'd walked Melinda's note to the local FBI office and told them how I came to have it. But I'd never heard another thing from them—no follow-up, ever. The interviews had ceased a month after Melinda's body was discovered. Even they seemed to have forgotten about her.

Daya Patel had stopped coming to work six months before Melinda disappeared. It had taken a week for her to be declared missing. Her boyfriend and she had fought often. He was out of the country at the time, so the theory had been that she'd left town to get away from him. That possibility ended when her car was found abandoned in a desolate area. No sign of her had ever been located, and after Melinda's death, it became pretty clear to me what her fate had been.

I'd been transferred upstairs to replace Patel, and had even been assigned her old cubicle, a detail I hadn't known until after I started on this floor.

"Kell, let's get moving." Kirby pushed my shoulder and jostled me back to reality. The meeting was over.

I stood and shuffled down the line of chairs.

"The biggest waste of time ever," she said. "Can you believe he wants to start another inventory?"

"Huh?"

"An inventory again already. How do you spell anal-retentive? K-R-A-U-S-E."

"Yeah, a waste of time," I agreed.

The Smithsonian had over a hundred and fifty thousand items, many of them packed away in storage, and an inventory was a monumental task.

I stumbled on the way out, but caught the doorframe before I ended up on my ass.

Mark grabbed my elbow to steady me. "Careful there, Kelly. You okay?"

I forced a half laugh. "Damned heels."

He released his hold and left with a wink. "They do look hot, though."

The compliment pulled a half-smile from me. He wasn't a bad guy, easy-going it seemed, but I'd learned my lesson about dating someone from work. That wasn't a mistake I was about to repeat. Instead I'd found lots of new ones to make.

Kirby pulled me toward the bulletin board on our floor. "Hey, there's a supervisor position open in finance that would be a step up for you. You should take a shot at it."

I read the posting with fake enthusiasm. "It looks good, but I don't think I'm right for that one." My current job was nice—no calendar pressures, a boss I could deal with, and responsibilities I could handle. Stability was underappreciated.

Back at my desk, I turned on my computer and signed in. I blinked, but the icons on the screen swam back and forth, refusing to stay in focus. My thoughts went back to the two dead women and the note in my drawer.

Kirby reappeared. "Coffee? You look like death warmed over after that meeting."

"Sure." I stood. I could use the distraction.

Kirby stuck her head around the corner to speak to my cubicle neighbor, Evelyn. "Ev, you want to join us?"

"No. I don't feel so good."

I stepped out of my cube.

"I got a killer hangover cure, if you need it," Kirby told her.

Evelyn looked like crap this morning, and it wasn't the first Monday that hadn't agreed with her.

"It's not that," she said. "I think I'll go home."

Kirby started toward her caffeine fix, and I followed. "Wanna try the Columbian blend? It's better than the regular stuff," she said.

She was a superstitious sort and had decided I needed to break old habits if I was ever going to get laid.

I chose an English Breakfast teabag and added hot water. "No thanks. I don't need anything to clean the rust off my bicycle chain."

She laughed. "It's not that bad."

"It's not that good either."

Back in my cube, I closed my eyes. Melinda's face reappeared, and the newscaster's voice played over and over in my head.

Act normal, I kept telling myself. If someone was watching, I shouldn't do anything out of the ordinary. Today was not the day to take Kirby's advice.

After spending the entire morning working on a spreadsheet that should have taken me a half hour, I couldn't take it anymore. I stood and walked to the restroom, then to the coffee room for another cup of tea, and back to my desk. All the while I looked around the office. Nothing seemed out of place. I didn't detect anyone watching me, following me, or paying any attention at all. Only when I noticed the little black spheres at opposite corners of the room did my blood turn cold.

Any of us could be watched by the eyes behind the black plastic. It was impossible to tell which way the camera within pointed, or who was at the monitor on the other end.

As I sat, my skin started to itch. What could I do to keep from being the next victim? Or was it too late?

I pulled the note from my drawer and opened it on my lap, away from prying eyes. Whoever this was wanted me to change the entrance code on the southwest doorway.

Could it just be a prank? Or could this be a test by Protective Services to see if I was trustworthy? If I was being watched and Melinda's killer was part of OPS, I couldn't go to them.

Closing my eyes, I shook my head at the impossibility of my position. I didn't know who to trust. My boss, Mr. Heiden, was a nice enough guy, but very by the book. He'd only refer the matter to OPS.

What if Melinda had taken the note to the wrong person instead of doing what it demanded and that had sealed her fate? My face could be the next one on the evening news if I made the wrong choice.

I needed to talk to someone, and the only people I could trust without reservation were my family. Unfortunately, none of them lived anywhere close. All but me and Vincent were still in California.

If I called my father, or any of my overprotective brothers, I'd be grabbed up, shoved into Daddy's jet, and on the way back home in a matter of hours. I'd come to DC to get away from LA, and away from Daddy's control, although I hadn't put it that way when I talked to him. The last thing I wanted to do was give him a reason to pull me back there.

My sister-in-law, Ashley, was in the FBI. She might have good advice, but she'd probably blab it to my brother, who'd tell Daddy, and I'd be snatched back to California by dinner time.

My sister, Serena, was the clear choice. She'd listen and help me puzzle through who to talk to and what precautions to take. To be safe, I couldn't call until lunchtime when I could be out of the building.

The note went back into the drawer after I'd taken a picture of it with my phone. I would call Serena when I went out to eat, someplace I wouldn't be overheard.

I checked the time again—a half hour to lunch.

~

Adam

My phone vibrated with a text message.

HARPER: Be about ten late

Sal Harper was always late. The motto of the FBI didn't include punctuality, he'd once joked. If it had, he'd no longer be with the Bureau.

I'd gotten stuck with the midnight watch on this stakeout, and not once in the last week had he managed to relieve me on time.

The word *relieve* was not a good one to have go through my head. I'd already filled the bottle I was peeing into in the car, and my bladder was about to burst. Leaving my post for a break at the coffee shop two blocks away was not an option. The last DC agent who'd been caught doing that was now in Anchorage. Our field office was only a few blocks from HQ, so more was always expected of us.

I started to type a text back to Harper.

ME: get here on time for a change

I deleted it without sending. He was not only senior to me, but he played weekly poker with our boss, which is why I'd gotten the overnight duty in the first place, and he got the day shift. Pissing Harper off would likely lead to even worse assignments. Shit ran downhill in the Bureau, and I wasn't far from the bottom.

Harper finally pulled up behind me in his minivan and waved through the windshield. He'd even been assigned a minivan with enough room to stand up when he had to piss. I had to contort myself to get it in the bottle without dribbling on my pants.

I pulled out my keychain with the big C.

Dad had given it to me as soon as I was old enough to drive—a constant reminder of the one thing that mattered—C for Cartwright.

My piece-of-shit undercover car started right up and rattled its way down the street, past the location we were watching. I was careful not to look left at the rundown house containing the dirt-bag human traffickers. Our intel said they were expecting another "delivery" soon, and we had to catch them in the act when the girls arrived, before they all got sent off to other cities.

DC's finest, the Metropolitan Police Department, had handed the case over to us when they realized the operation crossed state lines, and HQ always had us prioritize these trafficking cases.

I made it to my place, and the bathroom, without bursting. In the kitchen, I ground a scoop of my special St. Helena beans and loaded the French press. A few minutes later, the smell of the coffee filled the kitchen as I decanted it into my mug.

I was going to need several cups to make it through another day. We were short staffed for the case load, thanks to more budget wrangling in Congress. While they debated priorities, we didn't have the manpower to properly handle the crimes that came our way. But that's what we had the top brass for: to deal with the elected jerkoffs.

Upstairs, I shed my undercover outfit of intentionally dirty clothes. My coffee cup came with me into the shower. That and the hot water eased the soreness of sitting in the car all night.

I hadn't joined the Bureau to make a living. My family had plenty of money. I did this to make a difference, and that meant making sacrifices. Sacrifices that mattered.

From a very young age, I'd known that pushing papers around the way my old man did was never going to be my future. Today's assignment was the kind of admission I had to pay to get a chance at the New York Organized Crime Task Force.

There was evil in this world. It had to be confronted, and I meant to make a difference doing just that. I felt for the telltale bulge of the keyring in my pocket. When I was done, the Cartwright name would no longer be shorthand for screw-up in the FBI.

CHAPTER 2

Kelly

The little Indian restaurant was one of my regular haunts. It had only two tables on the sidewalk separated by the walkway to the door. The far one was already occupied by an older couple.

Normally I sat inside, but today I chose the nearer sidewalk table and took the seat with its back to the restaurant. There wasn't much pedestrian traffic on this street, and I could see well in both directions.

The waiter brought water, and I ordered my usual lunch—Diet Coke, naan, and chicken tikka masala—without bothering with the menu.

After checking in both directions, I dialed my sister.

Serena picked up. "Hiya. Miss me?"

"Always." That was certainly true. "Do you have a few minutes? I need some advice."

"I always have time for you. What's his name?"

I laughed. "It's not a man." Even with my worries, it lifted my spirits to talk to her.

"That's too bad." She went silent, waiting for me.

"I have a problem at work."

"Yeah?"

"I got a threatening note, and I'm not sure what to do."

"You could take it to HR, I guess."

"This is worse than that."

"How much worse?"

"Here's what it says." I'd memorized the words and repeated them verbatim.

"Who's Brooks?"

The waiter arrived with my drink.

"Just a sec…" I thanked him and continued after he left. "She used to work here. She was murdered six months ago."

An audible gasp came across the line. "Who have you told about this?"

"Nobody, yet." I explained the problem with going to OPS, HR, or my boss, hoping she'd have a better idea.

For about five seconds, all I got from Serena was silence. "I'd call Ashley."

"But she'll tell Vincent, and that will end up being a wone-way ticket back home."

"I know she's not allowed to talk to him about work. If you make it an official FBI question, that should keep it from him. I'll send you her direct number. Let me know what she says. She's the expert when it comes to shit like this."

I thanked her before we hung up, and I only had to wait a minute for my food to come.

After more checking of my surroundings and a bite of my food, I dialed Ashley.

"Benson here." There was a lot of background noise, but her voice was familiar even though I'd only met her at the wedding.

"Ashley, it's Kelly Benson. Serena gave me your number."

"Kelly, I'm about to go into a meeting. What can I do for you?"

"If I talk to you about something FBI related, can we keep it from Vincent?"

"I don't discuss active Bureau business with him, if that's what you're asking."

"Let's call it active FBI business then. I've gotten a threatening note, and I need help."

"Give me a sec to get to a quieter room…"

I heard a door close, and the background noise died away.

"Okay, can you send me the note?"

"Sure." I texted her the picture I'd taken.

A moment later she'd received it. "Is this Melinda Brooks they're referencing?"

"How'd you know that?"

"The abduction and murder of a federal employee is a high-priority case at the Bureau."

That made perfect sense.

I looked up as the older couple at the other table left.

She sighed. "I have to be honest. In a case like this, which looks like the perp wants to get leverage, and it's not personal, you have two choices. I won't judge you regardless."

I took another bite of my food as the waiter appeared to bus the other table.

She continued. "You could remove yourself and let the Bureau and the museum look into it, or we could get you some security and start up an operation to catch this guy."

"So you don't think I should go to our security people?"

"This has to be handled by the Bureau, no question about it. How did you get the note?"

"It was in an interoffice envelope on my desk after the weekend."

"Okay, here's what we do. I'm going to call the DC Field Office, and they'll figure out a plan to get you protection. I'll call you back on your cell. If you can talk, call me Ash. If you can't, call me Ashley. Got it?"

"Okay."

"It'll be all right. The Bureau will take care of you. I'll make sure of it."

I thanked her profusely, and we hung up.

Relieved, I took a bite of my tikka masala. Serena had been right. Ashley would take care of me.

~

Adam

My morning at the DC Field Office had been monotonous—no call outs to break up the video watching. My partner, Neil Boxer, and I had just finished lunch.

I relaunched the video player on my machine. "I'm at T minus eleven days."

"I'm still on minus eight," he replied.

He had the even days, and I was doing the odd ones as we made our way through the bank surveillance video, combing for a glimpse of the man who'd become our masked robber. "The Fawkes Crew" we called him and his partner because of the Guy Fawkes masks they wore.

It was the second bank job in a month by the same pair who'd shot up the bank in Gaithersburg, Maryland. This one had gone down in Falls Church, Virginia. The woman drove and stayed in the car. The man had gone inside, fired two shots into the ceiling, and was out in less than a minute. No one had gotten hurt, but a robbery with someone recklessly firing off rounds was a dangerous situation. An itchy trigger finger meant anything could happen on their next job.

The man wore a mask during the heist, but he had a limp. We hoped to use that and his general body type to ID him casing the location. Even your average bank robber wasn't stupid enough to rob a bank he'd never been inside before.

Television shows made it look simple, but that was far from the truth. We were doing the grunt work. An hour in, I caught my eyelids closing for more than a blink, and I stood to stretch. My knee cracked again.

Fucking ACL.

I twisted my ring. It was a constant reminder of what could have been—what should have been.

I started for the coffee machine. "I need another cup."

Neil hit pause and leaned back in his chair to stretch. "Knock yourself out."

Two other guys from the floor below were ahead of me when I arrived at the machine. I'd bought the expensive machine on my own dime, and now a lot of the agents in the office made the trip to our floor for the good stuff. Each of the other floors had a government-issue coffee maker that dispensed brown liquid that could hardly be called coffee.

The double shot I'd programmed in was brewing when our ASAC, Assistant Special Agent in Charge, Jarvis Dempsey yelled for me and Boxer to join him.

At last, something to break up the video scrolling. I headed for his office and Neil followed.

"Close the door," he barked as we entered. Something had riled him today.

I did as requested and took the second seat across from him.

"I hate getting these calls," he complained. He passed us each a copy of a typewritten note.

I looked at Neil, who didn't seem to have a clue either.

"AD Donnelly just called. We have to drop everything for some hotshot in Boston."

Dempsey didn't often get anything straight from the Assistant Director, so it didn't pay to take it lightly.

He punched the hold button on his speakerphone. "I've got Boxer and Cartwright here with me now."

A woman's voice came over the box. "Did you get the note I sent?"

"Yes," Neil said.

"This was received this morning by an employee at the Smithsonian. The Brooks mentioned on the note is Melinda Brooks, the second of two Smithsonian employees who've been abducted and murdered in the last year."

"We know," Dempsey said. "They're our cases."

I recalled the Brooks murder. Neil and I hadn't been on it, but a lot of agents in the office had. The trail had quickly gone cold, and it was unsolved so far.

"We believe the note writer is SMK from the two previous cases."

Neil hit the mute button. "Why is she telling us our business?"

The Smithsonian Museum Killer had been our case from the beginning.

ASAC Dempsey ignored him and took it off mute. "You want us to interview this employee?" he asked.

"No. She needs undercover protection in place to let this play out until we can get a handle on the Unsub."

Neil shook his head. "What does museum security have on this?"

"The Unsub could be in their security, so we don't think we can loop in anyone in the building."

"Who is we?" Dempsey asked.

There was a hesitation on the other end. "The director and me."

She'd just pulled out the biggest trump card in the deck, and Dempsey's face showed it. A case involving the death of a federal employee in DC was a big deal, two murders was a bigger deal, but one with the director's attention was the biggest. Dempsey wasn't fool enough to argue with her if she'd already brought it up with the director. Being assigned a case by the AD was serious; mentioning the director took it up another notch.

"The previous abductions were both offsite."

Again, she was telling us things we knew.

"If this follows the pattern, she should be secure in her building. We need you guys to go under to cover her off premises."

Neil huffed. He didn't like being told what to do, and she'd already decided how we were going to run our operation.

Dempsey ignored Neil. "We'll get right on it."

"Thanks, guys. I'll send over the meeting detail," she said.

Dempsey punched the speakerphone off. "Needless to say, this is your top case starting today."

"She's got some brass ones, telling us what we're going to do. Who the hell was that?" Neil asked.

"Ashley Newton. Now she's Ashley Benson."

Neil nodded and wisely decided to shut up. He and I had heard the same rumors about her. You didn't argue with someone who had the director's ear.

I hated the name. But she was good. Singlehandedly taking down a corrupt Assistant US Attorney and keeping it out of the papers was a major coup, even if she'd had the poor taste to marry a Benson later. At least she wasn't a Benson by birth.

Dempsey pointed at me. "Cartwright, you're up. Neil will provide backup."

This would obviously entail a lot of hours, and Dempsey always favored Neil in these decisions.

Once again, I had no choice in the matter. "Great. Who's the protectee?"

Dempsey passed over the thin file. "Rich girl. Just your type."

I dreaded opening the cover. He was probably kidding, and it would turn out to be a middle-aged cat lady.

The name surprised me: Kelly Benson. I knew that name. Now Ashley Benson's involvement became clear. Kelly was her sister-in-law, and the younger sister of the man who'd ruined my knee, and my life.

I slammed the folder shut. Protecting a Benson? I couldn't think of a worse punishment.

"Is there a problem?" Dempsey asked.

"It's just..." How could I explain and get out of this?

"Cartwright, the AD is all over this. Fuck it up like your uncle, and I'll personally see to it that you never make it to New York."

That settled it for me. "Sure, boss."

Dempsey shook his head. "Keep your head in the game, Cartwright." He waved us off. "Now get outta here, you two."

Neil and I left and took over the small conference room to work out a plan. The Bensons were fucking everywhere. They'd ruined my uncle's life and gotten him killed. Now they were screwing with me. Again. They were a pestilence, but it seemed I had no choice.

CHAPTER 3

Kelly

At the end of the workday, I unlocked the drawer I kept my purse in and rummaged through the extra-large handbag I carried. It took a minute, but I found the eyeshadow I brought along for just such an emergency. A girl had to be prepared, and I could almost always find what I needed at the bottom of this bag. It had *nine* pockets, and I loved it so much, I'd bought a second one.

My cube neighbor, Evelyn, made do with a purse barely large enough for her phone and was always asking to borrow something I carried. To her, small and stylish was the way to go. But what was the use if you didn't have what you needed when you needed it? Being prepared beat her way every day.

I checked the drawer after re-locking it. We'd had a rash of purse thefts a while back, and I wasn't taking any chances with my black beauty.

I headed off to the bathroom, and Kirby walked in as I was finishing my first eye.

"What are we getting all pretty for?" she asked.

"Another SuperSingles date. Sooner or later I have to find the prince among the frogs." A harmless lie.

"Want some professional help?"

"No thanks. I'm keeping it simple." I wasn't attempting anything like what she could do with makeup brushes.

"You know what you're doing wrong?"

"You think it's too dark?"

She looked at my reflection. "You need to try dating guys that do different things. Take a risk. Date somebody who isn't in accounting."

I'd expected makeup advice and gotten something entirely different.

"I've dated insurance guys."

She pointed a finger at me. "Or insurance."

"Accounting is safe. Ever hear of an accountant turning into a serial killer?"

She turned on the water to rinse her mug. "I have a nice cousin in Alexandria I could set you up with."

"Yeah? What does he do for a living?"

She rinsed her mug again before answering. "Assistant mortician."

"I'll pass." The idea of even shaking hands with a guy who'd been touching dead bodies made me cringe.

"He's not a frog."

I switched to my other eye. "Still pass."

Mortician, give me a break.

She left, and I was alone again with my apprehension about tonight.

Ashley had promised me FBI protection. I owed it to Melinda to give this my best shot. This maniac had to be stopped.

I'd picked the restaurant, and my instructions from Ashley were to get a table and wait to meet my "detail," whatever that meant.

I ARRIVED AT ANGELICA'S EARLY, AND THE HOSTESS SEATED ME AT A TABLE NEAR the window. Without any names, I was left to look for men who showed up in off-the-rack dark suits, white shirts, thin, plain ties, probably sticks up their asses, and definitely super-short hair. Or maybe they were sending a woman as well. What did female FBI agents wear? Pants for sure…after that I drew a blank.

One guy too attractive to be an FBI prospect arrived. Blond, tall, and well-muscled, he was also underdressed for an FBI dude. Blondie briefly looked in my direction, but then took up residence at the bar. Definitely lick-worthy, he ranked several points above any of the recent dates I'd been on. How come there weren't some like him on SuperSingles?

A minute later an attractive redhead with the world's deepest cleavage joined him. Lucky girl.

Maybe that was my problem—not enough cleavage in my SuperSingles profile picture. While I waited, I thought through the tops in my closet.

I glanced down. Definitely insufficient cleavage to be fishing in this pond. I undid a button.

An even taller, more muscled guy walked in. Mr. Muscles stopped to take in the room. The leather flight jacket over his button-down shirt still didn't fit the FBI dress code. His eyes landed on me, and a hint of a smile tugged at the corners of his mouth before his scan moved on to the other tables.

At least showing a little more cleavage had gotten me noticed, a real improvement.

He continued past the bar to the bathrooms.

I went back to watching the front door for my detail.

"Kelly?"

I turned. It was Mr. Muscles, and this close, he looked oddly familiar.

He moved around to take the other seat. "Your profile picture doesn't do you justice."

He knew my name, and I realized why. He was Adam Cartwright from years ago in LA.

I blushed and cringed at the same time, if that was possible. Daddy would kill me if he knew I was even talking with a Cartwright. Daddy had been at war with Adam's father forever, and my brother Dennis and Adam had serious bad blood between them for some other reason nobody had ever explained. The Hatfields and the McCoys had probably been friendlier.

He pulled out the chair. "It's been a long time. How have you been?"

I fumbled for the right words. "Okay. But... But I'm expecting to meet some people, actually."

He sat down. "I know. I'm your date. Adam Carter." He said the last name slowly.

My mouth fell open.

"What's good here?" He acted as if this was a real date, and our families didn't hate each other. Or maybe he was pretending not to remember.

"You?" I couldn't believe it. The feud had never made any sense to me, but Daddy would have a heart attack if he knew I was sitting across the table from one of the hated Cartwrights.

He skipped my query. "What do you recommend?"

I'd picked this place because it was close to work. "I've only been here once before, so I don't really know." I paused. "Are you...?" I didn't want to say *FBI* out loud.

"Ashley asked me to dine with you, if that answers your question."

That did answer one of my questions. If Ashley sent him, he was in the right place.

"You and...?"

"I think a dinner for two is much more intimate, don't you?"

That answered my other question. My detail was apparently a single protector.

As he scanned the menu, I took in the person across from me. No longer the high school senior I'd last seen, this was a man—light blue eyes, an angular chin that could probably cut glass, and shoulders Apollo would be envious of. The too-short dusty blond hair was the only part I'd gotten right about him.

His eyes came up to meet mine, and a smile formed on his lips. "I meant it."

"What?" I squeaked, self-conscious at having been caught checking him out.

"Your picture doesn't do you justice."

The heat in my cheeks went up a notch. I looked down and took a sip of water. "Thank you."

A waitress arrived to break the embarrassing silence. "Can I get you something to drink? A cocktail? Wine? A beer?"

I ordered a chardonnay, but he stuck to lemonade.

"How is this going to work?" I asked.

"Usually you order first and eat second."

I let out an exasperated sigh. "Really?"

He looked around before leaning forward. "We should talk later."

The hint was clear. I hadn't spotted anybody from the office, but I didn't know everybody in the building either, and being overheard wouldn't be good.

"What is it you do, Adam?" That was the most innocuous, date-like question I could come up with.

He put down the menu. "I work at the State Department. Did you bring the item with you?"

I nodded. I'd brought the note in a plastic bag.

"Hold on to it 'till we get outside."

"Okay." I couldn't control my curiosity. "And what do you do for the—"

He stopped me with a raised finger. "I'm a guidance counselor."

"That sounds interesting."

"Frustrating is more like it. Sometimes I get the most spoiled children assigned to me." His eyes bored into me with the words *spoiled children*. "And I have to keep them out of trouble."

Charming had been replaced by insulting.

The waitress returned with our drinks, stopping him before he really got on a roll. She departed after taking our dinner orders.

"Do you end up whipping them into submission?" I asked.

A smirk appeared. "Only the ones that like it."

"And if they don't appreciate your approach?"

He sipped his lemonade. "They don't get a choice. They do as they're told, or very bad things happen. That would also get me in trouble, so I don't allow it. But we should talk later."

Protection was starting to sound like confinement, and locked up didn't appeal to me.

I played with my fork. "Do they get field trips?"

"Solo, no. Only supervised." His hand came across to cover mine. "I take very good care of my clients."

The electricity that shot from him to me was unmistakable. I willed my hand to move, but it froze, welded in place by the warmth of his touch and the look in his eyes. Antagonism was now nowhere to be found in those light blues, only softness. Once again, heat accumulated in my cheeks.

He took his hand back, and I missed the touch more than I should have, particularly given his family name. I really did need a date.

Our food arrived, and the conversation transitioned to a familiar, date-like pattern. He answered my questions about his life since we'd last seen each other, using euphemisms for this current job, but being truthful about college. At least I thought so, anyway. In turn, I relayed my path from Los Angeles to the Smithsonian.

I didn't need to make up terms or job titles as he had. I had no reason to hide being a museum rat.

Every time I looked up, I saw a bit more of him, with less of the filter of my brother's or father's animosity tainting the image.

"What's that smirk I see every once in a while?" he asked, catching me in one of those moments.

"Nothing."

He pointed his fork at me, and his grin turned into a grimace. "There are a few rules. The first is you have to follow my instructions precisely and without question. The second is that you have to be completely honest with me. Hiding even the smallest thing can be dangerous." He leaned forward and whispered the next words. "It's the only way I can protect you."

Even whispered, his words conveyed conviction. I believed he really did want to protect me, almost as if he were family.

I looked down. "I was just thinking you're not so bad."

"Thank you," he said, spearing a piece of meat. "Not that *not so bad* is such a great compliment, but for being honest." He pointed the meat-filled fork at me. "You're not so bad yourself."

I felt like throwing something from my plate, but I kept it together. "Thank you."

I recovered my composure, and we finished the dinner without any more insults.

After I declined dessert, he put down his menu and didn't mention the key lime pie he'd asked the waitress about. I was anxious to go somewhere we could talk frankly about what to expect, and whether I should do what the note had asked.

We split the check and walked outside.

"Can we talk out here?"

Instead of answering, he asked, "Did you drive in today?"

"No, I took the Metro." I didn't add that I hadn't remembered to gas up.

He pointed toward the garage down the street. "My car is this way. I'll drive you home, and we can talk on the way."

I followed him. "You know where I live?"

"Of course."

What was I thinking? They probably had a three-inch file on me. "What's my favorite color?"

"I don't know yet."

Maybe it wasn't three inches thick after all.

He slowed and took my hand, interlacing his fingers with mine.

The shock of his touch made me pull away.

"To anybody watching, we're on a date," he said, offering his hand again.

I moved my heavy purse to the opposite shoulder and intertwined my fingers with his.

This time, his grip was stronger.

In a move that surprised me, he shortened his stride to match mine.

I looked up at him. The streetlights gave his chin an even more chiseled look than earlier, and I liked it.

~

Adam

Kelly Benson had been instantly recognizable when I entered the restaurant. Not as obviously seductive as the redhead at the bar with her tits hanging half out of her top, but a sophisticated, beautiful girl somewhat insecure about her looks, by the way she dressed. Although, that could have been dictated by her work environment.

She'd been watching the door, but hadn't recognized me. Her surprise when I took the chair across from her had been real. The girl had filled out in all the right places since I'd last seen her when I left for USC—full tits and a smile that could kill, when she let it loose. Her emerald eyes were striking against the light brown of her hair, and they carried a twinkle that hinted at an intelligence that wasn't to be underestimated.

Neil had entered and taken a seat at the bar a few minutes after we ordered, to provide another set of eyes and so he'd recognize her more easily if he needed to later.

I'd had to keep reminding her we couldn't talk freely with people around, and because I hadn't prepared her, she'd reacted poorly to my taking her hand outside.

But the sidewalk was empty, and we weren't likely being watched.

She adjusted her purse, took a deep breath, and took my hand again.

"That's the idea," I told her.

She looked up with a smile. "Does your job keep you very busy?"

"The client I just started with is getting my attention twenty-four seven."

This fox could run the entire spectrum from seductive to playful to cunning. If she weren't a Benson—and this were a real date—I'd be having her for breakfast, lunch, and dinner by the weekend. But that brought me right back to the facts: she was a fucking Benson.

I escorted her into the garage and to my car. For this assignment I'd switched from last night's junker to my Lexus.

She swung her legs in as I held the door for her—legs that had been out of view during dinner, killer legs.

I rounded the car and climbed in. "I'll take that note now."

She fished a plastic bag with a paper inside it from her purse.

"And the envelope?"

"I didn't keep it. It was just a brown interoffice envelope."

"And who was it from?"

"It said our security department, but I don't believe that."

Neither did I. The evidence went in the backseat, but before I could hit the start button, the interrogation began.

"Is it just you?"

I pulled my finger back from the starter. "No, I have a partner. He was at the restaurant as well, but you won't see Neil unless he's needed, and I can call in more people as required. This doesn't work if the Unsub sees you surrounded by agents."

"Oh."

"I'm really tired. Can we go now and talk on the way?"

She nodded, but my phone vibrated immediately, and I took it out to check.

NEIL: No tails from here

After showing her the message, I put it away and started the car. "Neil doesn't think we were followed."

"You expected to be followed?"

"Didn't expect it. That was just a precaution. The note you got implied you're being watched, and to be safe, we have to assume that can include away from work."

"You're scaring me."

I turned right out of the garage and moved a hand briefly to her shoulder. "Be strong. I'll keep you safe. I promise." When I looked over, she was smiling.

"Thank you."

I returned my hand to the wheel and navigated toward her house. "Tell me what you know about the Brooks case."

"Melinda got a note just like the one I got, telling her to change the door code, except it referenced Daya Patel, the previous victim, and then Melinda ended up dead. That's all I know."

The note had been turned in a month after the murder, and hadn't provided us any forensic evidence. "Did she really get it on Halloween?" I asked.

"I told them when I brought it in, she never said anything to me."

"When did you get your note?"

"Like I told Ashley, it was on my desk this morning. What do you think this is about—I mean, the door code part?"

I had to be honest. "I would think it's a test."

"And Melinda refused?"

I turned left and sucked in a breath. "I don't know if she thought it was a joke or refused. Either way, she disappeared two days after Halloween."

She wrapped her arms around herself. "I'm not sure I can do this."

CHAPTER 4

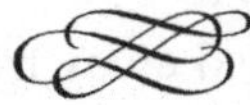

Kelly

Adam pulled the car over and put his hand on my shoulder again. "It's okay to be scared. It's your choice, but it's one you have to make by tomorrow."

I turned to him. "What can I do? He has to know where I live."

He took my hand in his. The strength and warmth were comforting. "You can leave town. If you do, you'll be safe. Patel didn't help him, so he picked Brooks. When she didn't help him…"

I finished the sentence he'd trailed off. "He picked me. Why me?"

"We've got no idea. But he still wants something, and he needs your help."

"If I leave, you think I'll be safe?"

"Yes. If you leave, you won't be of any use to him, or a threat either. So he'll probably…"

I sniffed. "He'll pick someone else in my building, won't he?"

"That's likely."

The word *likely* was meant to soften the blow, but it didn't.

I shivered. "I don't have a choice, then, do I?"

He squeezed my hand. "Yes, you do. You can choose to do this or not, and nobody's going to judge you."

Even in the limited light from the street lamps, it was clear he meant it.

I took a breath. "If I stay, how do we do this?"

"You have until tomorrow afternoon to make up your mind. That's when he expects you to reset the door. If we do this, you have to commit to following my instructions completely."

I nodded. "I think I want to do it."

He let go of my hand and pulled away from the curb. "Think about it overnight. If you decide to move forward, you'll follow the instructions on the note tomorrow, and we'll see where this leads. Once you pass that test, I expect you'll get more instructions."

It sounded simple enough to start with. "Okay."

This was a decision I'd have to make on my own. One word to my family, and Daddy would choose for me.

"You need to explain how this protection is going to work," I said. "Are you driving me to work and stuff?"

He looked over briefly. "It's simple, and it's complicated. Your Smithsonian building is well secured, so while you're at work during the day, you'll be safe. Outside of work, it's my job to keep you safe."

"What are you going to do? Shadow me everywhere?"

"Pretty much. Yolanda's out of town, right?" Somehow he knew my housemate had left on Saturday.

"How do you know about her?"

"We do our research, and her itinerary is on her Facebook page."

"Oh." That made sense. Yolanda was always oversharing.

"And you don't have a boyfriend right now, do you?"

"That's pretty personal."

"Do you?"

Since he'd checked out my SuperSingles profile, I was pretty sure he knew the answer. "No. Not right now."

"Good. Then I won't have to shoot him to win your affections. I'm your new boyfriend."

I pulled back. "Nobody's going to believe that." *Boyfriend* and *Cartwright* were two things that didn't go together in my world.

"I need to be around you all the time, so we need to make them believe it. Everybody needs to believe it."

This just got a whole lot more complicated.

My new fake boyfriend reached over and took my hand. After a few blocks, we hit a red light. He looked over. "I had a very nice time with you tonight. I think you're an incredible lady."

I couldn't tell if this was him getting into character or being serious. I decided he was acting, and responded accordingly. "You're not so bad yourself."

He smiled. "Think hard about whether you're prepared for this. You have until the end of work tomorrow. After that, changing your mind is a problem."

The blocks went by quickly, and he stopped in front of my house.

He pulled a business card out of his pocket after setting the parking brake.

The card read *Adam Carter* and looked to be an official State Department business card.

"My cover job, if you need to explain to anybody. And if you have any concerns at all during work, use that cell number and call me right away." He shocked me by snaking a hand behind my neck and pulling me to him. "The other part of my cover." He leaned over and kissed me quickly on the lips before letting me go. "Call me tomorrow."

The tingle on my lips disoriented me for a moment. I grasped the card tightly as I opened the door and climbed out. "I will."

I had a long night of thinking ahead of me.

~

Adam

I ARRIVED BACK AT MY PLACE, DOG TIRED AND READY FOR MY FIRST REAL NIGHT of sleep in a week—one I planned on taking advantage of. I poured a glass of scotch, which I wouldn't need to fall asleep, but just because I felt like it.

Kelly was a typical Benson, unfamiliar with the rigors of the real world, and probably spineless when push came to shove. Tomorrow I figured she'd bug out for the safety of her daddy's castle. She'd leave the real work, the dangerous work, to someone without her money and privilege—a typical Benson move.

None of them had enough courage to do the right thing if it involved effort or sacrifice. Encounter a problem, get out the checkbook, and presto, problem solved.

The Bensons had always been able to buy their way out. There was nothing their wealth and connections couldn't get for them, no obstacle that couldn't be overcome.

My dad had started with nothing and built his business from the ground up. Our family was not quite as rich, but more impressively, none of it was hand-me-down money from a previous generation like theirs.

Her father had tried and failed to bury my dad years ago. I could see the anger still burning in Dad whenever the Benson name came up.

Pity that Kelly would likely bail, and I wouldn't be able to see the combination of horror and anger on her brother Dennis's face when he learned I was undercover with his younger sister. *"Hey, Dennis, do you like it as much as Kelly does? Taking it in the ass, I mean."* The line I'd prepared for the occasion would completely unhinge him. Cuffing him for assaulting a federal officer would make my day. Too bad I wouldn't get to use it.

Sipping my drink, I wondered what it would have been like tailing such a nice piece of ass around. She was quite a looker. Her tits had filled out nicely, and those legs had always been mighty fine.

I fantasized for a moment about how grateful she'd be after I saved her from that psycho SMK and the way she'd want to repay me. Did she even know how to suck dick? Or was that beneath her? It didn't matter. As a Benson girl, she'd probably never had a proper fucking. My dick got hard at the image of her fine ass bent over for me. Grabbing those hips of hers would feel so good as I gave her a pounding. I rubbed my dick through my pants as I imagined slamming into her until she couldn't walk straight.

I got up, grabbed a few tissues, loosened my belt, unzipped, and jerked off imagining her beneath me, her eyes looking up at me, wanting me. I would teach her what she needed to know.

After cleaning up, I finished my drink.

Fucking fantasy.

She'd be on an airplane and in California by Wednesday, touching up her nails and leaving people like me to deal with SMK, who'd already killed twice. She'd leave and not look back as the next girl was threatened and murdered by this Unsub. After the next kill, we'd up his status to serial killer.

When we caught this guy after his fourth or fifth or whatever kill, would Kelly even care about the other victims—the senseless killings we could've prevented if she'd had the guts to work with us?

No fucking way. She'd be safe in California, sipping her latte and planning her next spa weekend.

It sucked that she could walk away like this, but that was life in the real world. The undercover sting would only work with someone who was committed and would stick it out. Doing it half-assed, the Benson way, would be worse than not even trying. The Unsub would be warned, go underground, change his tactics, and we'd be back at the beginning again.

This was our one shot at him. Neither of the previous two victims had come forward. How many more would die because Kelly didn't have what it took to catch him? I guessed three.

After pouring another drink, I walked to the window and only saw dozens of people on the street going about their lives without a clue that a killer was among them. He was out there somewhere, and he had the advantage. The realization that another body would soon drop sucked, but nothing could change that. Tomorrow night, I'd be back in the shitmobile on another overnight stakeout, and Kelly Benson would be on a plane back to Daddy.

I finished my drink and headed to bed.

CHAPTER 5

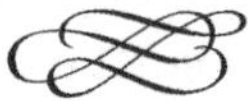

Kelly

When my alarm sounded Tuesday morning, it was a relief to actually give up trying to sleep.

I'd thought sleep would come eventually. I'd been wrong. It had hardly come at all. The news broadcasts about Melinda had played over and over again in my head. Even turning up the sound machine in my bedroom hadn't helped. The image of the threatening note had so burned itself into my brain that it was painted on the back of my eyelids every time I closed them.

As much as I wanted to do the right thing, I didn't see how I could go even a day or two wondering if the monster who'd taken Melinda and Patel was behind me, or around the next corner. Cop shows were full of instances where the detectives promised to protect someone and the criminal eventually got to them anyway. Even on an empty stomach, I almost puked in my bed thinking of what this guy had done to poor Melinda.

Padding down to the kitchen and making my first cup of tea was a welcome distraction. Forcing myself to be active rather than lying in bed momentarily banished the demons. I silently counted the ten dips of my teabag in the hot water before discarding it in the little bowl I pulled from the cupboard for that purpose. I emptied the bowl into the trash and set it in the dishwasher.

As a minor bonus, Yolanda wasn't here this morning to complain about how my habit filled up the dishwasher unnecessarily.

I climbed into the shower with my hot mug. The warm water running over me slowly relieved the restless tension my sleeplessness had caused.

I hurried through my morning routine after remembering I hadn't gone out to get gas last night like I should have. Finally, after mascara I was ready. The girl in the mirror begged to differ. When I looked carefully, the lack of sleep showed under my eyes, but I didn't have the time or the energy to deal with that.

After locking my door behind me and stepping toward the sidewalk, I spied Mr. Dark Suit coming my way. I turned left toward the Metro station and silently wished for a life as routine as his.

He probably got up every day on time, got to work on time, home on time, and all with no threatening notes to punctuate his day with terror.

Kirby was wrong. Predictably boring monotony could be good. Routine kept me grounded.

If somebody offered me a key to rewind the clock a day or two and go back to boring, I'd jump at the chance. I'd even go out with Harold again if that would get me out of my current predicament.

Without that magic key, escape seemed my only alternative.

I'D BEEN AT WORK AN HOUR WHEN I CLOSED THE SPREADSHEET AND RUBBED MY eyes. Last night, the prospect of working with Adam had sounded dangerous. This morning, putting myself in the crosshairs of a killer seemed clearly a bad idea.

My brothers would all have more colorful ways of putting it, starting with something like I was *fucking stupid beyond belief.*

After my talk with Ashley, it had seemed manageable because it was the right thing to do. But I'd overestimated myself. After a sleepless night remembering what I knew had happened to Melinda and what I imagined had happened to Daya Patel, I couldn't handle the fear anymore. Now helping the FBI seemed both dangerous and unrealistic. How could I help if I couldn't even function at work?

Leaving wouldn't be so much running away as running to safety, running to my future. It was a future I wanted to be alive for next month and next year—a future where I was free to be predictably boring, or even change to almost slightly adventurous. Didn't I deserve that much?

None of that would be possible if I stayed.

Sure, Adam could keep me safe for a month, maybe longer, but if we didn't catch this guy right away, at some point, the Bureau would call Adam back, and by waiting us out, the killer would win in the end. There was a reason he hadn't been caught yet. He wasn't stupid or impatient.

Somewhere in the building he could wait for months, or years maybe, to find the right time to cut my future short, the way he had Melinda's. He would be in charge. He would decide the timing, and all I could do would be dread the end.

It didn't have to play out that way, of course. I could leave the Smithsonian if I helped Adam but he wasn't able to catch the guy. Then I could look over my shoulder forever, wondering if I'd made him mad enough to come after me when I settled down somewhere else.

Like Adam had said, if I left today, before the test, I wouldn't pose a threat, and the killer would forget about me.

If I left today, I'd have to leave behind this job, but I didn't have to go back to California and my family's control. I could go to Chicago, or New York maybe, and still be far enough away to be comfortable. I'd been to Chicago once. It would be a good place to end up.

I smiled. A fresh start was the ticket. No killer stalking me—and a fresh batch of accountants to check out on SuperSingles would be a bonus.

"Kell."

I flinched.

"You okay?" Kirby asked as I turned around.

I worked at a smile. "I didn't get much sleep last night."

"How about a coffee run then? You look like you could use a pick-me-up."

I bet I looked like I could use a dozen pick-me-ups. "Why not?"

When we got there, she took a minute choosing today's poison, while I knew what I wanted and poured the hot water over my usual teabag.

The world was so fucking coffee-centric. There were coffee shops, coffee breaks, and even our mugs were called coffee cups. No love for us tea drinkers here. I'd tried the concoctions they poured in their cups a few times.

Sumatran, Columbian, Kona roast—it was all mud to me. The British had it right, as far as I was concerned. Tea had coffee beat by a mile.

This morning she switched to Kona roast. "You need to get back on the horse after getting thrown, and a mid-week date is less pressure than a weekend one." She was back to date counseling. "Change something, maybe your hair or your makeup. Be adventurous; break out of your normal routine. Kiss the guy, and see if the frog turns into a prince."

I followed her back toward our corner of the building. "Maybe. But I'm not starting by switching to coffee." And I definitely wasn't kissing the frog.

"I'll convince you sooner or later."

Probably not, since I might soon be leaving for Chicago.

For the rest of the morning, I kept myself busy checking out job prospects in Chicago and a few alternative cities, just to be safe.

San Francisco had good opportunities, but was a little too close to the family.

Seattle seemed far enough away, but it rained too much for my taste.

New York and Chicago both had good possibilities. Manhattan would be exciting, but in the end the windy city probably made more sense. If the killer considered coming after me, at least I'd be farther away than a short train ride on the Acela.

Len, one of the building guards, stopped outside my cubicle. "Kelly, how about lunch today?"

This had to be the fourth time he'd asked.

I let him down easy, hoping he'd get the hint at some point. "I can't today. Thanks for asking, though."

Shortly before lunch, my boss, Mr. Heiden, called both Kirby and me to his office. "We have a candidate down in HR coming in to interview. I'd appreciate it if you two could take her to lunch and give me your impressions after you hand her off to Todd. I'll wrap it up after that."

Kirby looked at me and nodded. "Sounds good."

It was a bad idea to turn down something our boss said he wanted.

"Sure," I agreed.

Kirby deserved my support. Also, at least now I had a solid alibi for not having lunch with Len.

"How's your mother doing?" I asked Mr. Heiden now that business was out of the way.

His face didn't show his normal enthusiasm. "About the same. The doctors are recommending another new drug and something they call proton therapy. Thanks for asking."

His mother had been diagnosed with advanced colorectal cancer about two years ago. Numerous treatments had each been successful, but only for a while before the disease adapted and re-attacked. Her situation took him out of the office occasionally, but even Krause wasn't cold-hearted enough to complain about it, given the reason.

"What position is this woman applying for?" Kirby asked, getting us back to a lighter topic.

"Melinda's," Heiden answered.

I tried to keep my surprise from showing as we stood to go.

All during lunch, Tiffany Snow struck me as a terrific candidate.

She had good answers to Kirby's questions, and she asked insightful ones about the job. She didn't seem as averse to becoming a government employee as some people were. We were funded by Congress, so most of us got our paychecks from Uncle Sam.

With every glance at her, I was consumed by the specter that if I left, she could become a target. I ended up letting Kirby do most of the talking and not posing any questions of significance.

"Is something wrong with the salmon today?" Kirby asked.

"I'm just not very hungry," I lied.

The real problem was my stomach. I felt ill sitting with these two, realizing that when I left, one of them could end up being next to get a note and feel the paralyzing fear that had gripped me from the moment I opened that envelope. One of them could end up the next face on the news.

Kirby was a friend. How could I do that to her and live with myself?

I'd just met Tiffany, but now that I had, leaving became that much more difficult. If the killer had needed Melinda's help, that would surely translate to Tiffany being on his list, since she was taking Melinda's spot.

Warning them was out of the question, but I also couldn't let them become targets. The situation was all fucked up.

Nausea welled up, and I stood. "I don't feel well. Please excuse me." Rushing to the bathroom, I barely had time to kneel before the little I'd eaten came up and decorated the toilet bowl.

After several dry heaves, I was rinsing my mouth at the sink when Kirby came in to check on me.

"Can I get you anything?" she asked with the concern of the genuine friend she was—a friend I couldn't leave at the mercy of a killer.

"No. It's my fault. I shouldn't have touched those leftovers at breakfast. I'll be fine."

"I've got some Maalox back in my desk."

"That would be great. Go back and finish up with Tiffany. I'll just be a minute."

Luckily this was a high-end restaurant, and they stocked mouthwash and little paper cups in the bathroom. I swished and spit a few times before I felt halfway normal again.

Kirby called for the check when I rejoined them.

"I'm super excited about the opportunity to work with you guys. It sounds like quite a place," Tiffany said.

I silently vowed that I wouldn't let the monster target these two. Adam and I were their best chance.

Although it terrified me, keeping them safe was the only choice.

For Kirby's sake, I needed to step up and take a chance. I needed to help Adam help all of us.

Leaving and letting the monster target these unsuspecting women would haunt me for the rest of my life. How terrible would it be to one day read my friend Kirby's name in the news and know it was my fault? To know I'd had lunch with her and left town that evening, sentencing her to such a terrible fate? How would I ever be able to go to sleep again without seeing her face in my nightmares asking me why I'd done that to her?

I might not think I was brave enough to stay, but I certainly wasn't brave enough to endure a pain like that for the rest of my life.

I selected Adam's contact and typed out my text.

Staying wouldn't be easy, but I didn't have a choice.

Adam

On Tuesday after lunch, Neil and I were working through more bank camera footage, looking for the Falls Church pair. We still had no faces for either of them.

The second robbery in Falls Church had only involved one warning shot, and overall had seemed more professional than the first. If they weren't the amateurs we'd initially thought, we might have to go back a long time to catch sight of them casing the banks. It was monotonous but important work.

I looked over as a guy I didn't recognize came out of Dempsey's office.

The ASAC pointed to me, and the man strode my way with Dempsey in tow.

"Cartwright." The five-pointed star on the creds he flashed marked him as Secret Service. "Special Agent Zanelli. I need a minute of your time."

I had no idea what I'd done to interest the Secret Service. "Sure. What's up?"

"In private," he responded.

He joined Dempsey and me in the small conference room.

He shut the door behind us and pulled out papers that he placed on the table. "Sign this."

I looked at the SF 312 non-disclosure agreement. "What's this for?"

I knew perfectly well that it was for access to something requiring a security clearance above my current level, but had no idea what it could be.

"Good. If you refuse to sign, I'm done here." He didn't seem too eager to complete his task.

I put pen to paper and scribbled my name, birth date, social security number, and FBI badge number.

Dempsey signed in the witness box, and Zanelli filled out his section.

"That will be all," Zanelli told Dempsey.

Dempsey reacted as I expected. "Really?"

"Special Agent Cartwright only," Zanelli told him.

The boss left, shaking his head, and closed the door behind him. As ASAC, he wasn't used to being out of the loop.

Zanelli took a seat, and I did as well.

"So what's the big secret?" I asked.

He slid a small cloth pouch across the table. "Your protectee is a woman, is that correct?"

"Yes." At least I had a clue now that this had to do with Kelly Benson.

He pointed at the pouch. "That is a tracking medallion disguised as jewelry."

I opened the pouch and poured the contents into my palm.

"She should wear it at all times, and if she feels threatened, she should press the center stone. Try it."

I pressed in the middle of the necklace and felt the click of a button.

His phone started chirping. He punched the screen and stopped the noise. "This is normally only given to assistant-cabinet-secretary-level protectees and above. Its existence is to remain secret. You are only authorized to give it to her if she signs the 312." He removed another form 312 from his pocket and slid it over. "I don't agree, but I've been told to authorize you to give your protectee this, if and when you are certain she can be trusted with it."

I accepted the form and returned the necklace to its pouch.

"Are you positive she can be trusted?" he asked.

I gave him the honest answer. "I don't know yet." At this point I didn't even expect her to stick around. "I won't give this to her until I'm certain."

That assurance seemed to put him more at ease. "And not without the 312," he reminded me as he rose. He pulled a phone out of his pocket, punched the screen, and handed it to me. "Use this app if you need to locate her. And, that phone is covered by the 312 as well. Nobody else gets access to that."

I nodded. "What's the range?" I asked, turning the small pouch over in my hand.

"Anywhere in DC. Outside of the district and surrounding counties, range is limited."

"Who do I have to thank for this?"

"Your director. And if the existence of this leaks out, even he won't be able to protect you from us. Your hide will be on my wall."

A minute later he was gone, and I was back at my desk.

Ashley Benson had more influence at HQ than I'd imagined if she had pulled this off. The Secret Service did not share well with anyone.

An hour later, my phone dinged with an incoming text.

KELLY: I'm in

She'd surprised me. I let out a relieved sigh. I knew the longer it took her to decide, the more likely it would be that she'd rabbit, and we'd lose this chance to catch the Unsub before the body count went up.

Neil looked up. "News?" He knew I was waiting on a decision from Kelly.

"Benson's in. So we're a go." I pulled out my wallet and handed over a twenty. "I didn't figure she'd have the balls."

He plucked the money from my hand as I went to tell the ASAC the operation was on.

What still remained to be seen was if Kelly would have the guts to stick it out for more than a few days.

"Better not screw this up, Cartwright," was Dempsey's reaction to the news. "If this operation goes south, I'm feeding you to the AD." He clearly had hoped Kelly would decline, and he wouldn't have the AD breathing down his neck.

"Look on the bright side," I told him. "Neil and I are going to catch this guy, and you might get your own FO to run."

He smiled. Dempsey was itching for a promotion to SAC of his own field office. "Get outta here and get busy, then. And don't take any chances."

I left without argument. His statement was Dempsey speak for *don't tell me what you're doing*. If it works, I approved it. If it doesn't, I didn't, and it's your fucking fault. Standard Bureau procedure. Being bottom of the food chain sucked.

Back at my desk, I composed a text to Kelly.

ME: Take care of the door before you leave

Her response was quick

KELLY: OK

ME: Pick you up out front at 7 for our date

I waited, but no immediate response came back, which was a relief. I didn't need an argument.

And now I had the additional task of evaluating her trustworthiness for the necklace Zanelli had given me. If I guessed wrong and she screwed me, it would be the second career a Benson had ruined for me.

CHAPTER 6

KELLY

WHEN WE RETURNED FROM LUNCH, I'D LET KIRBY REPORT TO HEIDEN THAT WE liked Tiffany for the job, while I brushed my teeth.

Having made the decision to stay and fight relieved me of the guilt I'd been carrying around. No more upchucking at lunch. I'd made the right choice.

It was done. I erased my message history with Adam on my phone.

The message that came later reminded me of the overall plan.

ADAM: Pick you up out front at 7 for our date

Seven was a bit later than I wanted to leave today, but I could use the extra time. Now that I was no longer weighed down by my internal debate, I could finish what I hadn't gotten done this morning.

I hadn't made much progress before I was interrupted by Adam's next message, which made me laugh.

ADAM: Did you dress sexy for me?

The true answer to that was a solid no. My normal work attire didn't move the sexy needle. I'd wasted a better outfit on Harold.

Adam was really serious about the boyfriend bit as a cover.

ME: No

ADAM: Wearing your smile would be just super sexy

I had to read it twice to be sure I had it right. The man was flirting, and I could use more of the feeling that gave me. But once again, who'd said that? The cover persona or the real Adam?

ME: Thank you

ADAM: I meant wearing just your smile would be super sexy

I giggled, but didn't dare respond to that. Did he mean a smile and nothing else?

"Hey, what's so funny?" Kirby asked.

I hadn't heard her coming up. "Nothing."

She'd seen me reading my messages. "I saw that. What's so funny?"

"Just a guy." If I was going to have a fake boyfriend, it made sense she'd be the first to know—after Yolanda, of course, if she were in town.

"Not Harold?"

I shook my head. "Definitely not Harold."

"So?" she asked, her hands on her hips. "Is this the guy from last night?"

"He's someone my sister-in-law hooked me up with." Best to stay with the truth where ever possible. Saying Ashley had gotten us together was easy to remember.

"Are you going to see him again?"

I smirked. "We have another dinner tonight."

I didn't have answers prepared for her barrage of questions.

"And you didn't tell me?" she demanded.

"I wasn't sure where it would lead."

She held her hand out. "So let me see what's funny."

I handed over the phone.

Her eyes bugged out. "I'd say you have a live one on the line. I like his sense of humor." She handed back the phone. "Is he hot?"

I didn't need to lie about that. "Only if you like tall, blond, and handsome."

"Way to go, girl." She tapped the top of my cubicle wall. "I'll expect all the details tomorrow. And no more day-old food for breakfast, you hear me?"

After she left, I reviewed Adam's flirty messages again. Kirby was right; he did have a sense of humor.

The afternoon went by slowly. I kept remembering that the door needed to be programmed before I left.

I closed my eyes. *Think positively, Kelly. The power of positivity can overcome any obstacle.*

After several deep breaths, I opened my eyes. *Note writer*—I couldn't keep using that name for him. I was determined to not be intimidated. Scared, yes. Intimidated, no. I could be in control of my emotions. He hid from view, watching and threatening, while I was in the open, in the sunlight.

Ghost—that would fit. He hid in the shadows like a ghost, refusing to show himself.

We were going to win this game of cat and mouse and bring the Ghost into the sunlight he feared. Sunlight was more powerful than darkness, and we would prevail. We had to.

The Ghost thought he was hunting me. When in fact, Adam and I were about to turn the tables on him. He would be the prey for a change.

Six forty-five finally came around. I packed up my purse and headed for the stairwell in the southwest corner instead of the elevator bank.

"Benson," Mr. Heiden called as he emerged from his office and caught sight of me. It was unusual for him to stay this late.

I stopped and turned. Pretending to not hear him had never worked.

He waved, and I walked back, away from the door I needed to get to.

"We made an offer to Snow this afternoon."

I waited to hear the rest.

"She starts on Monday. I'll be out, so you and Stackhouse can start showing her the ropes."

I nodded. "Great."

He gave me a thumbs up. "Take good care of her. Candidates like her aren't easy to come by."

"I will." Now I was officially fighting the Ghost to save two people instead of just Kirby.

Mr. Heiden checked his watch and turned back toward his office.

The stairwell at the far end was empty, and the sounds of my footsteps down the concrete stairs echoed against the cement walls. Descending floor by floor, I reached the ground floor exit door, took a deep breath, and swiped my keycard.

It flashed red.

Fuck.

I swiped again, and the green light came on and the lock clicked open. With shaky fingers, I entered my override code and set the combo to four ones. Then I froze. Ghost hadn't told me how many entries or what time to program it for. The mechanism could handle anywhere from one to ninety-nine openings over a period of one to twenty-four hours.

The lights went yellow and red, then red. I hadn't finished the programming soon enough for it to take.

I heard the sounds of shoes on the stairs, and then a conversation started just above me.

I quickly swiped again and reprogrammed the code. I set it for one entry over twenty-four hours.

The bright sunlight of the street blinded me for a second as I exited and shut the door behind me. The Ghost didn't know how the locks worked. He knew I could set a temporary code, but he didn't know the details. That didn't tell me much about him, but it was a start.

Blinking in the light, I turned left toward Maryland Avenue. At the corner, I looked left. All the metered spaces in front of our building were full, and no gray Lexus, so I walked to the intersection by the entrance and leaned against the stoplight pole. My watch said I was three minutes early and no Adam, so now I knew something about him as well.

The light turned, the crowd surged past me to cross, and my fake boyfriend's car magically appeared in front of me.

I let myself in and closed the door.

Before I could get the seatbelt from behind the seat, he pointed discreetly toward the Metro entrance. "Who's the girl watching you?"

When I glanced over, she waved. "Kirby. I work with her." She had obviously staked out the street to get a look at my new boyfriend.

Adam pulled me toward him, his hand behind my neck, and his lips crashed down on mine.

I pushed against him in surprise, but his hands held me in place.

We traded breath, and I gave in as the tingles returned. Running my hands up to his shoulders, I let myself relax and savored the feel of him, the taste of him, the smell of him. The feel of his stubble was a new sensation for me.

His grip loosened, but then, as suddenly as it had begun, he broke the kiss. "Did you get the door?"

I nodded. "Yes."

He let me go.

Settling back in my seat, I didn't know what to think of what had just happened. Instinctively, I fastened my seatbelt.

Kirby smiled at me as we pulled into traffic.

At the next light, Adam turned left and looked over. "Don't do that again." His tone was cold, bordering on angry.

"Do what?"

"I told you anytime people are around, you have to sell them on the idea that we're together. Anything less is dangerous."

The gall.

I crossed my arms. "You could have warned me."

"Have you made all your boyfriends ask before kissing you?"

"Have you always been this rude?"

A block later, he offered his hand as the light turned green. "Truce?"

Reluctantly, I took his hand. "Truce." I'd have to keep in mind he'd been brought up a Cartwright, and that meant the manners of a warthog.

"Now, is that so hard?"

The hand holding wasn't, but the unexpected kiss had been. "I guess not."

"It's for your own safety, Kelly." He squeezed my hand.

I returned the gesture. "Sorry, you just surprised me."

He pulled his hand back and turned left on Independence. "When you see your boyfriend, you smile. You can't wait for him to hold you. You can't wait to kiss him."

"I got it. High school romance. Maybe we should pass notes in class."

He gritted his teeth briefly and turned quiet. My sarcasm hadn't been appreciated.

He turned right across the Mall.

"Where are we going?"

"I made a reservation at a nice little Italian restaurant I know."

The tourists in their T-shirts and shorts had thinned somewhat from the mid-day peak, but many were still on the Mall and Constitution Ave.

"I learned something," I told him, "about the guy who wrote the note."

"Go ahead."

"He doesn't understand the locks, because he didn't tell me how many entrances to set the temporary code for."

Adam nodded but didn't say anything.

"So he's probably not one of our security guys."

"Or the omission is intentional, because otherwise it'd be obvious he's in security."

I hadn't considered that. Cat and mouse might be harder than it seemed.

A block later, I glanced left, trying not to be obvious. I decided that even if he was a Cartwright, Adam was a damned sight smarter and better looking than Harold.

I snickered at the comparison. Adam's hair might be too short, but at least he wasn't prematurely balding.

"What's so funny?"

"Nothing."

"Go ahead. I can take it."

"A boyfriend of mine would let his hair grow out a little."

He nodded. "I can do that." He looked over for a second and smiled. "And my girlfriend would let her hair down."

I pulled my purse off the floor and started releasing my chignon. I deposited the pins in the purse pocket I dedicated to them. A purse could never have too many pockets. Sweeping my hair around one shoulder, I gave it a quick brush. "Better?"

He nodded as he turned into a garage near City Center Plaza.

Back on the street, he turned north and took my hand. "It's a few blocks. Are you okay walking?"

"I can keep up." I'd chosen lower work heels today.

We crossed to the shady side of the street.

"Why'd you volunteer for this?" I asked.

"I didn't," was his curt answer.

I let go of his hand. "Oh." Of course he didn't want to do it, me being a Benson and him a Cartwright.

"I don't get to pick my cases."

We stopped at the next intersection.

The light turned green, and he urged me forward with a hand at the small of my back. "I would have if I could, though. I mean, who wouldn't want to spend time with you?"

"You don't need to patronize me."

His expression stiffened. On the other side of the street, he pulled me to a stop. "That's another thing you need to stop doing."

"What?"

His eyes held mine. "A lady graciously accepts a compliment," he said softly.

"And who says I'm a lady?" I shot back as soon as an elderly couple passed us by.

"And that too. You can stop putting yourself down. No wonder you don't have a boyfriend."

I huffed. "I'll have you know I have lots of prospects. I'm just picky." The manners of the warthog were back.

He smiled at me with no idea how insulting he'd been. "Shall we go?" He offered me his fake-boyfriend hand again, and I took it like I was supposed to, like I'd been ordered to.

As we walked, the feeling of holding hands with him became progressively more tolerable. I caught the occasional glance in my direction, accompanied by a smile that didn't look forced. The man was a natural-born actor.

A lady? That'll be the day.

CHAPTER 7

Adam

I led Kelly down the steps from the sidewalk to the recessed entrance of the restaurant. The place was small, but the food was excellent.

The usual hostess was at the front.

"Adam—reservation for two, and the alcove, please." I'd requested specific seating for tonight.

She nodded. "This way. I have your booth ready."

I urged Kelly ahead of me.

She took one side of the booth, and I took the other.

Kelly waited until the hostess had left. "They know you here?"

"I've been here a few times."

"This is cozy," she remarked.

"I like this place for the food, and the privacy."

She opened the menu. "What do you recommend?"

"If you want to be adventurous, the black ink crabmeat ravioli."

She made a face, not seeming to like my suggestion.

I put my menu down. "I haven't found a mediocre thing on the list yet."

When our waiter came, I asked for a bottle of prosecco and the tri-color salad to start. Kelly chose the baby spinach salad.

"My favorite color is peach, by the way," she said, answering her test question from yesterday. "What's yours?"

"Blue."

She tilted her head. "Figures."

"What's wrong with blue?"

She ran her finger up the condensation of her water glass. "It's so predictable."

"You mean manly."

She smiled.

The bubbly arrived, and our waiter poured us both a glass. He took our food order before departing.

She chose fettuccine alla Bolognese. Not that exciting.

I decided on the braised lamb ravioli.

"What are we celebrating?" she asked when we were alone again.

I raised my glass. "How about a successful assignment?"

Her smile dimmed with the word *assignment*.

I should have chosen a different toast. This dinner was meant to put her at ease, not get her uptight.

The critical period in a case such as this was always the first several days. Kelly had chosen not to bolt yet, which was encouraging, but there was still a danger she might if she got too anxious. Once she'd invested a week in working with me, it would become much less likely that she'd get cold feet and pull out.

After a week, she'd be invested in the outcome and not want to look like a quitter. It didn't even matter that I'd judge her that way if she bailed. She'd apply the label herself regardless.

She raised her glass, but didn't repeat the words.

"What do you do when you're not escorting scared ladies around?" she asked.

I thought I detected a bit of humor there. A good sign. I considered what I could tell her. "I've been mostly on two cases recently. A set of bank robberies that could turn deadly because the guy likes to shoot his gun."

"That's terrible."

Our salads arrived to interrupt us.

I forked a bite. "So far it's only money, and nobody's been hurt. It could get worse though in a hurry."

"Are you close to catching the guy?"

I twisted my glass. "It's a pair. A man goes into the bank—he's the dangerous one—and a woman waits outside and drives. And no, we don't have anything to go on yet. No fingerprints or faces, and nothing definitive from the witnesses."

She finished chewing and took another swig of her rapidly emptying glass of prosecco. "And the other case?"

"Human trafficking."

"Here in DC?"

I nodded. "DC isn't immune. It's all over the country, in communities you wouldn't suspect."

"Oh."

"This group specializes in young girls brought in from eastern Europe."

"I don't think I want to hear any more."

Her reaction was typical. We dealt with the seedy underbelly of society that most people were happy ignoring. They didn't mind hearing about bank robberies, money laundering, or even drugs. But mention human trafficking, and curiosity left the building.

"You asked."

She shrugged. "What happens to those cases while you're looking after me?"

"I've been on overnight stakeouts on the trafficking case, and obviously I can't do that while I'm watching you, but the bank case I can help with while you're at work."

We finished the salads without more discussion. Something I'd said had bothered her.

The salads were bussed, and our dinners arrived.

After a few bites she opened up again. "This is fantastic."

"I thought you'd like it." The food here was always delightful.

She nervously stirred her fettuccine around.

I took another sip of bubbly. "Kelly, what's the problem?"

"If you're watching over me, who catches those other bad men—the traffickers, I mean?"

"We have other people in the office to pick up that case."

The answer seemed to calm her as she took another forkful of food.

"Are you going to give me a gun?"

I failed to stifle a short laugh. "No. That's not part of the program. Look, I'll be there for you if it comes to that, but the basic plan here is to not leave you alone where you would be vulnerable. This guy's objective is not to hurt you. The note you got makes that obvious. He needs your cooperation for something. We need to find out what that is and catch him that way."

She ate a few bites and seemed at ease with my answer.

"I'll get you pepper spray to carry in your purse, if you like."

"Does that stuff work?"

"Mostly. It's better than nothing."

She shrugged, which I took as acceptance.

After I'd taken another bite, a man came in and looked around the tables. His eyes rested on Kelly for longer than they should have.

I pushed my plate toward the end of the table.

She cocked an eyebrow. "What?"

I left my side and joined her on the other side of the booth. "Scoot over."

She slid farther in and moved her plate and silverware to make room for me.

The next move would test her resolve. I slid in until our thighs touched and snaked an arm around her. "You need to trust me, Kelly."

She didn't shy away. "I heard that part already."

I picked up my glass. "Now pick up your glass and smile," I said softly.

The guy was doing a bad job of not being obvious as he looked toward our end of the room.

"What?"

I turned my head toward her, smiled and spoke softly into her ear. "Do it now, and smile while you look at me."

She did, and I held her eyes with mine.

I clinked our glasses. "Now giggle and drink."

The giggle was halfhearted, but she did take the sip I'd asked for.

I put down my glass, put my hand to her cheek, and moved in close. "We're being watched."

Her eyes widened.

"By the door, blue shirt."

She glanced over, more overtly than I would have liked.

My hand guided her chin to look back to me. "Smile. Do you know him?"

She gave me just the slightest shake of her head.

I moved closer and brushed my lips over hers.

Her eyes closed.

I gave her a brief kiss, which she didn't resist.

I pulled back. "You taste wonderful."

That got the full giggle I'd wanted earlier.

I glanced toward the door again. Blue Shirt was gone.

I kept my arm around her, speared a piece of my ravioli, and offered it to her.

She sucked it in. "That's good too." She reciprocated by feeding me a bite of her fettuccine.

I didn't get quite all of it, and a drip of sauce fell onto my shirt, which resulted in another giggle from Kelly.

After another two bites I asked, "Did you recognize him?"

"No. And he's gone now."

I smiled and fed her another bite. This was actually more fun than I'd thought it would be. "He might come back in."

KELLY

I HADN'T RECOGNIZED THE MAN IN THE BLUE SHIRT, BUT THAT DIDN'T MEAN much.

Adam and I kept up our playful feeding routine. On the next forkful I got an honest to God laugh out of him by threatening to miss his mouth.

He'd backed me into the corner of the booth, and with all the touching and giggling, our fake date had turned into something more fun than any real date I'd been on. He'd maneuvered us into a fun spot without me even noticing he was doing it.

I pulled his mouth close to mine. "Can I tell you something?"

He arched an eyebrow. "Only if you remember the rules."

After my third glass of prosecco, I had to think hard about that. "Okay, I'll do anything you tell me."

"I want you to slip your panties off and hand them to me."

I jerked back. "What?"

He grinned. "I'm kidding."

I let out a breath and relaxed.

He slid a finger under my chin and whispered. "I was kidding this time.

But a reaction like that could get us both in serious trouble. If you can't play along, we shouldn't start this. Are we clear?"

I nodded. "Yeah. Sorry."

He moved in so close, now only a breath away. "Sorry doesn't cut it. Next time we're in public and I tell you to do something without saying please, no matter how dumb it sounds, follow my instructions immediately and exactly."

I closed my eyes and nodded. It took a second to register. "Like a reverse magic word?"

He pulled back. "Exactly."

"That's screwy."

"Can you remember that?"

"Sure. If you say please, you're being nice. If you don't, you're being DA."

"DA?"

I smiled. "Dictatorial Asshole."

He shrugged. "Not how I would have put it, but it's important to keep you safe. You have to be one-hundred-percent certain you can go through with this."

"I am."

He gave me a questioning look.

"Are you trying to talk me out of this?"

"Only trying to be clear. Once we start, there's no turning back. Do you understand that?"

"Yes. I need to do this."

Our waiter came to remove the empty dinner plates and offered us a dessert menu.

"Now, the rule I meant earlier was the one about absolute honesty. What did you want to say?"

Ah, right. Honesty had been one of his rules. "Okay. I am honestly having a good time."

He closed the distance between us.

I closed my eyes.

He brushed the lightest of kisses on me. "Me too."

I put a hand on his thigh, hoping for another. Fake or not, I could go for more of his kisses.

He looked toward the door to the street. "Go powder your nose." He slid out of the booth.

I picked up my purse, slid out after him, and huffed my displeasure. "Sure, DA." I trotted off to the ladies room as ordered, with no idea why.

He was walking toward the cashier when I turned back to look.

I pushed open the door to the bathroom. He could have just said he wanted to leave. I was sure I wanted to do this, but the way he ran hot and cold unnerved me. It was as if he hoped I didn't want to help. I'd have to prove to him I could handle anything he could dish out.

When I returned, he was back in his seat on the other side of the booth, looking over the dessert menu. I sat across from him.

He put the menu down. "I wonder what the chocolate salami is like. That's new."

"I thought you wanted to leave." I opened my copy of the menu and found what he'd asked about. "Never heard of chocolate salami, but I'm pretty full anyway."

He ignored my comment about leaving. "Want to split a tiramisu?"

That offer was too good to refuse. "Sure." I lifted my glass and emptied the last of it in one swallow. "Why'd you send me away?"

"Shhh, not so loud."

I sighed, but did lower my voice. "Really?"

He looked around. "I had to talk to Neil."

"Your partner? I would have waited here."

"No, you don't understand. It's better if you don't know what he looks like."

"I don't get these stupid rules of yours. Wouldn't it be easier to just tell me?"

The waiter arrived, interrupting us again to take our dessert order. He assured us the tiramisu was excellent.

Adam checked around again. "If we're being watched by someone, he'll be in the best position to notice it, but not if you give him away by always looking at him."

"So he was here?"

He nodded.

I mulled that over a moment. Hot had turned to cold to get rid of me. After a bit, I thought I understood his twisted logic. "You still could have explained it up front. A little trust would be nice."

"Maybe next time."

Our dessert arrived, and he moved it to the center of the table.

We each attacked with spoons from our respective sides.

Finally, I let him take the last spoonful and sat back. "Why did you choose this?"

"Who doesn't like tiramisu?

I giggled. "No, silly, I mean the job."

The smile disappeared, and he pulled his wallet out of his pocket. He handed me a small, worn photo. "My Uncle Jack."

I smoothed my finger over the picture of a handsome man with a resemblance to Adam—clean cut, similar short hair, and smiling with a beach in the background. I took a guess at the significance. "Is he in the FBI?"

"Was."

"Retired, and now you're carrying on the family tradition?"

"He went undercover with the mob in New York." The words took an obvious toll on Adam's mood. "His cover was blown. He never got out." He blinked back what could have been a tear.

I laid my hand over his. "I'm sorry." There was no way I could really understand that level of pain. We hadn't lost anyone in our family, except Debbie years ago.

He twisted his glass and stared at it. "My goal is to eventually get into the New York Organized Crime Task Force and do what I can to make my mark. That's why I joined the Bureau."

I handed him back the photo. "I'm sure you will."

His hand came behind my neck to pull me in for another short kiss. When he pulled back, his eyes bored into mine. "I also joined to meet the pretty girls."

I pulled away, unable to hold back my laughter, and punched his shoulder. "You're terrible. Why do you say stuff like that?"

"It made you laugh, didn't it?"

I nodded. "Yeah."

"You're prettier with a smile on your face. And it's easier than tickling you."

I smiled again. "Thank you." It was the oddest way to give me a compliment. Cartwright or not, he was charming. Looking into his eyes, I sensed a good man, one I could trust, and besides, it was Daddy's feud, not mine.

"If you're on a date, you should be happy, shouldn't you?"

I nodded. "I am."

He smirked. "What affectionate nickname do your boyfriends give you?"

I couldn't come up with one that stuck out. "I don't know. Honey, I guess."

He huffed. "That won't do. You deserve something way better than that." He was going all out with this fake-boyfriend routine.

"And what do the girls call you?" I countered.

"Studmuffin."

"They do not."

"Maybe not." He shrugged. "But they're all thinking it."

I laughed again. He was probably right.

After another hour of banter, he asked for the check.

I pulled out my credit card, but he insisted on paying, just like a date—a better date than I could remember in forever.

He followed me out to the street. "Last chance. Are you sure you're up to this?" It had to be the fifth time he'd asked how certain I was.

Fishing in my purse, I grabbed the proof. "Hold out your hand."

He smiled as I handed over the panties I'd removed in the bathroom earlier.

"As ordered. Any more questions, DA?"

He chuckled and slid them into his pocket. "No. I think that answers it."

I was committed. I'd set the combination, and there was no turning back. I was the bait on Adam's hook to catch this bastard.

CHAPTER 8

ADAM

THE LACY UNDERWEAR IN MY POCKET ANSWERED THE QUESTION.

She hadn't displayed the Benson cowardice I'd expected. This girl had spunk.

After a quick glance each direction, I didn't see anyone tailing us, but I took her hand just in case. "Tell me about your job."

"Nothing much to tell. I'm an auditor in OIG, Office of the Inspector General."

"Basically the same as Melinda Brooks?"

Her smile deadened. "Yeah. She worked in our department."

I squeezed her hand. "Sorry to bring her up."

She nodded. "I get it. It's just hard every time I hear her name. I'd rather not remember what she must have gone through."

I stopped us and turned her toward me. "Just remember, this is all about catching the guy so it doesn't happen to anyone else."

She sucked in a breath. "Ask away, then."

I started us walking toward the car. "Did her job and yours overlap in any specific area?"

"No."

"Does your job give you special access to anything worth stealing?"

"No. I don't handle any accounts that have money in them. I don't handle any of the exhibits. Paper pushing is my stock in trade. All I do is make sure things tally up. It's mostly spreadsheet work—checking the wording of contracts, stuff like that."

"But you would be in a position to let somebody get away with stealing something, right?"

"On paper, I guess, but it's not like I have the keys to anything of value. And, the system is designed to catch that. We rotate areas of audit so a different set of eyes is looking at things every so often."

I punched the button for the crosswalk. "A lot of money must flow through there."

"Our budget is about a billion a year, but three quarters of it is salaries, and a lot of the rest goes into building upgrades and maintenance."

"Do you have access to buildings other than yours?"

"Of course, but it's not like I can walk out with anything. We don't have a mint with money laying around. I mean, we have the Hope Diamond on display in Natural History. But it's in a case no one person can open, and there are always guards around. Lots of people have access to the buildings."

I was out of questions for the moment. Her answers didn't provide anything that stood out. Her mention of the Hope Diamond was a thought, but how would an auditor help someone carry off a heist like that?

The killer's note was clearly a test to see if Kelly would cooperate. But what did he need her to help with? Nothing was making any sense yet. With two bodies in the ground, the only thing clear was he was a sick son of a bitch.

"Isn't that where we parked?" she asked as we walked past and kept going south.

"Our date isn't over yet."

She leaned into me. "Really?"

"I hope those are good walking shoes. They say the Washington Monument is pretty at night."

"I can handle that."

"Good. We need to get our history straight."

Her brow knitted with confusion. "Like what?"

"Do you bring guys home on the first date?"

She let go of my hand. "Get real."

"I'm moving in, so our story needs to be that we're getting back together after having been an item in California."

She thought for a second. "An item?"

I took her hand again. "How else are you going to explain our relationship going from zero to sixty in a day or two?"

"I guess that would work."

As we walked, we started to hash out a history together we could both remember.

Passing E Street, Kelly nodded toward the J. Edgar Hoover building. "Is that where you work?"

"No such luck. That's headquarters. I'm out of the field office on Fourth."

Turning right on Constitution, we still couldn't get a good view of the brightly lit monument until we'd gone another several blocks. But once we did, it was an impressive sight. We paused to take it in for a few moments, and then circled back the way we came.

We alternated discussion of our backstory with her playing tour guide for me as we passed several of the Smithsonian buildings on the way to the garage.

Back at the car, I opened the door for her.

"I had a nice time tonight," she said, laying a hand on my arm before she settled into the seat.

I closed the door, walked around, and climbed in the driver's side, all the while wondering why those words struck me as they did. I shouldn't have cared. This was a protection assignment, pure and simple, and she was a Benson no less.

I started the car and looked over. "I've had a nice time too."

As I backed out of the parking space, she said, "You're not at all like Dennis said."

I put the car in drive and rubbed my bad knee. The mere mention of her asshole brother pivoted my mood one hundred eighty degrees.

"He said he'd be out in a few weeks," she continued. "We should get together."

"No," I told her—without the vitriol I felt at hearing his name. No fucking way in hell was I sitting in a room with him for even a single minute.

She put a hand on my shoulder. "Oh, he's not that bad."

I slammed on the brakes, pulled to the curb, and looked over. "I said no, and I meant it."

Her mouth dropped open for a second. The mood between us shifted instantly to full-on frosty.

"Take me home." She crossed her arms and looked straight ahead.

She didn't get it.

~

Kelly

I stayed silent during the rest of the drive to my house. The glances I chanced in Adam's direction showed an angry, jaw-clenched version of him so unlike the amiable version dinner had brought out.

The bad blood between my brother and him obviously went deeper than I knew.

"I'm sorry," I ventured. "I didn't know how strongly you felt. I won't suggest it again."

He took in a loud breath through gritted teeth, but held his tongue.

"Do you want to talk about it?"

The glance he shot me told me the answer before his words arrived. "No. I do not."

We arrived at my house, and he parked on the street, shutting off the engine.

I reached for the door handle.

His hand went to my shoulder. "Stop." It was another command from DA.

I pulled my hand away and turned to him. "What?"

His eyes softened. "I apologize for barking at you earlier. It's a sensitive subject, okay?"

I nodded, happy for the thaw in his mood. "You need to work on that boyfriend routine of yours. My boyfriend would open up to me about things important to him."

He snorted. "And my girlfriend wouldn't push me before I was ready. Truce?"

"Truce," I replied. Learning the borders he put around things was going to take time. "Can we go in now?"

"Sure. Just let me check things out first."

The implication made me shiver. "You think the Ghost might be in my house?"

"Ghost?"

"The note writer."

"I'm responsible for your safety, so I check rather than assume." He opened his door and exited the car. "You come with me."

I left the car and joined him on the walkway to my door.

Back in fake-boyfriend mode, he put his arm around me as we walked to the house.

After I unlocked the door for him, his gun came out.

I followed him around as he checked all the rooms, doors, and windows on the first floor and then the second. He even opened the closets.

"Satisfied?" I asked after he put the gun away.

"It pays to be thorough."

I walked toward the stairs. "Let me show you your room downstairs." I assumed he planned on sleeping in the house rather than in his car.

He followed me down. "Sure."

"I've got a nice bottle of scotch if you want to join me for a nightcap." I still hoped to get us back on better terms after misjudging the Dennis situation in the car.

"Why not?" He followed me down the stairs.

Before we reached the kitchen, the doorbell rang.

His gun came out again. "Are you expecting anybody?"

I headed for the door. "No."

He followed me as the bell rang again. "Tell me if you recognize who it is." He stood to the side while I used the peephole.

I flipped the deadbolt open. "It's my housemate, Yolanda."

She rushed in as soon as I opened the door to give me a hug. "Can't find my keys. I missed you." She gasped and released me. "Oh. I didn't know we had company."

Adam extended his hand. "Adam Carter."

She took it. "Yolanda Hamilton."

"Adam and I know each other from school," I explained. "We didn't realize until yesterday that we're both in DC."

Adam kissed my cheek as he passed by. "And I'm so glad you called, Sugarbear."

I blushed at the affectionate nickname. "I thought you weren't back for a while," I said to Yolanda.

Adam continued outside and picked up the two suitcases she'd brought with her.

She checked Adam out briefly before turning back to me with a smirk. "Me too, but my boss called me back, so here I am."

Adam hefted the suitcases inside and his arm came around me, pulling me tightly to him and nuzzling my ear.

"I would have called earlier, if I'd known," Yolanda said.

Adam planted a noisy kiss on my ear before letting me go.

Yolanda lifted an eyebrow.

He picked up the suitcases again. "Where to?"

"Upstairs, first door on the left," Yolanda told him. She leaned close when we heard Adam open her door upstairs. "He's cute."

I followed her into the kitchen and recited my rehearsed lines. "We went out for a while in California, but haven't seen each other for years—till yesterday, that is."

"Went out, like…?" She raised an eyebrow.

I nodded. "Until—well, anyway, the geography didn't work." Being too specific could trip me up if I wasn't careful. "But maybe now it's not an issue."

"I could see that." She opened the fridge. "I hate long flights. A glass of wine, and I'm off to bed."

Adam appeared at the doorway. "Kells was just offering me a scotch. Want to join us?"

I'd accumulated a second nickname in as many minutes.

She closed the fridge. "Sure, but not for long. I've been up since three this morning."

I pulled the bottle of Macallan 18 from the back of the cabinet, along with three tumblers. "Why'd your boss pull you back early?"

"Another stupid traveling exhibit coming to town—Hollywood movie shit, if you believe that. Susie was supposed to handle it, but she went out on maternity early, so here I am."

I poured Yolanda's glass first and handed it to her. Adam's was next.

He accepted it. "Kells tells me you also work at the museum."

"Curator in Natural History. About as unglamorous as it gets."

I poured my glass and lifted it for a toast. "Welcome back."

We clinked all the way around, and I took a sip. I welcomed the soothing warmth in my belly that would soon lead to relaxation.

"So you get to play with T-Rex heads and stuff?" Adam asked.

"No. They only let me touch things that never lived—gems and rocks, the inanimate stuff."

Adam looked over his glass. "Well, a moon rock is pretty exciting."

"We have those, and meteorites too, including one that came from the moon." She took another not-dainty gulp, almost draining her glass.

Adam nodded. "Kells says you're very good at what you do."

Yolanda's face lit up. "Did she now?"

I shrugged. "An unintended compliment might have slipped out."

She downed the last of her drink. "Adam, I like you. You're already having a good effect on her."

Adam clinked his glass against mine. "See? Someone thinks I'm not all bad."

I rolled my eyes. "Don't let it go to your head."

Yolanda put her empty glass down. "I'll be asleep in ten minutes. You two kids have fun, and don't worry about making noise. I'll be dead to the world."

I blushed at her assumption that Adam and I would soon be banging my headboard against the wall.

Adam placed his arm around me again. "We'll be good, won't we?" His body heat was distractingly nice up against me.

I nodded, and it hit me. With his rule that nobody could know, not even Yolanda, that meant we had to share my bedroom—and the bathroom. He couldn't sleep downstairs like I'd planned.

My face heated at the thought.

CHAPTER 9

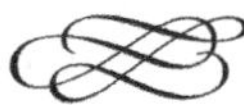

ADAM

I POURED MYSELF ANOTHER ROUND FROM THE BOTTLE WITH MY FREE HAND AND hovered it over her glass. "Another?"

She nodded.

Her glass got a smaller portion than mine.

She lifted her glass. "Where the hell did Sugarbear come from anyway?"

I kissed her temple. "I think it fits you."

I didn't admit that I'd had Golden Crisp cereal the morning I first saw her back in LA, and the name stuck in my mind. That was when she was just a pretty face, before I learned she carried the dreaded Benson family DNA.

It struck me that being affectionate with Kelly was becoming more natural by the minute. This acting shit wasn't that hard. Or maybe it was because she was doing such a good job of acting non-Benson.

I let go of her and took the bottle back to the cabinet she'd retrieved it from. "This go here?"

"Anywhere over there is fine."

I returned to her but didn't initiate contact again. It wasn't necessary without an audience.

She took a long gulp. "You know what this means?"

"What?"

She fidgeted with her glass and finished it with another gulp. "Yolanda being back."

I knew exactly what was bothering her but wanted her to broach it. "No, what?"

"We have to, you know…"

"What?"

She shot me the you're-full-of-shit look. "Share the bedroom. I mean, I can't very well make my boyfriend sleep downstairs when I bring him home."

I scratched my chin. "Yeah. I hadn't thought about that. Trust me, I can be a gentleman if I have to."

"Can be?"

"Will be." I finished my glass and offered my hand. "Shall we go figure it out?"

Her nervousness was obvious as we took the stairs and entered her room.

I'd checked it quickly when we first came in, but hadn't paid attention. Peach was definitely her color.

She went to the closet and pulled out an extra bedspread. "Where's your stuff? I mean, clothes and things?"

"When a boyfriend comes over for the first time, he doesn't bring a suitcase with him."

She handed me the bedspread. "I guess not. I have extra sheets here too."

I pulled her panties out of my pocket. "I'll trade you for a pillow." The thought of her bare next to me had been distracting as hell downstairs.

She shook her head. "I can't believe you told me to do that." She pulled a pillow from the bed and threw it in my direction.

I caught it and tossed the panties on the bed. "It's important that you do what I tell you without question."

"I guess."

That cavalier attitude could get her killed.

"Don't you get it?" I rounded the bed to her and stood inches away. "Slap me."

~

KELLY

. . .

Slap him? What the hell?

He grabbed my shoulders. "You still don't get it. You have to trust me and do what I say. Questioning is going to get you, me, or both of us killed."

"But I didn't expect you to—"

"Don't think," he said, cutting me off. "There are only two things I won't tell you to do."

"Only two?

"Stomp on my foot with your high heel, because I value walking, and knee me in the balls, because I want kids one day."

I laughed. "Too bad that second one's off limits. It's the one I've practiced."

"This isn't going to work if you question what I tell you. So now you have three choices. A: I can put you on a plane back to Daddy, B: you can stay and follow the rules to the letter, or C: you can do what you're doing, and get yourself killed."

I broke free and gave him a slap. "B."

He backed up and rubbed his cheek. "Better, but you have to be quicker."

I nodded. "Yes, DA, I get it. Be faster. Hit harder." I wound up to give him a bigger slap.

He caught my wrist just before I connected. "Once is enough." His grip on my wrist was strong as he moved closer. "Are we done?"

"I think we're just getting started." The words slipped past my mouth filter before I realized how flirty they sounded.

His eyes held mine as his mouth slowly turned up in a smile. "That we are."

I returned the smile, but didn't have any words to go with it.

His eyes froze me in place. His mouth opened slightly, and he licked his lips.

The simple gesture sent a rush of liquid heat to my lady parts.

An instant later, the moment evaporated. "Just remember the rules." He let me go and turned back to laying out the comforter.

Should I say something? If so, I had no idea what.

Pulling a nightshirt from my drawer, I took the first turn in the bathroom.

My pre-bedtime routine included makeup remover, a hot washcloth on my face to open the pores, a thorough wash, and finally a moisturizer.

He knocked before I was done. "You okay in there? It's been twenty minutes."

I rubbed in the last of my moisturizer. "It has not."

A loud huff came from the other side of the door before I opened it.

His eyes fell momentarily to my chest before rising to meet mine. "Done?"

I'd changed into a Dodger's T-shirt for bed, and my nipples were visibly pokey against the thin cotton.

I backed up. "The blue toothbrush is a clean extra if you want to use that."

"Thanks."

After he walked in, I started out, but I looked back and caught his eyes dropping to the hem of my T-shirt, which barely covered my ass.

He moved to shut the door. "You can turn off the light. I'll find my way in the dark."

I set my noise machine to rain and flipped off the light. Stepping over the comforter he'd set out on the floor, I slipped under the covers in my bed. Settling back into the softness of the mattress, I wondered for a second how well Adam would do on the floor.

He'd signed up for this. It wasn't my fault if he wasn't comfortable. Neither of us had known Yolanda would come back, screwing up the plan.

Slowly my eyes acclimated to the dim light from the fluorescent star dots on my ceiling.

I listened to the flush, the washing, and the spitting from the other side of the door, more nervous than I should have been.

He was the FBI guy sent here to keep me safe, so why was I apprehensive? I was in my own bed, in my own room, protected by a gun-toting fed. What could go wrong?

It shouldn't matter that my family wouldn't approve. Hell, they'd have a fit if they even knew I'd eaten dinner with a Cartwright, much less invited him into my home. It took more than two hands to count the times Daddy had cursed out the Cartwrights in my presence. I'd asked why twice, and been shut down both times. I wasn't old enough, I'd been told.

Hating the Cartwrights was a given in our family. Daddy was never wrong about such things.

I suspected Dennis knew Daddy's reason for hating them, but he must've been sworn to secrecy because I couldn't get it out of him, even when he was drunk.

The fan in the bathroom went silent, the sliver of light under the door went dark, and Adam came out.

With the light given off by my star dots, I could see everything—absolutely everything.

He was naked.

The image of him seared itself into my brain. I turned away and rolled to face the window. Closing my eyes didn't help; the vision remained.

My God. He slept in the nude.

Even with only the dim light, it had all been on display: the breadth of his shoulders, the prominent pecs, the six-pack abs, the defined V leading down to…down to his…his package.

"You okay?" he asked.

I rolled onto my back. "Uh-huh, why?"

"I can hear it in your breathing. Are you scared?" Having just come from the bright light of the bathroom, his eyes surely hadn't adjusted. He couldn't have caught me staring at him—all of him.

Scared, no. Surprised, yes. But I couldn't admit what I'd seen. "A little."

"That's understandable."

"You think he's dangerous, don't you?" I asked.

"Yes, but I'm more dangerous."

"What if I do the wrong thing?"

"We'll get through this. I'll keep you safe. In the end you'll have an exciting tale to tell the grandkids."

"I hope so." What I really hoped was that this would end on a boring note. *Exciting* sounded like code for *dangerous.*

This was really happening. I had a man with a gun sleeping in the same room with me, and a Cartwright no less. I'd changed the code on the door at work, and tomorrow I'd go in as the bait in Adam's trap.

He was quiet for a moment. "What's with the dots on the ceiling?"

"They let me feel like I'm falling asleep outside, under the stars."

"Sort of bright."

"They dim after a while."

"And the noise?" he asked.

"I like the sound of the rain."

"You're an odd girl. If it's raining, you're not going to see the stars. You're just going to get wet."

I giggled. I hadn't thought of it that way. "I can change it to ocean waves, if you want."

"It's good to hear you laugh, Sugarbear. Your room, your choice. I just didn't take you for a romantic."

I didn't have anything to say to that, so I stayed quiet. It wasn't until then that I realized how deftly he'd steered the conversation away from the Ghost, chasing me to something lighter.

"I didn't mean it as an insult," he said. "You just surprise me, is all."

"Why? Because I'm not a mean Benson?"

He didn't respond.

I'd clearly stepped over the line again, just as I had in the car. A minute later, I couldn't take the awkward silence anymore. "I'm sorry. That was uncalled for."

"I don't want to talk about it. It's best if we keep family out of this."

He obviously intended to keep ignoring the elephant in the room in hopes it would evaporate with time.

"Why are you the one they sent?"

"The truth of the matter is that most of the guys in the office are too old to pull off being your boyfriend. That left only Jerry and me, and nobody would believe he'd landed a fox like you."

I turned back toward him, smiling in the dark.

"I mean, he's so butt ugly, we were sure that the first time you met him, you'd be booking a flight out of town just to get away."

I laughed. "So we're back to you didn't have a choice, then?"

"I could have refused, I guess, but I'm not stupid. The chance to hang out and kiss a girl as pretty as you doesn't come along every day."

He'd shifted again from cold to complimentary.

I scooted to look over the edge of the bed at him.

He looked up and smiled. Luckily the rest of him was covered by the sheet, and I didn't have to resist glancing below his face.

I could sense the sincerity in his smile. "Thank you. You're not so bad yourself."

He took a finger, kissed it, and lifted it to my lips. "There's nowhere I'd rather be. Goodnight, Sugarbear."

I kissed his finger. "Goodnight." I rolled back over and raised my thumb to trace my tingling lips. Just the memory of the kisses from my protective knight excited me.

I gazed up at my starlit sky and traced over my lips again and again. Before long, the sound of his breathing settled into the rhythm of sleep. I closed my eyes and listened to the rain. Safety was within my grasp for the first time since I'd opened the envelope with that horrid note.

In time, the familiar noise of my sound machine soothed me. I listened carefully and consciously matched my breathing to Adam's. Slowly, sleep overtook me.

CHAPTER 10

Kelly

I woke to the sound of the shower in my bathroom. The door was closed, and it took a second for reality to penetrate the fog.

Adam Cartwright was in my shower.

Through the bedroom door, I heard Yolanda's morning music.

She was up already, and playing rock to get herself going. Blocking out her morning music was one of the reasons I set my noise machine to play the rain so loudly.

If she was up and about, using the hall bathroom wouldn't work. I'd have to wait for my turn here.

Last night's scotches had taken a toll on my bladder, and after five more minutes of listening to the splashing water, I wasn't waiting any longer. I rolled out of bed, determined to be an adult about this. I was sharing my bathroom with a strange man—what the hell was wrong with that? Liberated women did it all the time.

My sister Serena had even had a guy as a roommate after college for a while. I smiled to myself, remembering that had only lasted until Daddy found out. The guy miraculously got a job offer across the country that was too good to refuse. Odd coincidence? No way. Daddy had his ways of getting what he wanted, and the resources to pull them off.

Padding to the bathroom door, I decided against knocking. This was my house. I didn't need permission to use my own damned toilet.

The sight that awaited me as I silently pushed open the door stopped me in my tracks.

My own Apollo clone faced away from me, the view only slightly blurred by the water droplets on the glass. The strong legs I hadn't noticed last night led up to a tight, white ass, then tapered out across chiseled back muscles to the broad shoulders I hadn't forgotten. The scene was right out of a movie, rising steam and all, as he held his head under the stream of water. In spite of willing myself to dash past the shower, I stood there, mesmerized by the view.

"Morning, Sugarbear," he said.

Fuck.

I hurried past and into the toilet closet, turning on the light and closing the door. "Good morning." I was sure I hadn't made a noise, yet somehow he knew.

After finishing up, I purposely avoided looking toward the shower as I made my way to the sink.

"You let the cold air in when you opened the door," he noted.

"Sorry." I grabbed my toothbrush, loaded it with toothpaste, and looked up to see him in the mirror, facing me this time.

He was covering himself with both hands. "I can bring swim trunks over to shower in, if that will make you more comfortable."

I shook my head while brushing, admiring the strong arms I'd also missed last night. My gaze raked down his torso to his…his hands hiding his equipment. "No need. It's nothing I haven't seen before, and we're both modern adults here. It's fine with me if you're—"

"Naked as a jaybird?"

"Yeah." I sounded like an imbecile. And, yes, I'd seen a guy naked before, but not a man like him. I needed a bigger thesaurus. *Hunk* didn't go nearly far enough in describing him. Keeping my eyes on the sink, I finished brushing.

He turned off the water, and seconds later was toweling off beside me. "Your turn."

"I'll wait till you're done." No way was I stripping off my nightshirt right here and stepping into the shower with him watching me.

"Suit yourself."

I left, and a few minutes later, the door opened and he emerged wearing the same clothes as last night. "I'll gather up some things to bring over while you're at work. What do you normally have for breakfast?"

The question dumbfounded me for a second.

"You eat breakfast, right?" he asked. "Like you said, we're modern adults, so I won't insist you make *me* breakfast."

I moved toward the bathroom. "How enlightened of you. I'll have oatmeal." I hadn't eaten a bowl of oatmeal in ages, but it was the first thing that came to mind I thought he could cook.

"You gotta spice up your life, girl."

Soaping up under the hot spray, his words came back to me. I closed my eyes and imagined his hands gliding the bar of soap over me. Up my sides, under and over my breasts, and then down my legs and back up again, not stopping until they reached my heat. That would certainly spice up my life.

Get a grip, girl.

The man was a Cartwright, doing a job. He'd said as much last night. He'd drawn the short straw, they didn't have anyone else for the job—however you wanted to look at it. He had no choice but to be here with me. His only interest was preventing a black mark on his record. Failing at witness protection had to be devastating for one's career.

My hormones were pulling me in the wrong direction. Being interested in him was off the table. I was a career stepping stone to him and nothing more.

Or maybe a career speed-bump was a better description.

He probably figured that being a Benson, I'd screw up his career any way I could, and it would justify his hatred of us. That's how a Cartwright thought.

Running my thumb over my lips, I recalled the finger kiss from last night, and the smile it brought back made a liar of me. Even if it wasn't logical to want to get closer to him, my hormones disagreed.

But, does he like math?

He was a natural born actor. Underneath the charm ran a river of hatred for me and my family a mile wide.

I'd almost believed he meant the romantic gesture.

Sugarbear, he called me. Closing my eyes again, I ran the soap bar over my body some more and allowed myself to wonder what it would be like if my name wasn't Benson. How would he treat me, and how lucky would that girl be?

I can dream, can't I?

I'd read studies that showed an active imagination and visualizing yourself in a happy place were good for your mental health. I deserved that, didn't I?

My hands made another few circuits of my body, and I let my imagination run wild. It had been a long time since I'd had a guy's hands on me—too long, way too long. I washed between my legs and for a moment considered going further, but that was a later exercise for my dirty imagination.

I put the soap back on the wall, rinsed off, and started on my hair.

It couldn't be real between us, but I could wish to be whoever had been special enough to first earn the name Sugarbear and imagine how she'd felt. *Positive visualization, good for one's mental health*, I repeated silently.

As a dinner date, he'd been head and shoulders above any of the guys I'd met so far in this town—a good listener, and quick with a compliment. Even though we both knew I was in the crosshairs of a stone cold killer, he'd put me at ease. He projected confidence that he could and would protect me from the Ghost.

Turning off the water, I wrung the excess out of my hair. This had been my most enjoyable morning shower in an overly long time.

Adam had already spiced up my life.

Too bad he was a Cartwright.

Adam

THE PILLOW WENT BACK ON THE BED AND THE PILE OF THINGS I'D SLEPT ON WENT under the bed before I opened the door to head downstairs. My aching back was going to have me popping a few pills today.

Yolanda had beat me down to the kitchen.

I stretched and headed for the fridge. "Good morning."

"Hiya, Adam. There's pods under the machine if you want coffee."

"Thanks." I located a container of orange juice on the top shelf of the refrigerator. "What does Kells like for breakfast these days?"

"Today is Wednesday, so egg and soldiers."

"Not oatmeal?"

She rolled her eyes. "My God, no. Monday is scrambled, Tuesday is over easy, and like I said, Wednesday is egg and soldiers, Thursday French toast—like clockwork. Never a change, and never, ever oatmeal."

I worked my phone to find out what the hell I was supposed to cook. I poured water in a shallow pot and started it on the stove.

"Egg cups are up there," Yolanda said, pointing to the cabinet on the left. "So she wasn't like this back in California?" The question was a loaded one.

I pulled down the egg cups she'd pointed out. "Not so much, but college life can be pretty hectic at times." I really had no idea if Kelly had always been this regimented. "You want some OJ?"

Yolanda busied herself brewing another cup of coffee. "No thanks."

I poured juice into two glasses for us and located the silverware drawer.

When Yolanda's java was done, she poured it into a travel mug. "Did you guys both go to UCLA?"

Best practice here was to stick with the truth as much as possible and keep the lies that had to be remembered to a minimum. "No, I was across town at USC. What about you?"

"Columbia undergrad and doctorate."

I consulted the instructions on my phone again. "New York girl, then?"

"Rhode Island. Columbia was as far away as my parents would let me apply."

I pulled two eggs from the carton in the fridge and plopped them in the water, which had just started boiling.

Yolanda checked the clock on the oven. "I gotta get an early start. The boss wants a plan for the traveling Hollywood exhibit. Then, of course, he'll want to change it."

Apparently I wasn't the only one with a boss who liked to micromanage.

We said our goodbyes, and I was alone trying to decipher the recipe instructions for breakfast. It said to start a timer for six minutes, but I hadn't read that part when I put the eggs in, so set it for five and a half minutes on my phone.

White bread toast was the next item, followed by two cups of coffee for us.

Cut the crust off the toast? What the hell was that about? This was as stupid as mushy peas.

No wonder there were fine restaurants for French, Italian, and even Spanish food, but not English.

A creak of the floor sounded behind me while I tended to the coffee machine.

I turned, and there she was—the liar.

CHAPTER 11

Kelly

When I turned the corner into the kitchen, the sight surprised me: egg cups and toast strips, my normal Wednesday breakfast.

He turned from the coffee maker. "I warned you about following the rules." His tone was decidedly harsh.

"What?"

"You lied to me."

"I did not."

"You said you normally have oatmeal."

"So what? I picked something I thought you could cook." The words escaped before the inherent insult struck me.

He glowered. "I know you Bensons have a tough time understanding rules, but in this case they are non-negotiable. If I'm going to stick my neck out, you have to do your part, and that includes complete honesty."

The Benson insult cut deep, but my shoulders slumped with the realization that he was right. I'd taken liberties with the truth, but breakfast hadn't seemed like such a big deal.

I took my seat in front of the egg and soldiers he'd prepared. "I'm sorry. It won't happen again."

"How'd you know what I eat on Wednesdays?"

"Yolanda isn't a liar."

The plate he'd prepared looked perfect. He'd even cut the crust off the toast—impressive. He brought over the mugs of coffee he'd made.

"I only drink tea." My aversion to coffee hadn't come up in our discussions.

He shrugged. "Your loss."

I rose, poured the brown sludge in the sink, and started a cup of tea. Somehow, my trying to make breakfast an easier task had resulted in a confrontation. "Can we stop arguing and you tell me the plan?"

"Sure. I take you to work, and we wait for your pen pal to send you the next instructions." He sipped his coffee, but he hadn't started eating yet.

"And if I get another note, what do I do?"

"We don't want to chance an email, just in case he has access, and calling might be overheard. Can you text from your desk without anybody knowing?"

I pulled the finished cup from the microwave. "If I'm sitting in my cube, sure."

"Then that's what we do. And, if you have to call, use your cell, not the office phone."

After stirring, I threw the used teabag in the trash. "You don't need to wait for me."

He sipped his coffee again, but he hadn't started eating yet. "A gentleman waits for a lady."

I sat down with my tea. "And what makes you think I'm a lady?"

He put the mug down, and his eyes bored into me. "We've been over this. If you were, you'd be quicker to accept a compliment and slower to argue." His eyes held mine a second more before he went back to sipping his coffee.

Somehow he brought out the argumentative side in me. I cracked open my egg to find it perfectly done. I dipped the first sliver of toast into the creamy yolk.

"How'd you come to eat your breakfast this way?" he asked.

I dipped another slice. "I had it once while visiting London, and it stuck with me."

He smiled over a spoonful of egg. "Interesting."

"How so?"

"You're able to change after all."

I chose to take the high road and ignore the comment. "Thank you for making breakfast."

He stretched his shoulders with an obvious grimace. "My pleasure. I'm always up for learning something new."

I hazarded a guess. "Stiff?"

"A little."

"Now who's not being honest?"

"Okay, more than a little. I'll get used to it."

I scooped some of my egg out with a spoon. "How is lunch supposed to work?"

"You can't go out alone."

"What about out to the food trucks out front?"

"Is that your normal lunch?"

"Tuesday and Thursday, yes. The other days I either microwave something to have at my desk or go out with some people from the office."

He put his coffee mug down. "Make today a microwave day then. You've got a new diet—soup only, something like that."

"I'm not on a stupid diet."

"You are today. That way you have an excuse not to go out with anyone. Tomorrow I'll meet you for lunch, and we'll figure it out after that. Does that work?"

This was feeling less like protection and more like prison. "I guess." I'd have to find a suitable, boring, diet soup to bring, but it was a workable idea, I supposed.

We finished breakfast with only a few more words between us as I contemplated how he'd committed to sleeping on the floor without complaint.

~

ADAM HAD DRIVEN ME IN TO WORK IN MY CAR AFTER BACKTRACKING NORTH TO get gas.

Hal checked his watch as I slid my handbag over for his x-ray perusal. "You're early today."

I shrugged. "It happens."

Upstairs, Mr. Heiden's office was open, but Kirby and Evelyn's cubicles were both empty as I passed by.

After retrieving my phone and putting away my purse, I ventured to open the first interoffice mail envelope in the stack on my desk. It was from the National Zoo. I took the time to read the contents well enough to know they'd included everything I'd asked for.

The next two were both from Air and Space.

The fourth, though, had OPS in the *from* column. I let out a relieved breath when I released the red string and out popped the normal access logs I'd expected.

The next envelope wasn't as thick, and also being from OPS, it had my heart racing as I opened it.

This note was more complex than the last. I shivered as I read it, and re-read it.

> Follow your instructions to the letter and don't end up like Brooks.
>
> Log into the email account Griffin1897 on webhost.ua and follow the instructions in the message in the drafts folder. Password:rememberBrooks.
>
> Check the drafts folder every day for further instructions. When you have read a message put an X in the From line.
>
> Remember Brooks.

How could I forget Melinda? I photographed the paper with my phone.

"You're in early." It was Kirby behind me.

I quickly slipped the note back in its envelope and turned. "You're the second one to tell me that."

She checked her watch. "It's true."

I shrugged.

"Our horoscope says it's not a good time to change routines." She'd learned shortly after I started here that we had the same sign. "Want to get coffee?"

Keeping to a routine was a normal state for me. "Sure." I tied the envelope shut before I left to follow Kirby for my cup of tea.

"You look tired."

"Maybe a little."

She put her cup under the machine and punched in her choice. "How'd the date go?"

I smiled and felt heat rising in my cheeks.

"Come on. That well, huh?"

I had to say something at this point. I shrugged. "A guy I knew in California."

"That smile of yours says more than that."

I added hot water to my cup. "I like him. But, my brothers wouldn't approve."

"Do they ever?"

I snorted. She had my brothers pegged. "No, not my brothers. But, he works at State, so he must have passed a background check."

She poked around a little more about Adam, but I managed to keep my answers simple and short, except I did tell her his name.

The note was still waiting for me when we got back from our trek to the coffee room. With nobody walking by, I texted my picture of the note with a message to Adam.

ME: New note arrived - what do I do?

~

Adam

Sitting at my desk at the field office, I paused the dreaded bank video and read the text from Kelly slowly. When I'd finished, I held up my phone. "Neil, we got another communication from the Ghost."

"Who's the Ghost?"

"SMK." I'd fallen into using Kelly's name for him rather than the Bureau's.

He hustled over. "Yeah?"

I handed him the phone.

"Smart fucker using a Ukrainian website. We won't be able to get squat from them. And a sadistic son of a bitch with that password."

He was right. No way would we get any cooperation from the Ukrainians, and we had no way to track any traffic coming or going from that country either. No longer using the interoffice mail also eliminated surveillance cameras in her building as a source. This guy was no idiot. Making Kelly type "rememberBrooks" every morning was a pretty sick reminder of the stakes.

Neil went back to the bank case while I typed out my response to Kelly.

ME: Very smart to use a Ukrainian site. Login and check for a message.

Five minutes later, another text arrived.

KELLY: Here's the message - what do I do?

The attached picture of the message gave us the first hint of what he was after.

> TO: GRIFFIN1897
> FROM:
> SUBJECT:
> Scan the inventory schedule and attach it to this message.
> Check every day for additional instructions.
> Remember Brooks.

"Whatever it is has to do with an inventory check," I told Neil.

"Does she know what that means?"

"I'll find out tonight." I sent a message back to Kelly.

ME: Do it

At least now we knew more than before.

KELLY: Done - what now?

ME: Nothing

The Griffin1897 struck me as odd. It meant something, but I couldn't place it. It was going to be a waiting game now. I put my foam earplugs in and went back to bank reality TV without another message from Kelly.

While the bank video threatened to put me to sleep, I inhaled another two cups of coffee. I'd caught three limpers this morning, but none of them was close physically to our robbery Unsub.

In the middle of the next day's video, it came to me. I paused the footage and looked up the reference on my browser. I was right.

SMK had a sense of humor. Griffin was the name of the invisible man in H. G. Wells book of the same name, which was published in 1897 —Griffin1897.

I went back to the video while I worried about what SMK's endgame might be.

Neil had pointed out what I hadn't considered when we'd been tasked with this. With the director taking an interest in this case, there would be hell to pay if we screwed up in any way, and with Kelly being related to Ashley Benson, it would be even worse if anything happened to Kelly.

I stopped the video. What if we scared SMK into hiding for a while and he came back out later and hurt Kelly? That scenario made my position even more precarious. On any normal case, the original protection detail wouldn't be faulted, but this case wouldn't be handled normally. With Benson's connection to HQ, I'd be fucked royally if we didn't catch SMK and he came back later to hurt her. The thought chilled me.

My future at the Bureau was more tied to the outcome of this case than I'd realized when I'd said yes.

I started the video again. Moving forward was the only option open to me.

Kelly's inability to take the rules seriously loomed even bigger in my mind than it had earlier. Would she screw up and get herself hurt? If so, Ashley Benson would surely see to it that I got the blame and a one-way ticket out of the Bureau.

If I'd refused the protection assignment on Monday after learning her name, the damage would have been contained, but I hadn't thought that far ahead. Now if I pulled out, and anything went wrong for any reason, Ashley Benson with her pipeline to the director would ruin my career, claiming my actions had alerted SMK.

It was time for another two pills. Pulling open the drawer, I chose Advil this time.

An hour later, Dad's face showed up on my phone as a call came in. "Dad?"

"How's life treating you? Got a girl for us to meet yet?" Our calls started the same way almost every time. Mom was itching to spoil some grandkids.

"Not this week."

"I'm calling because I could use your help."

"Sure. What with?"

"I'm in a bit of a battle with one of the Bensons." That was nothing new. "One of the sons this time. Your old friend Dennis."

I couldn't stop myself from reaching for my knee.

"Anyway, we have a whistleblower with some information on him, but she's afraid to come forward."

It was about time somebody blew the whistle on those people. "What can I do to help?"

"She's scared to go to the SEC herself—you know, job security. So I'd like you to pass the information on and see that it gets to the right people."

I thought about possible blowback on this and couldn't come up with any right away. "I'll have to ask around to see how to go about it, but I should be able to do that." Since it was outside the Bureau, helping to take the Bensons down a notch might not help my career here, but if anyone deserved to be cut down to size, it was Dennis.

"Great," Dad said. "I don't know how long it'll be, but I'll forward the information when I get it. And be sure to let me know when you find her."

The *her* was the proverbial one who was good enough to bring home to the parents—the one I would be proud of, and the one who could endure my mother asking her about future babies.

After what Dennis Benson had cost me, payback would feel good.

CHAPTER 12

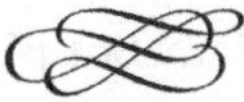

Kelly

The Ghost wanted the inventory schedule.

It had arrived yesterday afternoon, and he knew it. That most definitely put him in this building.

I'd been careful that nobody was watching while I scanned the schedule and attached it to the email message, per his instructions.

But I was still wondering what it all meant. *What does the schedule have to do with anything?* When we did an inventory, the buildings were packed—with more people around, not fewer. The museum even x-rayed everybody's bags as they left to make sure nothing walked out the door.

This was for those FBI geniuses to figure out, I guess. I had to wait for the Ghost to tell me what door to unlock, or what to steal for him.

If he wanted me to take something, he damned well better tell me how to get it, and how to get it out as well, because I certainly didn't know. Our procedures had been honed over the years to prevent exactly that.

We knew the risk of theft was highest during an inventory, and we were prepared. During normal operations, with guests in the buildings, anything that could be carried out was locked up and behind glass. We had alarms and surveillance galore, not to mention guards at all the doors.

The Ukrainian address connection still bugged me.

A little before lunch, Kirby and Evelyn appeared together at my cube.

"Wanna try the gyro truck today, or barbecue?" Kirby asked.

"Or Peruvian?" Evelyn asked.

Since there weren't as many restaurants south of the Mall as there were on the north side near all the hotels, the lunch trucks congregated outside our building on Maryland.

"No, thanks. I'm staying in and doing soup today," I replied.

Kirby tilted her head in disbelief. "Soup?"

Since I'd promised Adam I'd stay inside, I was stuck. "New diet."

Kirby giggled. "Adam, huh?"

I shrugged.

"What did I miss?" Evelyn asked.

"She claims he's nothing special, but one date and she's on a diet," Kirby told her.

"How come you didn't tell me?" Evelyn asked.

I stuck to the storyline. "Old friend. Just found out he worked in DC."

Kirby nodded toward the elevator. "Sure. That's why she looks like she didn't get much sleep last night. Let's go."

The two marched off with Kirby mumbling in hushed tones to Evelyn—no doubt regurgitating everything she'd learned from me about Adam, and probably making up additional details. The girl was a one-person gossip machine.

Turning back to my monitor, I realized this was probably good. Having Kirby spread the word about my new "boyfriend" would help Adam's cover if we were being watched by the Ghost.

I closed my eyes and transported myself back to our nighttime walk to the Washington Monument. It had been a quintessential date moment—an arm-in-arm romantic stroll to see a romantic sight after a romantic dinner together. Romantic times three: a Hallmark moment.

I opened my eyes and shook my head to rid myself of the thoughts. The romance was all fake. It was a mirage intended to confuse.

Adam was playing a part, doing a job, carrying out a responsibility, putting up with me.

Opening my drawer, I pulled the soup can out of my purse and headed off to the microwave in the coffee room.

Kirby had gotten the motivation wrong, but she was right that I was doing this for Adam.

As the seconds ticked off the microwave, I thought back to the image of Adam naked in the shower. How bad would it be if the romance were real instead of fake? I could have joined him in the shower and soaped up his back before he turned around and returned the favor—soaping all of me with his strong hands. Just the thought hardened my nipples.

My mind raced a mile a minute. Would he bend me over and take me in the shower? A shiver ran through me. That would be a new experience. To call my bedroom exploits plain vanilla was being too kind. The romance novels I kept in the back of my dresser drawer had descriptions of dozens of things I'd never done or had done to me.

Shower sex would be a good way to start expanding my horizons. I'd heard Yolanda and Bogdan in the shower before, and the noises they made were off-the-charts naughty compared to what I was used to.

Or, would Adam lift me up, carry me out to the bed, and have sex with me while I looked into those luscious eyes and screamed his name? Maybe he would be the one groaning my name. Guys sometimes did that, didn't they?

I was getting way ahead of myself. We'd fake kissed, and I was imagining he wanted to have sex with me? I wasn't homely or anything, and I had all the right parts, so why wouldn't he want to?

Now I was making no sense at all.

The brief time we'd spent together had already scrambled my brain.

The microwave's ding killed my diversion from reality.

The hot bowl threatened to burn my fingers as I retrieved it. A pair of paper napkins allowed me to carry my steaming liquid lunch back to my desk without dropping it. Next time, I wouldn't set the timer for as long.

Blowing on the first spoonful, I realized the soup wasn't the only thing that had heated up in the coffee room. The thought of a more-than-professional relationship with Adam had warmed up my insides as well. The evidence tingled between my legs and made me smile, if only to myself.

My words to Kirby came back to me. *"My brother wouldn't approve."* Dad had disliked Adam's family forever, and my brothers would take Dad's side on something like this without a doubt. *Disdain, disgust, hostility,* and *loathing* were all too mild. *Hatred* was the closest word to describe Daddy's feelings about the Cartwrights, and even that wasn't strong enough.

I tried to imagine the conversation. *"Daddy, I have some good news and some bad news. The good news is that I finally found someone in DC I like. The bad news is he's a Cartwright."*

The Daddy explosion following that would rival Mt. Vesuvius.

I for sure wanted to be judged by who I was and what I'd done, not by the actions of a previous generation. I was my own woman. Shouldn't that translate to Adam being his own man, and not a carbon copy of his father?

ADAM

"BOXER AND CARTWRIGHT," DEMPSEY YELLED.

Pausing the sleep-inducing video, I happily followed Neil to the ASAC's office.

He handed Neil a piece of paper. "Looks like the same crew you two are after. Just hit a bank in Bethesda. This time we have a casualty. Take Gleason and Sams with you."

My gut tightened, hoping we didn't have a DB.

"How serious?" Neil asked.

"Paramedics are on scene is all I know."

A few minutes later, we were in the car on the ramp up from the underground garage, waiting for the barrier to lower. Gleason and Sams were in the second car, and forensics was getting a team together.

With lights and siren, Neil quickly navigated the traffic toward the bank. "This was bound to happen," he said as he steered around stopped cars. "Hopefully it's not fatal."

"Yeah," I agreed.

We'd been on this case for a while now, and if we lost a victim to a shooting, we'd be second guessing whether we could have caught the guys sooner and prevented it.

I checked the traffic on my phone. "Connecticut is faster than Wisconsin for the first mile or two." Time was always critical in these situations.

Most people had no concept of how quickly memories of the little things could evaporate if we didn't interview the victims soon after the event.

We pulled up to find five local units on the scene and checked in with Captain Ellis from the Bethesda Division of the Montgomery County Police.

"The victim?" Neil asked.

"Just transported. Conscious, and it doesn't look life threatening to me." He opened a notepad. "She was just standing there when he turned toward her and fired. According to her and the closest person to her, a teller by the name of…" He checked his notes. "Skates, the lady didn't do anything to provoke it. They'd all been following orders, and the cash had been collected by the woman. It happened just before they left."

"A woman?" I asked.

"Yeah. Two inside. One woman with no mask, one man. The male wore a Guy Fawkes mask—you know the hacker, Anonymous type. He's the one who opened fire, and there was a driver outside by the door. Three in all."

This was a change from before. The masks were the same, but they'd added someone to the crew.

Neil looked up from his notepad. "Dye packs?"

"The manager said they stopped using them a year ago after a rookie teller set one off by mistake."

This was another similarity. They were always lucky enough to hit banks that didn't have exploding dye packs hidden in the cash.

"We'll start inside," I told Gleason. "You guys start interviews."

I pulled booties from my pocket, and Neil followed me inside after donning his.

The scene didn't tell us much. We found the normal disarray of a shooting—blood on the floor, two cartridge casings for forensics, and two smeared puddles of urine where scared customers had been lying on the floor. The medical debris from the paramedics treating the victim had been shoved to the side.

Outside, Gleason and Sams were interviewing customers, and we started on the tellers.

The bank loan officer, who actually hadn't been close to the shooter, gave us the best clue. "She spit on the floor before leaving."

"Who?"

"The woman who collected the money."

I urged our witness toward the front door. "Could you point out where?"

Approaching the glass door, she pointed to the right hand side about ten feet in, where a wet spot showed on the floor.

"And you're sure it was the woman?" Neil asked.

"Absolutely. It was as they were leaving."

"I'll get forensics on it," I told Neil.

He took her away from the door, and I went inside.

The forensics team was concentrating on the row of teller stations when I pulled aside the lead and pointed out the spit smear. "Spit from the female Unsub. We need DNA on that expedited."

"We can't expedite every damned sample," she shot back.

"Tracy, have I asked you to expedite anything in the past two weeks? I just need this one fast."

She snorted. "Right. It's been three weeks. I'll put it in to the lab, but you know how backed up they are." She leaned over. "You're in luck Adam."

"How so?"

"There's blood in this. It'll run well."

We had run through a half dozen interviews before Dempsey called.

"Cartwright," I answered.

"Tell me we have a solid lead on this Fawkes Crew."

"We have a face this time, and possibly DNA from the third Unsub."

"I thought there were only two."

"This time they brought along a third."

"Because of the shooting, this one's all over the news, and you and Boxer are making us look bad by not catching these guys. This is our home turf. You're the lead on this one, Cartwright. You need to work it harder and close this."

He'd said all there was to say about who was getting the blame for the case still being open.

"We're on it. Like I said, we now have a face and DNA." Thinking positively, I didn't hedge it as *possible* DNA.

He let me go after another admonition that the clock was ticking.

We finished interviews and were reviewing the surveillance video in the back room when the text arrived.

KELLY: What time are you picking me up?

I checked my watch and put the phone away. "Neil, I gotta get going."

"Sure thing, Romeo. I wouldn't want you to be late for date night. I'll catch a ride back with Gleason."

Gleason ran the tape back again and restarted the shooting sequence. "I still don't see anything that triggered it."

A few minutes later, I texted Kelly after starting up the car.

ME: Will call when close

Given the state of traffic, that wouldn't be soon.

Now I was on duty twenty-four hours a day between Kelly in the off hours and the other cases during the day. I dialed Neil.

"What's up, Romeo?"

The ribbing was already getting old.

"If you send me a copy of today's video, and a few prior days, I'll get started on it tonight."

"Are you sure that won't cramp your style with the lady?" Sarcasm dripped off his words.

"Bite me."

"That's her job."

"We could switch, and I'll stay home while you stay up all night keeping the little princess safe."

He sighed. "Just kidding. I'm sure it's hard work."

The only kidding part was that he didn't actually feel a single ounce of pity for me.

"The video?"

"Sure. I'll send it when I get back to the office."

Tonight he'd be curled up at home with a beer and a soft bed while I had to work around the clock, and sleep on the floor.

CHAPTER 13

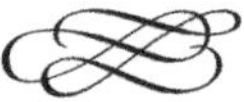

Kelly

I'd been waiting almost an hour when Adam finally texted.

ADAM: Outside now

I loaded my umbrella and phone into my purse and started down.

As promised, Adam was directly outside, leaning against his car with his arms folded. He opened the door for me as I approached. "About time."

I stopped mid-stride. "You're the one who's late."

He held the door open. "You should've been ready."

I slid into the seat and pulled the door closed without his help.

He climbed in and started the car, still without an apology.

After two blocks of silence, I couldn't take it any longer. "What's your problem?"

"I don't have a problem."

That was utter bullshit.

"I forgot, Cartwrights don't have problems. It's only the rest of us who are mortal."

His jaw clenched, and he glanced over. "That's a very Benson way of looking at the world."

"I'm not the one who arrived in a piss-poor mood."

He looked straight ahead without answering. His jaw ticked again, but he didn't open up.

I took a stab at the issue. "Not have a good day at work?"

He drove on without any reaction.

Settling back into my seat, I resigned myself to the silent treatment.

Two blocks later he spoke. "No. Not a good day."

I turned to him again. "Want to talk about it? I'm here to listen."

He pulled up in front of my house. "Stay here."

He hadn't said please, which put the command in DA mode, so I stayed put.

After rounding the car, he looked both ways down the street before opening my door for me.

I took his hand as I climbed out. "Thank you."

"You're most vulnerable between the car and the house."

The words were a reminder of the situation I'd gotten myself into—and that I was a job to him.

After entering, he had me wait by the entry as he went through his routine again of checking all the rooms for an intruder.

"All clear," he said when he returned from upstairs.

Passing through the dining room, I dropped my heavy purse on the table and made my way to the kitchen. "What would you like for dinner?"

He opened the fridge. "Whatever."

"Stop it," I shot back.

"Stop what?"

I threw my hands up. "This *nothing's wrong* routine when you're obviously pissed at something."

"It *is* nothing."

"Right. This is the real you. The nice you is just an act. Be sure to bring him out when Yolanda comes home." I turned and left for the dining room where I pulled out my phone. With the app, I ordered a personal size pepperoni pizza and a salad.

He was still in the kitchen, beer in hand, when I went upstairs to change. The business clothes came off. Yoga pants, a sweatshirt, and sandals completed the transition to relaxed. I paced back and forth a few times.

Why was I letting Adam's fit get to me? He was only hired help after all—free hired help, to be more precise—a temporary interloper in my life to deal with the Ghost. What was the big deal? It didn't matter in the cosmic scheme of things if he was happy, sad, or inconvenienced.

He was a big boy and could take care of himself. He didn't need or want me fussing over him, or even appearing the least bit concerned about him.

I waited upstairs.

The jerk could stew in his own juices downstairs where I didn't have to put up with his spoiled-child routine.

I clicked on the television and Judge Judy was in full swing. It would do to distract me while I waited for dinner. Judge Judy started interrogating the girl who had taken and wrecked her now-ex-boyfriend's car.

I imagined the judge interrogating Adam instead to get the truth out of him. Judge Judy didn't tolerate any shitty non-answers in her courtroom.

In my head, the judge was just about to get the truth out of Adam when the doorbell rang.

When I reached the top of the stairs, Adam was nearing the door, gun in hand. "I ordered pizza. Please don't shoot the guy."

He checked through the peephole before tucking the gun in his waistband at the small of his back and opening the door. Adam had his wallet out before I reached the bottom, and he tipped the guy while accepting my dinner.

"Thanks," I called to the delivery guy as Adam closed and locked the door.

Adam's eyes lingered on my legs before returning to the box. "What do we have here?"

"*We* don't have anything." I took the box and bag from him. "*I* have dinner."

His brows creased as he got my meaning.

I waited for another just-like-a-Benson comment, but it didn't come. What was that anyway? "*A very Benson way of looking at the world*," he'd said with obvious disgust. It was as if I were a subspecies or something, based on my family name.

A delicious cheese-and-pepperoni aroma erupted from the box when I opened it on the kitchen counter. I salivated as I gathered a plate and silverware to attack my prize.

Adam followed me into the kitchen after snagging his beer from the family room. He opened the fridge and peered in, followed by the freezer. "What do you have to eat around here that isn't diet?"

"You weren't interested," I reminded him.

A grunt was all he sent back.

I eased a piece of the pizza onto a plate. "You can always cook two Lean Cuisines if one isn't enough for you."

He nodded, but the grimace on his face said *no* as he continued his search.

I opened the salad container, poured it into a bowl, and added half the container of dressing. "There's a squirrel in the trees out back if you want to shoot it and have some fresh meat."

That got a laugh out of him before the sternness returned. "Very funny."

With two pieces of my pizza on the plate, I added the salad, silverware, and napkins to a tray and ventured into the family room. Instead of Judge Judy, I found a *Friends* rerun to start.

The ding of the microwave sounded from the kitchen. He'd chosen something frozen instead of my squirrel suggestion.

Good thing. I didn't want Mrs. Hammond next door calling the SWAT team on us.

A few minutes later, he carried a tray in, took a seat in the wingback chair, and started eating without a word.

I finished my first slice. "When are you going to tell me about you and Dennis?"

He shook his head. "When are you going to stop asking?"

"Why do you dislike me so much?"

"I don't."

A typical guy answer.

"Then why won't you talk to me?"

He stood. "Nothing to talk about." He carried his tray into the other room.

I was alone with my salad and *Friends*. Collecting another piece of pepperoni from the box solved that. Now there were four of us: me, the pizza, the salad, and the TV.

After scarfing down the remainder of the warm, gooey pizza, but not all the salad, I cleaned up. Walking past Adam without a word, I went up to my room and dialed my sister Serena. If Adam wouldn't talk to me, maybe she had the answers.

"Hey, Kelly, I was just going to call you," Serena answered.

"Do you have news?"

"Yeah. Dennis has a new girl."

That was an interesting change. Since his marriage collapsed, my older brother hadn't had any women in his life that we knew of.

"Who?"

"He hasn't admitted it yet, but I think it's the girl who started working for him recently."

"What's her name?"

"Jennifer, but you didn't hear it from me. Anyway, enough about him. What's new with you?"

I'd called to pump her for information, not the other way around. "Tell me what you know about Dennis and Adam Cartwright."

"You should ask Dennis that question."

"You know he won't tell me, so I'm asking you."

"Why the interest in Adam Cartwright?" She'd always been stubborn about releasing information without getting some in return.

"I saw him at a coffee shop, and I was curious."

"Curious like you think he's cute?"

I was still getting nothing from her. "Are you going to tell me or not?"

"Well, there's another issue between Dennis and Adam, and it's not pretty."

I waited for her to continue.

"They got in a fight in college, and Adam came out of it injured. The worst part is that Dennis was in the wrong, and he's never apologized, so this one is on him. I'm sure Adam hates Dennis for it, and he's right to. But Dennis despises Adam as well, probably projecting his guilt is all I can figure. He refuses to talk about it."

"Why?"

"Pride, I guess. You know, one of those I'm-too-manly-to-discuss-my-feelings kind of things. Let's just say it was not one of our brother's best moments."

"Oh." That was all I could muster as my heart sank.

"Now are you going to tell me why you're asking?"

"I said I saw him and was curious." Both things were true, even if the explanation was incomplete.

"You know I'm going to bug you until you tell me the truth about this."

That was her way.

"I am telling the truth. Gotta go. There's somebody at the door."

"Later then, but I'm not letting you off the hook."

We hung up, and I lay back on the bed.

Now the animosity made sense. Dennis had hurt Adam, and it had been my brother's fault. No wonder Adam despised me. Guilt by association: same last name, painted with the same broad brush.

As I returned downstairs, I heard Yolanda's voice coming from the kitchen. "What exactly do you guys at State do anyway?"

Adam

I rinsed my plate at the sink. "Same as any other government employees. We shuffle paper, mostly."

Yolanda scoffed. "No, really. Do you have some specialty or something?"

Kelly reappeared at the doorway.

I opened my arms to her. "Have a nice nap, Sugarbear? Your roomie wants to know if I even work for a living."

Kelly shrugged as she walked my direction. "They won't let me into his building to see."

I took her in my arms and rubbed her back. "Missed you."

She looked up at me and offered her lips. "I'm back now." She closed the distance for a kiss.

I kept the kiss appropriately short, given our audience. "And it couldn't make me happier." The press of her breasts against me and the taste of her had blood leaving my brain and heading south, where I didn't need it right now. The distracting strawberry scent of her hair lingered with me after we broke the kiss.

She turned to Yolanda and moved away enough to slow the stirring of my cock. "He won't answer my questions either. Everything is top secret or something."

"I do have a security clearance," I said, trying to keep it truthful.

Yolanda took a swig of the beer in her hand. "You guys at State probably spend half your time causing problems so you have something to fix."

I pulled Kelly to my side. "Not me. Right now I'm working on something very important and quite dangerous."

Yolanda's face scrunched up. "Like a war in the Middle East?"

I looked down at Kelly and back to Yolanda. "Not that serious, but lives are at stake." The warmth of Kelly against me only reminded me of the importance of this assignment.

Kelly's hold on me tightened. "And we're all very appreciative."

More contact was not what I needed right now. I let go of her. "I have to get back to work."

Yolanda put her beer on the counter. "At least my job stops when I leave the building. I'll be upstairs if you need my advice solving the world's problems."

My eyes followed the pretty Yolanda out of the kitchen, watching the sway of her ass. Maybe watching Yolanda was the way to get my mind off of the annoyingly attractive woman I was here to protect.

Unfortunately for me, Kelly was more than pretty, and whatever chemical signals she gave off that my conscious mind couldn't register were screwing with me in a way I didn't know how to combat.

Yolanda mounted the stairs.

Focusing on Yolanda hadn't worked. Kelly's strawberry scent was still with me. As I closed my eyes and traced a finger over my lip, the feel of her returned. Inhaling a deep, cleansing breath, I banished the memory and retook my chair. Work had to be the antidote. My laptop woke as I opened it in front of me.

Kelly found me a few minutes later with two glasses of wine. "Can I help?"

I paused the video. "No." Her being close was the problem, not the solution.

She offered me one of the glasses. "A peace offering."

I took it and set it down without drinking any.

She lifted her glass. "To getting to know each other better."

"Yeah," was all I said.

Getting work straightened out before the Fawkes case boiled over and burned me was what I needed. Getting further involved with a Benson, even a pretty one—especially a pretty one—was exactly the wrong prescription right now.

She raised her glass again and glared at me as I looked up. "To getting to know each other better."

I grabbed my glass and raised it a tad. "Yeah." I took a sip. "Now, I have work to do."

She stayed seated across from me, twisting her glass around.

I went back to my laptop and started the video I'd paused when she came in.

"Okay, but I'm sorry my brother was mean to you."

Her statement surprised me. Bensons didn't ever apologize—not in my experience. But then, women would use anything to start a conversation before turning it into the inquisition they really intended.

I didn't fall for the line. After pausing the video again, I looked up, forced a smile, and nodded. "Forget it."

Forgetting the incident was something I'd never accomplish, but discussing it and reliving it were two things I always avoided. As if on cue, a pang went through my knee.

"Can we talk about it?"

"No."

"I'd like to understand."

She wasn't getting it. Persistence was not a good quality at the moment.

I took a deep breath. "I said no, and I meant it. I get that he's your brother and all, but he's an ass. Just drop it."

She huffed and stood. "You don't have to be mean about it." She walked to the kitchen, and a moment later she was climbing the stairs with her wine glass in one hand and the bottle in the other. Why was *no* such a hard concept for her to grasp?

Words never helped when a girl got all emotional like this. She was lashing out, and I didn't have the time, the patience, or anything approaching the right words to resolve anything for her. One tap of the keys, and the video restarted.

FIVE HOURS LATER, MY EYESIGHT WAS BLURRING AND IT WAS DIFFICULT KEEPING my eyes open at all. Reality TV, bank style, was sleep inducing. I still hadn't found anything on the inside video of Gaithersburg that looked like our two Unsubs—the limper with the mask or the girl stupid enough to not wear a mask. Since the driver never got out of the car, we had even less to go on related to her.

Realizing we had nothing on the driver brought up an awkward possibility. We'd thought the Fawkes Crew were amateurs based on the gun play, but that could be a misconception. If they'd sent the driver in to case the locations, we'd never spot her on the surveillance videos. That would absolutely move them out of the amateur category.

After making note of where I'd stopped, I shut down and closed the laptop. I made a round of the doors and windows to check that everything was secure before heading upstairs. Two Advils down the hatch with a bit of water, and I was ready for another night on the floor. A stop in the downstairs bathroom to avoid waking Kelly finished everything on the first floor.

I turned off the hall light and waited twenty seconds for my eyes to acclimate to the dark before slipping into her room. With the stupid star dots she had on the ceiling, her room was brighter than the hallway. I pulled my sleeping cushion of a folded-over comforter from under the bed.

Kelly lay on her back, snoring lightly.

It would have been easy to slip in alongside her and spare myself the painful floor experience, and I considered it for a moment longer than I should have.

She looked angelic under the covers in the dim light with her hair spread across the pillow. But looks could be deceiving. As a Benson, she had evil in her genes in a way that couldn't be undone.

People liked to debate nature versus nurture, but one didn't have to look far to understand that nature always won. It didn't matter how lovingly you treated a tiger as a cub, it would always grow up to be a killer. Heredity always prevailed.

We were all slaves to our heritage. More than physical traits were passed from parent to child. In the Benson case, that included evil intentions and a lack of morals. We'd learned that when they'd forced my Uncle Jack's move to New York. Her father might as well have pulled the trigger.

I resisted the temptation to play the fake boyfriend to the hilt and kiss Kelly before I settled onto my hardwood torture bed.

CHAPTER 14

Kelly

I PRIED MY EYES OPEN THE NEXT MORNING TO THE SOUND OF THE SHOWER running behind the bathroom door. A fuzzy image of last night's wine bottle stared back at me from the nightstand. My leathery tongue and mild headache told me what my eyes couldn't quite make out. It was empty, and I remembered why—my obstinate house guest, or protector, or tormentor, whatever he was.

Adam had slipped in last night without waking me. Probably not a hard feat, given the empty bottle in front of me.

I rolled out of bed, padded over, and opened the door without bothering to knock. I could be as rude as him, if I chose.

He wasn't facing the wall this time, and his eyes were closed as he rinsed the shampoo out of his hair.

I scooted past and into the toilet.

He noticed me as I made my way to the sink. "Morning, Sugarbear."

Nobody was around, so he didn't need the nickname. I started brushing my teeth, with occasional glances in the mirror.

He hadn't turned around, and I was getting the full view this morning—the powerful pecs, the washboard abs, and everything else he'd hidden behind his hands before. He'd be sinfully delectable if it weren't for the awful personality.

Well, maybe not awful, but annoying at least.

I looked down at the sink and concentrated on scouring away the aftereffects of last night's wine with my brush. I bit down on the brush and pulled the Advil bottle from the drawer, laying two on the counter.

"Not talking to me this morning?" he asked.

I spit and rinsed before answering. "You don't answer when I talk to you." I popped the Advil and swallowed with a handful of water.

"I had work to do. And you're not my type."

I turned around and leaned against the counter, challenging him to stay facing me.

"What does that mean?" What the hell did being his type have to do with talking out his problem with Dennis? Or with my family?

"I know your type."

"And what type is that, Mr. Agent Man? Boobs too small and brain too big?"

He laughed. "There's nothing wrong with your boobs, Sugarbear."

Once again he was trying to avoid a direct answer.

"What is your type then?"

"Forget it. You're a nice girl. I'll be out in a minute, and you can have the shower."

"I don't want the shower; I want an answer."

He shook his head. "You can't handle the answer."

"Try me."

"Okay. You're an accountant—"

"Auditor," I corrected.

He waited several seconds. "There. You're doing it already. You can't stand to sit and listen to somebody's complete thought without arguing."

I lolled my head back and forth. "Go ahead." I was guilty of interrupting him, but he'd been wrong.

"You've lived a privileged, Benson life."

I almost interrupted him, but held back. His family was rich too.

"Everything's been handed to you on a platter. You've never had to work for anything, or had anything unfairly denied you, or taken from you."

There was a grudge hidden somewhere behind his words.

I gritted my teeth and waited a few seconds to respond. "I'll have you know that I worked my ass off to get my CPA. School, tests, and two years of slave labor at Arthur and Company. Nobody got me this job at the museum; I earned it. I had a plan, and I executed it."

"Sure, and your Daddy didn't make a call to smooth the way?"

"Of course not. He offered, but I wouldn't let him."

"So for once, Daddy didn't smooth out one of life's bumps for you. You Bensons are all alike. Got a problem? Write a check or make a call, and presto, no more problem."

"And you never got anywhere on your family name?"

His fists clenched. "I got into the Bureau in *spite* of my family name, not because of it."

There was a story behind the statement, but now wasn't the time to explore it.

"So tell me what day of the week today is." He seemed to be making an effort to be calmer.

I shook my head. "What? Can't tell the day of the week without your watch? It's Thursday."

"And that makes it French toast day."

I couldn't tell where the conversation was veering off to. "If you don't like it, you don't have to have any."

"That's what makes you not my type. You have a routine and a plan for everything. You made a plan to get the job. You make a plan for breakfast based on the day of the week."

I clenched my teeth, because he was spot on about my morning routine.

"You probably don't even allow yourself to fart if it's not on the plan. You're incapable of spontaneity, incapable of taking even the slightest risk. You're like a cyborg."

The fucker was smiling. *Smiling*, of all things.

"You think I don't ever do anything spontaneous and take a risk?"

"That's what I said. There's no rain in the forecast, and yet you pack an umbrella in your purse."

"That's called being prepared."

"That's called being anal. I bet you've never done anything outrageous just for the fuck of it. Daddy's perfect little girl, that's who you are."

Now he was being insulting. I huffed. "I can do something outrageous if I want. And as for risky, isn't being the bait on the end of your hook taking a bit of a chance?"

He nodded. "I'll give you that, but that's not what I'm talking about. When was the last time you went skinny dipping?"

I didn't have an answer for that, because I never had.

"I'll bet it's a big day for you when you wear shoes that don't match your outfit."

I crossed my arms and fumed.

"See? Daddy's little princess can't name one just-for-the-fuck-of-it thing she's done in her entire life."

He was being impossible. But his arrows hadn't missed their mark. It hurt to think how right he was about how I'd lived my life. But that could change.

I pulled my nightshirt over my head, strode to the shower door, and joined him. "How's this for just for the fuck of it?" Fear gripped me, and my knees shook as I stood in front of him, more vulnerable than I'd ever been.

His eyes went wide, lust burning in them.

I might have taken outrageous way too far. A quick glance down showed the effect my naked form was having on him. A vascular response they called it—tied to the sympathetic nervous system—something that couldn't be faked or hidden. Blood surged, and his cock grew, as if reaching for me.

My hardened nipples echoed his response, and it wasn't because I was cold.

He took my shoulders and spun me. "Turn around."

I shivered as I waited breathlessly. What would come next? Had I gone too far? He'd successfully pushed my buttons. I was on the knife edge of fear and excitement.

A moment later, he ran the bar of soap over my shoulders and back. "I take back the part about lacking spontaneity." His words were softer now, without the accusatory edge. "You're cold." He pulled me into the warm spray for a moment, mistaking my shivers of fear for a chill.

I pulled my hair out of the way over my shoulder as he washed me. Anticipation replaced fear as the tingles under my skin followed the movement of his hands. The wetness between my legs wasn't entirely due to the shower.

He urged my elbows up, and I raised my arms.

As he soaped my sides, he approached, but didn't reach, the sides of my breasts. Moving down, his soapy hands caressed my legs. "And I don't think your brain is too small either, Sugarbear."

Finally, a nice comment.

"I know you're smart."

And earlier he'd said he liked my boobs, or at least that there wasn't anything wrong with them.

His hands traced a path down my legs. "And a tattoo. You surprise me, Kells."

I giggled as his fingers trailed sparks to the inside of my thighs. I gasped as he came up higher.

He stopped before reaching anything taboo. "You have nice legs too."

It came off as a pleasant and sincere compliment, a distinct change from the way our conversation had started.

"Thank you." The movement of his hands across my skin sent a series of shocks up my spine.

He stood, and I couldn't see behind me, but I felt his cock brush against my ass as he rose. "Sorry."

I played dumb. "For what?"

He didn't answer for a moment. "I just don't want to talk about your asshole brother."

"I wanted to say I'm sorry for what happened to you." I turned around to look into his eyes.

They carried a hurt I couldn't fathom.

I put a hand on his chest. "I'll wait till you're ready to talk about it."

He removed my hand. "You'll have a long wait."

"I can be patient." My risk taking wasn't over yet. "Now will you help me with my front?"

"I better not."

"Scared?"

He leaned toward me.

I backed up.

"That might lead to me fucking you hard against the wall."

"And what if that's what I want?"

My words were completely off-the-charts un-Kelly. They were way beyond anything I'd ever said. And they were unintended, but I couldn't pull them back, and didn't care to try. I found myself inexplicably drawn to this annoying man. I couldn't help but answer his challenge with another of my own.

He offered me the bar of soap and exited the shower.

My shoulders slumped.

He started to towel off. "I don't do gentle. You deserve better."

It sounded like a compliment, and I decided to take it that way. I'd gone from never coming close to shower sex to propositioning my fake boyfriend to take me against the wall, and his answer had been that I "deserved better." What did that mean? His issue with Dennis wasn't the only thing I wanted him to open up about.

Looking out the shower door, I held back the giggle I felt coming up as I watched him work around his hard-on while drying off. He could have hung the towel on it. The man had impressive equipment, and I'd made a definite impression—one he'd managed to resist acting on, but an impression all the same.

He hung up the towel, walked out of the bathroom, and closed the door.

Now I knew where the term *swinging dick* came from. Adrenaline still filled my veins from the encounter as I washed and conditioned my hair. As much as I willed myself to calm down, I couldn't get over the thrill of what had just happened. It had been naughty and exciting—exhilarating even. I would have to get up the nerve to add a smidgen of risky to my repertoire. This morning I felt more alive than I had in months.

As I rinsed the last of the conditioner out of my hair and took up the soap again, I smiled at the progress I'd made with him. I'd gone out on a dangerous limb, and we'd almost had a conversation. The bar of soap glided over and under my breasts, and I closed my eyes and imagined it was his hand. What would it feel like after all this time to be caressed by a real man's hands? But, what did *I don't do gentle* mean?

He was a real man, all right—fast to act and slow to talk, a gun-toting modern cowboy. No, with the manners he had, knight fit him better than cowboy. He did carry a gun, but he wasn't the tobacco chewing and spitting type.

With my eyes still closed, I ran my knight's imaginary hand down between my legs, back and forth—a few times more than I needed to get myself clean.

If only.

He wasn't as bad as I'd made him out to be last night. He was just one of those macho, no-words types. But he had opened himself to the possibility of talking about things, and that was progress. He'd said I might have to wait a while, but at least *no* had left his vocabulary. I could be patient.

~

Adam

Kelly was a surprise and a half—a lot more ballsy than I'd figured, and even a small tattoo on her ankle.

I shook my head as I dressed quickly, re-stowed my sleeping setup under the bed, and trotted downstairs to fix breakfast.

She wasn't as simple to understand as she'd seemed. I'd have to keep that in mind going forward.

Yolanda was on the way out as I descended the stairs, and I wished her a good day.

Cyborg? I'd gone a little overboard in my criticism of Kelly upstairs, and it wouldn't pay to have the assignment go south because I'd intentionally pissed her off. I pulled eggs from the fridge and cracked them into a bowl. Her Thursday routine breakfast seemed like a reasonable way to broker a peace.

She arrived as I was turning the last of the toast in the pan. "You didn't have to make that. I could try something different. Yolanda has some Raisin Bran in the cupboard."

"I'll throw it out if you want."

"No. It smells delicious. I just meant..."

I understood her unfinished sentence just fine. We were both building bridges this morning instead of burning them down. "It's almost ready."

She set the table and brought out the maple syrup. "Where are you taking me?"

"Work, of course."

"I mean at lunch."

I brought the plate of French toast over to the table and sat. I'd forgotten my suggestion that we have lunch together today. "I can't. We had another bank robbery yesterday that I have to work on."

Her face fell. "I guess it's another soup day."

"Sorry. A teller was shot during the robbery, and Neil needs my help if we're going to catch these guys before someone else gets hurt."

She split the toast pieces between us and poured maple syrup on hers. "Want some?"

"Nah." I checked the fridge and found strawberry jam. The memory of her smell in my arms put a smile on my face and made the jam a clear choice for me.

"What are you smiling about?" she asked as I returned to the table.

"Nothing."

She accepted the lie and took a bite of breakfast.

"I'll try to make time another day," I added, meaning it.

"I understand. That's more important."

After cutting another bite, I tried another bridge-building question. "What's the story that goes with the tattoo?"

Her face dropped. "A reminder that life is short. My cousin died way before her time."

"I'm sorry."

We finished breakfast and made the drive to her work without either of us taking verbal jabs at the other.

"Sorry about the cyborg comment this morning," I said as I opened the car door for her to exit.

She climbed out, and the kiss we exchanged wasn't short or awkward.

As I drove toward the field office, I traced my lips with my thumb. She'd put feeling into the kiss, and I'd reciprocated. The scent of strawberry lingered with me.

Once I settled in at the office, Neil and I spent the morning reviewing the video of the latest bank job. We'd started working backwards, hoping to catch sight of the woman casing the location, but still came up empty. When I returned from a quick lunch, Neil waved me over.

"We finally got a lead," he announced.

I wended my way over to his desk. "Tell me the DNA got a hit."

He nodded and smiled. "Yeah, but you're not going to believe it."

"Does it give us an address to try?"

"She's in the missing persons database—a kidnapping case years ago in Phoenix." He handed me the single sheet from forensics.

I read the name and had to sit down.

Fuck.

Deborah E. Benson of Phoenix, Arizona. Looking farther down the page, the parents were listed as Seth and Marjorie Benson.

I could breathe again, and I relaxed back into my chair.

It wasn't the Bensons I knew and hated. Their father was Lloyd Benson, and they all lived in Los Angeles. Just a fucked-up coincidence—Benson was a common enough name. The problem with a hit on missing persons was that it gave us no addresses or associations to check to find her.

After a few more deep breaths, my heart slowed. I had to get better about this. Just the fucking name sent me up a wall—not exactly a calm, cool, professional response.

Neil stretched his neck. "I sent word to the Phoenix Field Office to notify next of kin that we got a hit." He laughed. "I wouldn't want to be the one going out to the family, though. *Hi, Mrs. Benson, we have good news and bad news. The good news is that your daughter is alive. The bad news is that she's turned to a life of crime and won't be out of prison before she's fifty*. Pretty weird, huh?"

"Yeah, weird is right."

Since I was the official lead, I had some discretion on tasks. "How about I redo the Falls Church video and you take Gaithersburg?"

"That works for me."

We had to re-review the video from both prior jobs now that we had the woman's face, to see if we'd missed her casing either of the locations. On the first pass, we'd only been looking for the guy with the limp. More boring but critical work lay ahead if we were going to catch the Fawkes Crew.

At the end of the day, Neil got off the phone and turned to me. "The team on the Phoenix kidnapping is flying out. They'll be here by lunch tomorrow."

Great, more time out of our day.

"And get this," he added. "There's another Boston connection."

I looked up. "Yeah?"

"One of them is Liz Parsons."

"The Boston bombing?"

"The same, so be nice."

Elizabeth Parsons had been injured in a bombing meant to kill both her and her partner, Ashley Newton—now Benson. It was the most significant bomb attack aimed at federal law enforcement since the Oklahoma City bombing, so everybody in the Bureau knew her name.

First Ashley Benson taking our SMK case up to the director and telling us how to handle it, and now Liz Parsons getting involved in the Guy Fawkes robberies? What was coming next—the director himself supervising our stakeouts on the trafficking case? This was unreal.

~

Kelly

First thing at my desk, I checked the email account.

I let out a relieved sigh when the page showed nothing new. How many more days would I have to dread coming to work?

Without an email from the Ghost to torment me, this morning's shower encounter took over my thoughts.

What was it about Adam that turned me on? He was so unlike any of the guys I'd dated, not even the same species.

"I don't do gentle. You deserve better," he'd said. The words ran through my brain on constant repeat. The *don't do gentle* comment reeked of a dangerous warning.

I left for an early lunch and dialed the one person I could ask about this.

Serena answered quickly, "Hey, what's wrong?"

"Why does something have to be wrong for me to call my big sister?"

She snorted. "This is only the second time you've ever called me during working hours, and the last time was because you'd gotten that creepy note."

Was I that predictable?

"Ashley said she got you fixed up with a bodyguard. Is that working out?"

I leaned against the building and sighed. "She was a big help."

"So what's wrong?"

I wasn't sure how to ask this. "What if a guy suggests..." I couldn't bring myself to say it.

She waited a few seconds before asking, "What?"

"Uh...rough sex?"

She laughed. "You think just because Duke has ink and ear gauges he's rough with me?"

I hung my head. "I didn't mean—"

"Messing with ya, Kell. He hasn't hurt you, has he?"

"No. No. Nothing like that. We haven't even... I just didn't know how to take it when he said something."

"Okay. Here's the deal. He can be rough for one of two reasons. If it's anger at you or women in general, he's mean, and you run like hell."

I shook my head, though she couldn't see me. "He's not like that."

"Good... Hard, rough sex can also be a primal, dominant-male thing—

him letting his passion loose. Here's the question for you: The dominant lion or wolf will fight to the death to protect his mate. Do you want that one, or the one that runs from a fight with his tail between his legs?"

When she put it like that, it sounded like there was only one possible answer.

"You think it's that simple?"

"If you're too scared to try, you don't deserve to run with the leader of the pack. Instead you should settle for the runt of the litter. Me, I'll take the passion of Randy Rough over Milton Milquetoast any day. You can't fight evolution. Give in to your inner cavewoman."

"I'm just not sure…"

"How will you know until you try it? For my money, any woman who hasn't enjoyed an occasional rough doggy session hasn't been properly mounted."

I thought for a moment. The word *rough* scared me, and *mounted* sounded more like elk rutting than bedroom sex.

"Who is this guy anyway?" she asked.

No way was I going there. "Just a guy I met."

"Good for you. It's about time you loosened up a little and met a real man."

After we finished talking, the lesson between the lines became clear. In Serena's terms, I didn't know what I was missing, because I'd never dated a *real* man.

CHAPTER 15

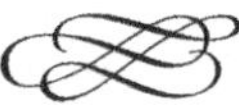

Adam

The next day, it was almost lunchtime when Boxer picked up his desk phone. "Sure. Send 'em up."

He turned to me. "They're here. Let's do the dog-and-pony show in three." Conference room three was small and set up for video on the screen.

A few minutes later, the two west coast agents arrived, looking for Neil and towing roller bags behind them.

He settled them in the conference room while I made a pit stop in the restroom.

When I returned, Neil was gathering up files from his desk. "A heads up, we're waiting for a family member—due at noon."

I shrugged. It was unusual, but not unheard of. Sitting down, I resigned myself to more bank reality TV watching. After another half hour on the video treadmill, I went to refresh my coffee.

Neil waved me over when I returned. "The relative is here. Let's get this over with."

I followed Neil into the conference room. I realized immediately that I'd been wrong to assume the Phoenix Bensons were separate from the LA Bensons—Dennis Benson was in the room. The scene knocked the wind out of me for a second. But fuck it, I could handle anything he could dish out. He was on my turf now. He had his daddy behind him, but I had the Bureau.

Neil and I exchanged cards with special agents Parsons and Newsom.

"Special Agent Adam Cartwright," I said as I handed my card to my nemesis, Dennis Benson.

After my ACL injury in the fight with him, my knee was never the same. I couldn't play my senior year, and any prospect of professional football evaporated.

He handed me his card with a phony smile. "It's been a while."

"It has," I replied.

Parsons' eyes narrowed as she took in our exchange. "Neil, why don't you run us through what you have?"

Neil sat. "Adam's lead on this."

She shrugged.

I rubbed my knee as I sat and opened my laptop to send the first video to the screen. "Let's start with the outdoor feed."

The image wasn't crystal clear, but it was what it was.

"Here's where they pull up." I stopped it where the suspects' car pulled up and then started again. "Two suspects get out, and the driver remains." The two moved across the frame to the area of the door. "One vehicle, three robbers this time. Two go inside, and one drives. Next we go to the inside feeds."

I changed it to the inside feed, which was a split screen with four camera angles. "Here we have a man and a woman. The woman is your vic." I moved the video forward a bit and stopped again. "Here they pull out guns and start issuing commands."

All four screens showed the panic that ensued. I stopped and started again. "He fires one shot into the ceiling for effect, and the woman goes to the tellers to collect the cash."

Looking over, I could see the concern in Dennis's face. He was getting the idea now. This was no school fight. His relative was carrying a gun in a serious crime and headed for real jail time. So much for the Benson reputation. It would finally get the update it deserved.

"Hold it," Newsom said.

I halted the playback.

She pointed. "Why is the man masked and the woman not?"

I shrugged. "She's not smart enough is my guess." I would have rather stated the obvious and said it was because she was an arrogant Benson, but I held that back. Nothing they ever did came back to haunt them the way they deserved.

I started the video again. "These three are amateurs, dangerous amateurs. The driver and the man have pulled off two other jobs nearby, but this is the first time they've brought her along." I pointed at the woman on the screen. "She's our best lead so far to get this group. Let's go on and see the rest."

The video continued as the woman put the gun in her coat pocket, then stopped, probably surprised, and looked straight at the camera for a second before going down the line, collecting cash in a duffle bag. That face shot and the DNA had given us our first good lead on this crew.

I ran it forward through the cash collection and stopped again. "This is where it went wrong."

When I restarted it, you could clearly see the woman bring the money back to the man, who then pivoted and fired at the teller, which caused the rest of them to hit the floor.

"What's the teller's condition?" Parsons asked.

"Stable," Neil replied.

"Good thing he was a terrible shot. We've been worried about exactly this, because the guy likes to shoot his gun," I added.

"Why did he shoot?" Newsom asked. "Get anything from the witness statements?" The question was a good one, but one we still couldn't answer.

Parsons leaned over to whisper to Dennis, who nodded at the comment.

I shrugged. "Don't know. Maybe she said something or moved too fast. So that's the first screw-up, and here's the second."

I restarted the video and on the screen, the pair left, the man followed by the woman.

"What did we miss?" Parsons asked.

I backed it up and went forward in slow motion. The man turned, and the woman leaned over a bit, then straightened and followed.

I would have missed it too, except that the loan officer had pointed it out.

"See it?" I backed up and restarted it.

On the second try, Parsons saw it. "She spit on the floor."

Neil spoke up. "That's right. Forensics pulled DNA from that spit, and that's when you got the call."

"Why did she do that?" Newsom asked.

I reverted to my previous answer. "Don't know. Like I said, stupid. Once we catch her, we've got a sure conviction on the robbery and attempted murder thanks to DNA, because we got no prints at any of the scenes."

Dennis cringed at the statement, which gave me a moment of satisfaction.

"The car?" Parsons asked.

Neil shook his head. "Stolen plates, no defining decals, and a dent in the right front is all we have to go on so far."

"Video of them casing it ahead of time?" Newsom asked.

I huffed. "As hard as it is for you west coast whiz kids to believe, we do know what we're doing. We've checked the old footage back six weeks. So far nothing, but we're still working it. Like I said, amateurs. This is a new crew. They got a little money out of the heists, so they'll be back and shooting other people if we don't find them first. Sorry you had to make the trip out, but we've got it from here, and we'll let you know when we catch her."

Dennis looked ready to blow, and he deserved it.

"Kidnapping takes priority," Newsom said.

"That was yesterday," Neil pointed out. "Already ran it up to the AD. Because of the shots fired, the robbery takes priority, and we have the lead." Neil hadn't wanted to get pushed aside after we'd done all the heavy lifting so far.

"Assistant Director," Parsons told Dennis, explaining what *AD* meant.

"What do you have that can help us find her?" I asked.

"Nothing at all," Parsons answered. "Kidnapped at five years old. At the time it was presumed to be a single kidnapper who died when we tried to apprehend him after the ransom pickup. When no further communications came, the child was assumed deceased. Until now."

Neil looked at Dennis. "And no communications with the family since then?"

Dennis shook his head. "Not a one."

If there had been, I wasn't sure he would have shared it anyway.

I shut down the video. "Thank you for your time, then."

Dennis Benson wasn't used to getting shut out of anything, and it showed. "I'd like updates as you get more."

I paused. "I'll let you know when we catch her." That was all I intended, and maybe more than he deserved.

"She's my cousin, and a victim here," he complained.

"She's a suspect," I shot back. "The victim is the lady in the hospital who took a bullet."

Parsons interceded. “She’s both. The kidnapping is still open, and she’s the victim in that. You can send me the updates, and I’ll pass them along.”

I gave in. “Sure.”

“And,” Dennis added, “I’d like a hard copy of the frame where we see her face.”

Parsons beat me to it. “Not a problem. I’m sure the family would like to see what she looks like after all these years.”

Ten minutes later, we were through with them.

I made a point of not shaking Benson’s hand as they left. If I’d known yesterday when we first got the results that the woman in the video was actually related to him, I probably would have skipped this meeting.

“You didn’t need to be so hard-assed with them,” Neil said.

“He’s an asshole.”

“Who?”

“Dennis Benson.”

He stopped me with a hand to my shoulder. “Is this more of the family feud you told me about?”

I nodded. “With him, yes.”

“Parsons was right. She may be the perp in this crime, but unless we have something that says otherwise, she’s still the vic in the kidnapping.”

I nodded. “Got it. Empathy for the vic’s family. I’ll write that down for next time.”

“Hold it right there,” Neil said firmly as he closed the door. “I’ll say it again. Parsons was right on this. You want to tell me what is really going on between you two?”

“Never met her before.”

He moved back and leaned against the table. “That’s not who I’m talking about and you know it. What is it between you and Benson?” He folded his arms.

I’d never shared that with anybody at the Bureau and wasn’t about to start now. “A beef when we were in college, is all.”

“Well, get past it or take yourself off the case. With your family name, you don’t have any spare goodwill to fuck up, and I’m not about to go down with you. After Boston, Parsons has ears in high places. You’ll get burned if you go pushing her buttons. You’ll lose that matchup every time.”

Of course he had to remind me of Uncle Jack’s legacy, which was now mine to live down. “You’re right.”

"Damned straight I am."

I opened the door to leave, but turned back to my partner. "Thanks. I'll keep it together."

"And I'm here for you when you want to lighten the load and tell me what happened between you two."

"Another time, maybe."

An hour later, my cell lit up. I'd entered the numbers for Parsons and Newsom after they'd left. The call was from Parsons.

I took Neil's advice to play nice with her. "Hi, Liz. I didn't expect to hear from you so soon."

"We're waiting for our flight, and I just thought I'd mention two things."

"Sure, what?"

"You might consider that there could be another side to the story you're not aware of."

"What story?"

"The reason my vic is now your suspect." Somehow we were back on the idea that the video lied and Deborah Benson wasn't an accomplice in the bank job.

"One doesn't come to mind. The video was pretty obvious." Parsons didn't know the Bensons like I did, or she wouldn't be suggesting bullshit like that.

"Just worth thinking about. And another thing..."

I waited.

"There's obviously some history between you and Dennis, and I wanted to get your side of the story."

My gut tightened as I sensed a trap. "Just an incident in college. It won't alter how we handle things with our suspects and your victim."

"That's good to hear."

Translation, I'd walked into the trap and said something she could use against me later.

"What did he say?" I asked.

"Nothing in particular. He joked that if he disappeared, we should put you at the top of the suspect list."

"Figures he'd say that, but it's not that bad," I lied. Messing him up someday had been on my long-term to-do list. Vengeance could wait, but it wouldn't be forgotten. When I got through with him, he'd know payback was a bitch.

"Good to hear. Also, the family would like to keep a lid on Deborah being found—at least for now."

Once again the Bensons were dictating terms to the Bureau, and it sucked.

"Is that all?" I asked as nicely as I could.

"For now. It was nice meeting you. Good luck, and please keep me up to date."

"Sure. Have a nice flight."

We hung up, and the reason for the call was crystal clear: Keep her informed or else. The fucking Bensons thought they ran the world.

Well, Patty Hearst had come from a powerful family, but in the end the FBI had been more powerful, and she went to prison. The Bensons were going to learn the same lesson. After being kidnapped at five, Deborah might have suffered a lot, but her actions now showed she was a true Benson: breeding trumped all.

Kelly

My phone rang with my big brother Dennis's picture on the screen.

"Hey, Dennis," I answered. "I hear from Serena you've got a new girl."

He ignored my comment. "I flew in last night for a customer meeting. Want to do dinner?"

He was always changing the subject on me. Whether it came from being the boss at work or just being the oldest among us, he always had to set the agenda.

I wasn't prepared for his question. "Dinner?" Having Adam shadowing me was a complication.

"Yeah, you know, food, wine, family."

I couldn't just refuse... "Sure." Adam could probably watch from outside the restaurant.

"Is everything all right?"

"Sure. I've just got work stuff going on." I couldn't bring up the Ghost.

"It's your town," he said. "You pick a place, and I'll call you later."

The Italian restaurant Adam had taken me came instantly to mind. Had I liked it solely because of the food, or also the company? I settled on the food. "If you like Italian, I've got a new place you might like. How's Josh doing working for Daddy?"

Dennis started filling me in on the latest.

Asking about Josh lowered my apprehension about dinner. It would make it easier to avoid my current predicament at work if I kept the topic on the rest of the family.

Dennis had a way of needling things out of me that I didn't mean to disclose—a big brother superpower of sorts. But I would be okay if I kept him busy answering my questions, and his avoiding the question of a new girl in his life gave me the tool to divert as needed. Poking at an area he didn't want to talk about always got to him—it was my little sister superpower.

He didn't mind dissecting *our* relationships, but his were a different matter. It wasn't fair. I could be as persistent as him, if I needed to. I'd get something out of him over the course of a meal.

He deserved a good woman in his life after how disastrous his marriage to Melissa had been.

CHAPTER 16

ADAM

AS I COMBED THROUGH THE FALLS CHURCH VIDEO AGAIN, LOOKING FOR THE Benson girl, I couldn't get Dennis's face and Neil's admonition out of my mind.

The fact that he'd brought that Parsons woman ate at me. Because of her I had to be deferential to Dennis Benson and treat him with kid gloves. The guy deserved to be treated like the ass he was, not some fucking prince of the realm.

My cell rang with the picture I'd taken of Kelly while she wasn't watching—even from the side she was stunning. "Adam Carter."

"Adam, my brother is in town," she started.

"Really?" I had no desire to go into anything regarding my earlier meeting with Dennis.

"He wants to have dinner, and I was wondering—"

I cut her off. "No!" I said it perhaps more strongly than I should have, but I'd had enough of the asshole for one day—fuck it, for a month, or a year.

"You didn't even let me finish. I already told him yes, and I wanted to know if you would join us."

"You're not meeting him for dinner."

"You can't just tell me that. He's my brother, for God's sake."

"I can, and I just did. Remember the rules."

"But you can't say that."

I hesitated. I knew only one thing that would get her to back down for sure. "If you want to terminate your protection right now and be shipped off to your daddy, just say the word." Giving up her freedom and being sent back to California seemed to be the only thing that truly terrified her.

"That's not fair. This doesn't have to do with keeping me safe or catching the Ghost. This is just you throwing a fit because you don't like him. You also can't do that. If you lose me, you've lost your whole case."

All the Bensons were totally fucking with me now. Dennis couldn't learn of my assignment with Kelly until it was over. It would send him into overload, and if he pulled his sister out of town, that would sink our chances of finding SMK anytime soon. It wasn't worth the risk.

"What would you tell him about me if we had dinner? You can't tell him about SMK. You can't tell him we're dating, so how would you explain me being there?"

"You could be outside, and watch from a distance."

"I'm not letting you out of my sight. That's the job, and besides, he'd recognize me."

"What about your partner?"

"No. He's not available tonight, and you know what I told you about recognizing him. He stays in the background." I didn't know for sure that Neil wasn't available, but I didn't want her meeting him anyway.

The pause indicated I'd stumped her, and for good reason. There wasn't a good way to handle it.

"Okay," she finally sighed. "I'll tell him I can't make it. You know this would be so much easier if you two would bury the hatchet."

I knew this was one grudge neither of us would give up. "Some things are easier said than done."

"I could help, if you'd tell me your side."

Once again she was picking at the scab, but I wasn't about to let her rip it off. She thought there were sides to what had happened, like an argument that could be negotiated.

"Maybe later." It was the easiest way to let her down. She hadn't been a part of it, and for some reason I didn't feel like telling her the truth that would surely shatter bonds with her family.

"Okay. Later."

~

KELLY

HE'D BEEN A JERK ABOUT DINNER WITH DENNIS, BUT WHEN HE BROUGHT UP THE problems, they did seem legitimate.

I dialed Dennis back.

"Sorry, Dennis. I can't do dinner tonight after all."

"That's too bad. I really wanted to hear what's wrong."

"Nothing's wrong," I told him. It was worth a shot.

"I can hear it in your voice, little one."

I took a calming breath to keep from blowing up. "I'm not little anymore."

"You'll always be my little sister, and I'll always take care of you."

"Fine. When I have twins, you can come over and be in charge of diaper changing."

"Are you pregnant?"

"Get real. What are you in town for anyway?"

He hesitated. "Customer meetings." The intonation of the answer wasn't the usual confident Dennis, and earlier he'd told me it was a customer meeting, not multiple.

"What are you hiding?"

He ignored my query. "Don't you want to tell me what's bothering you?"

"What's bothering me is that you won't tell me about your new girlfriend."

That got him to stop the attack for a moment. "How about if I stay another day and we do dinner tomorrow?"

I didn't even try to make up an excuse for tomorrow. "I'm busy."

"I get it. You don't want to talk to your brother."

"That guilt trip doesn't work on me. I'm glad you finally have someone in your life. Call back when you're ready to tell me about her."

He ignored my jab. "If not dinner, how about breakfast tomorrow?"

"And you'll tell me about her?"

He didn't respond to that. Pestering him about his girlfriend finally did the trick, and we got off the phone without another request to meet him before he left town.

What was it with guys anyway? Dennis refused to talk about the new flame he obviously had. He hadn't even attempted to deny it.

LATER THAT AFTERNOON, MR. HEIDEN CALLED SEVERAL OF US INTO HIS OFFICE.

"Inventory assignments," he told us, handing us each a sheet of paper. "We're working Natural History tomorrow. No sick calls, and be on time. We need all the positions manned." He used the word *manned*, even though we were mostly women here, but only Kirby had ever objected.

I checked the sheet. I was covering the employee entrance.

Heiden sat back down. "The facility will be closed to the public, and we need to keep this to a single day."

Several of us nodded, but nobody said anything.

"Benson, a word."

That was Heiden-speak for the others to leave, which they did.

He pointed at the chair.

I took the seat, unaware of what I might have done.

"You know," he started, "last year a moon rock went missing."

"I didn't know."

I'd heard a rumor, but nothing definite, and the moon rocks were a constant source of conjecture—everything from how many Neil Armstrong might have hidden in his socks and taken home, to if they were even really from the moon.

"Since all the alarms will be disabled during the inventory, the exit is our weak point. We're going to use an extra sensitive x-ray scanner, one of those airport types. It'll be manned by two guards from OPS, and I want you to oversee it."

I nodded.

"If either of them so much as coughs and looks away, I want you to demand a rescan. Everybody goes through the metal detectors, and everything, no matter how small, goes through x-ray. No exceptions. Understood?"

"Crystal clear."

I walked out of his office light on my feet. I was being entrusted with what he considered the most important of our tasks tomorrow. The rest of the team would be watching people check items off lists all day long.

But then I had a thought… After reaching my desk, I checked the Ukrainian email account again. I was relieved to find nothing had shown up. Being told to orchestrate something while hanging out all day with a bunch of guards would have been insanely difficult.

~

Adam

After the meeting with Parsons and Benson, Dempsey had decided I should take the afternoon watch on the trafficking case. Luckily, Harper had gotten approval for the rental of a unit across and two houses down from the suspects' location that had just become available, so we were out of our cars now.

The view of the street wasn't as clear, but my vantage point from the chair was more comfortable. The previous tenants had apparently not trained their pets well, and I'd already emptied the last of the air freshener spray.

Tomorrow I'd consider a nose clip instead.

A tipster had reported a tan cube van on its way here from San Diego, but the last tip on a vehicle headed here had come up empty. This house was consuming so many man-hours the ASAC was considering paring back the surveillance from physical to electronic only.

My phone rang, and I checked the street quickly before pulling it out. The screen held a Boston area code and a number I didn't recognize.

"Cartwright," I answered.

"Adam, Ashley Benson here. I wanted to follow up on your meeting with Dennis Benson."

Apparently the Bensons had already been communicating. "What about it?"

"He and Liz Parsons don't know anything about the SMK case and the protection you're providing for his sister."

"Okay?" It was good news that she hadn't told them.

"Have you told Kelly about her cousin?"

"I wasn't planning to. She doesn't need more on her plate right now."

"Good. Do you have a moment to discuss the kidnapping aspect?"

She didn't seem to get that it was irrelevant to the bank robberies.

"I guess. I'm cooling my heels on surveillance now."

"That sucks. Me too, but it's the job, isn't it? I'm sitting on a sex trafficking waypoint out here, and I have a few minutes, if you've got time to chat."

I was surprised to hear that with her exalted status she still pulled the same shitty surveillance duty as I did. "Same here, for the run-up to this year's Operation Cross Country."

Operation Cross Country was a coordinated nationwide sweep we'd started conducting annually in 2008 to get human traffickers rounded up. "What's up?"

"I'd hate for this case to cause your family any more grief." That hit a nerve, but I didn't understand what she was getting at.

I rechecked the street just as a van pulled up in front of our suspects' house.

"I gotta go, got activity here." I hung up immediately and dialed Neil while running downstairs to my car.

"Boxer," he answered.

"Tan van just pulled up."

"I'm on the way."

The phone went back in my pocket as I slowed to a walk and opened the door to the street.

Walking across the street, I made it into my car before the van driver restarted his vehicle.

One of the suspects came out of the house and started his car as the van pulled away.

Nobody else had gotten out to enter the house, but they could be going to a drop-off point somewhere else.

"Radio check," Neil's voice came in through my earpiece.

"Pulling out now," I responded.

At the intersection, the van went right, and the suspect's car went straight.

I chose to follow the van.

"I'm two blocks away," Neil said. If this guy went very far, we would have to trade positions or risk getting spotted.

I pressed talk. "The van turned right on Ninth."

"Got it."

A few seconds later, the van surprised me by stopping again. This time it was clear it wasn't our van. The driver opened the side door, carried a package to the door, tapped his handheld scanner, and remounted the van.

"Neil, false alarm. The van is only package delivery."

"Shit. Okay. I'm turning around."

Before I started back to my observation perch, a text arrived on my phone, and I stayed parked to read it.

PARSONS: Read the BENSNAP file. I'll get you access

She has a bug up her ass about something.

Another thing for my to-do list in all my free time.

Back on the suspects' street, it took two trips around the block before I found another parking space on the same side of the street as them, just not as close.

Upstairs, I settled in for more boring street watching and popped the top on another Pepsi. With nothing going on, I hefted my laptop and logged into records retrieval.

Looking up BENSNAP got me to the file with a surprise. It was marked *Special Access - Restricted,* meaning it wasn't available Bureau-wide. It was her kidnap case. The Deborah Benson kidnapping had apparently been high profile enough when it happened that the case merited a name from headquarters in addition to its case number—another parallel to Patty Hearst.

The system demanded I re-verify my badge number and fill in another field for referring agent name, which was something I'd never come across before.

E. Parsons didn't work. I pulled her card out of my wallet and entered her full name, which opened up access to the file. This was a level beyond what I normally dealt with.

It wasn't a large file as kidnapping cases went, and I started at the beginning with periodic checks of the street below.

The surprise came in the first pages.

Uncle Jack had been the lead agent on the case, something I hadn't known.

That he could have been on the case wasn't surprising in itself, as he'd been on a lot of cases in Phoenix before transferring to New York. What was curious, though, was that neither Uncle Jack nor Dad had ever mentioned it.

The stink of it had been that he'd screwed up big time on something and been run out of Phoenix, although I'd never gotten the details. Then, to add to his legacy, he'd been outed during his undercover with the New York mob. That wasn't the entire problem, though. Two other undercover agents had died the same week, and the Bureau's determination had been that Uncle Jack had talked, and his loose tongue had gotten the others killed.

Neither of the other agents had known about other undercover assets, which is how it was supposed to be, but Uncle Jack had researched the other cases before going in. He shouldn't have volunteered for the undercover. The rule was always to compartmentalize so one agent couldn't compromise another.

He'd knowingly broken the rule, and that was why my family name was mud in the Bureau. Two good agents down, and both of them his fault.

As I started reading the case file, I envisioned the five-year-old Benson girl, abducted, scared out of her wits. The image made my gut clench. But the face I saw wasn't what I expected. The face my mind put on that little girl was Kelly's. I blinked it away, but returning to the words on the page brought a younger version of my current protectee to mind.

She is just my current protectee, isn't she?

I closed the laptop and went back to my boring street surveillance. The thought of Kelly being abducted threatened to make me puke.

The file could wait.

CHAPTER 17

Kelly

Adam kissed my lips when I arrived at the curb.

This time I didn't resist, but wrapped my free arm around him and gave him more than a peck.

His arms tightened around me.

Being held close to him soothed my worries. If this is what I could look forward to with a real man for a boyfriend, I needed to get more serious about finding one after this was over.

Adam's hand ran up my side, and his thumb traced the underside of my breast. He held the kiss longer than yesterday—much longer as his thumb moved to circle my nipple.

A shiver of nervous excitement ran through me at the touch. I pulled myself closer and shifted to the side to rub my hip against his crotch. My heart thundered with the sheer naughtiness of doing this in public.

Serena's comment about running with the leader of the pack came back to me.

The boys at school had never made me feel like this. It was always just a hug and a kiss, and never in public. Kelly Benson had always been a proper girl, and proper girls controlled themselves. The guys I went out with had understood the meaning of *reserved* and acted accordingly. None of them had been leader-of-the-pack types.

If this was the most risqué I'd ever been in public. Maybe I deserved what Adam had accused me of in the shower.

He released me and opened the car door.

I slid in and closed my eyes to catch my breath, searching my memory for any time I'd done something as dangerous before. When I couldn't come up with anything, my eyes opened to the realization of how pathetically boring and safe my life had been up until now. Getting felt up in public didn't sound super risky, but it had felt that way to me.

I noticed Adam scanning the crowd as he walked around to the driver's side.

"Was that better?" I asked after he'd shut the door. I almost asked why he'd stopped. I hadn't wanted it to end. There was a feeling of safety in his arms that I couldn't quite figure out.

The smile Adam wore was contagious. "Much better, Sugarbear."

He nodded almost imperceptibly toward the Metro entrance. "The same girl is watching us. Do you think she bought it?" I still couldn't yet tell if he was acting, or if he felt what I did.

I glanced over in time to catch Kirby turning down the street. "She's not looking our way."

"She was." He pulled into traffic.

He turned north toward the Mall. "Anything new in the email account?"

"No. I checked before leaving."

He shook his head and sighed. "He wanted the inventory information for a reason. Isn't that tomorrow?"

"We start tomorrow with Natural History, but the whole process takes about two weeks. We do it a building or two at a time with a few days in between each."

"So that one's not his target if he didn't give you anything to do. What comes after that?"

"After that we move on to the African American Museum, and the National Gallery of Art on Wednesday."

We traveled several blocks before he spoke again. "How did your brother take it?"

"You mean me canceling dinner? Or the news that I'm dating you?"

He did a quick double-take at me before a chuckle overcame him. "Nice try."

"He suspects I'm hiding something."

"Maybe you're not as good a liar as he is."

My fingers dug into my thigh as I looked out the window and ignored him.

We stopped at a traffic light. "That's uncalled for, and you know it," I shot back.

He shrugged. "According to you."

I folded my arms and watched the people on the sidewalk go by—headed home after work or out to shop and get a bite to eat.

We passed a couple walking hand in hand, about our age. The next couple wasn't holding hands, but the expression on her face as she talked to him said it all. And the next couple looked the same.

I turned back toward Adam. "Why do you have to be such an ass?"

"Me the ass? You talked to him today. What did he have to say about what happened between us? He's the grade-A, number-one asshole."

"We didn't get into it. I wasn't supposed to talk about you, remember?"

He kept his eyes forward with a clenched jaw.

I kept after him. "I'm not supposed to even know you, so why don't you tell me about it?"

For about a block he didn't say anything. "What would you like for dinner tonight?" He twisted the silver ring he wore—the one with the star on it.

Back to square one. "I don't feel like cooking. How about Chinese? There's a place on P Street, to the left."

He nodded.

I texted Yolanda. If she was still at work, her boss didn't like her on the phone.

ME: Picking up Chinese - want some?

Her answer was prompt.

YOLANDA: Nanjing chicken pls

It didn't take long to reach the restaurant and order more than enough for all of us. Somehow Chinese takeout always created a ton of leftovers.

Adam hadn't said a word since I'd prodded him about Dennis. He twisted the ring again as we sat in the tiny waiting area's red plastic chairs.

"If your ring's too tight, I have a guy who can size it for you."

He pulled his hand away. "It's fine."

A two-word response was better than none. "What's the significance of the star?"

He looked away.

I waited him out.

"It's the Dallas Cowboys logo." He scanned the street again.

"I would have figured you for a Redskins fan."

He didn't answer.

"You played in college, right?"

"Until I tore my ACL."

"Do you miss it? Playing, I mean."

"I'll be watching the street." He rose and left, once again not answering a simple question.

Men.

~

Adam

I walked outside and looked up and down the street. Nothing out of the ordinary struck me, but I had the feeling I'd missed something on the way here. I hadn't seen anyone following us. The parked cars on the street were all empty. The foot traffic was what passed for normal in this section of the District, yet the itch didn't go away.

A few minutes later, Kelly came out with the bags of food, and I opened the door for her. "Smells good."

She slid into the seat wordlessly.

We had perfected the fake relationship. Anybody on the street watching us would know exactly what was going on: I was in the doghouse.

I got in on my side and started the car before speaking. "I'm sorry about what I said. I was out of line."

She didn't look over. "It's not a problem."

Bullshit.

I put my hand out to her. "Forgive me. I'll try to be better."

She took a deep breath before accepting my hand. "I get that I'm just a job to you. But when you attack my family, it hurts."

The words were hard to hear and harder to accept. "Kells, I'll do my best, and don't ever think you're just a job to me." I didn't say more, because that was already too much, and even I didn't understand what I meant.

She squeezed my hand before letting go. "We should go before the food gets cold."

I checked my mirror and pulled into traffic. Another careful sweep and I was doubly sure we weren't being followed, but the itch didn't abate.

Why had I just apologized to a Benson for telling her the truth? The girl was screwing with my mind. Apologies were for losers.

She pointed left. "The house is that way."

"Just making sure we're not being followed." My grip on the wheel tightened—screwing with my mind was right.

She nodded. "Just checking."

~

Kelly

Yolanda joined us shortly after we got to the house with the food. We gathered around the table and dug in. Before long she spooned more rice onto her plate. "This is hotter than I remember."

Reminding her that she'd had the same complaint last month wouldn't help.

"Try the beef with broccoli," Adam suggested.

Instead, she added another helping of the Nanjing chicken she was complaining about. "They must have changed the recipe."

I took a sip of my iced tea.

"Did you stop any wars today?" she asked Adam.

"If I did, I couldn't tell you," he replied with a smirk.

"I wish my boss had given me more of a heads up," Yolanda said, changing the subject.

I stopped my fork mid-flight to my mouth. "About what?"

"This stupid Hollywood traveling exhibit. I don't mean the exhibit will be stupid; it'll be gorgeous when I'm done with it, but I need to work all weekend to have it ready for the opening on Tuesday."

"Bosses can sometimes be unreasonable," Adam said. "Don't you agree, Kells?"

I shrugged. "Mine's not so bad."

Yolanda finished chewing. "You're lucky."

After dinner, Yolanda retreated upstairs, and Adam went back to the couch with his computer on his lap.

I joined him after finishing the cleanup. "Can you tell me about what you're doing? I mean, without having to shoot me or something?"

"No. I have to concentrate."

I scooted up against him. His warmth felt comfortable instead of intimidating. I whispered in his ear. "My boyfriend should share with me."

He nodded. "I guess. It's the bank robberies Neil and I are working. A group we call the Guy Fawkes Crew."

"How do you come up with names like that?"

"This one is because of the masks they wear."

I nodded. "And how is this helping you?"

"We're going over footage from the time before the robbery, looking to catch them casing the place so we can get an image of his face."

"If he wore a mask during the robbery, how will you know it's him?"

"He has a distinctive limp, and on this last job they brought along…" He paused. "A woman. She wasn't wearing a mask, so we might see them together, or maybe just her."

I decided on a challenge. "Can I see the robbery?"

"No. It's top secret."

"Now who's not being honest?"

He rubbed his chin before agreeing and switching windows again.

A screen divided into four frames started, and he ran it through until they'd just gotten money from the teller windows when he stopped it.

"Isn't there more?" I asked.

He put a hand on my leg. "You don't want to see the rest. He shoots a teller."

I gasped. "Oh my God, is she all right?"

"She'll recover. But that's why I need to spend evenings on this. We have to catch this crew before more people get hurt."

The robbery didn't sit right with me for some reason. "Can I see it again?"

"Why?"

"Please."

He sighed and started it from the beginning.

When he stopped it, I'd figured it out. "She's scared of him."

"They're all scared. The guy has a gun and fired it as soon as they came in."

"No. Not the customers." I pointed to the female robber on the screen. "Her. She's scared of the man."

He replayed it again. "I don't see it."

"Of course not. You're a man."

"You say that like it's some kind of defect."

"It's DNA. Women can read body language better. It's a fact."

He shook his head and ran it again. "You really think so?"

I nodded as I got up. "Thank you for sharing that." I decided to leave him be on a good note. "I'm going to check the email again."

The email account was thankfully a bust, which meant tomorrow would be a normal day without any interference from the Ghost.

"Nothing on the email," I called.

"Sugarbear, can we talk?"

Finally, the words I'd been hoping for.

When I returned, I found he'd put the computer away.

Adam

She joined me on the couch, and I put my arm around her.

Her mentioning honesty had gotten to me, and it was time to tell her the truth. "You know your tattoo? Your cousin?" I asked.

She pulled away just a bit. "I don't want to talk about what happened to her."

There was no way to ease into it, so I slapped the first truth on the table. "I'm not really supposed to tell you, but she's alive."

She pulled away. "You don't know that."

I grasped her shoulders. "Deborah Ellen Benson is alive."

Her eyes went wide, and her hand went to her mouth. "How? I mean, where? Where is she?"

"I don't know right now, but she's alive."

"I want to know how you know she's alive." She got up. "I've got to call Daddy."

I stood and grabbed her arm, pulling her back more roughly than I meant to.

"Let me go. I have to call Daddy. Are you sure?"

I took a breath, hoping that calming myself would rub off on her. "He knows. Sit down and listen to everything first."

"But—"

"Sit down," I commanded.

My tone seemed to get her attention, and she returned to the couch.

"How do you know? How can you be sure?"

Her idea of listening needed serious work.

"Why didn't she call us?"

When I didn't say a thing, my words must have finally registered, and she shut up.

I tilted my head. "Are you done?"

She crossed her arms defiantly. "I'm listening."

"The bank robbery we were just watching. That was her."

"Where?"

I ignored the interruption. "Deborah was one of the robbers."

"That's ridiculous."

"The DNA doesn't lie, and your brother thinks it looks like her."

"Which brother?"

"Dennis. That's why he was in town this week."

"Why didn't you tell me right away?"

I took a breath, trying to slow down the conversation she kept trying to accelerate. "Your family doesn't want the information to get out. When we got the DNA match, it came back to a kidnapping case from Phoenix—"

"Yeah, that's where she lived."

"I thought you were done." I waited a second. "Do you want to hear the rest of it or not?"

Her mouth formed a thin line. "Sorry. Yes, please."

I waited again to see if she was really done talking this time. "I had no idea she was related to you until your brother came out. Your family doesn't want the information released, but you're right about the honesty between us going both ways, so I needed to tell you. But you can't tell anyone else."

"I won't," she assured me. "Thank you for trusting me."

I took a breath. "You just said it looked like she was afraid of the man."

Kelly nodded.

"You got me thinking just maybe your brother was right, and she's not a willing participant."

"Duh. Of course not."

"But since she was part of the robbery, she's a criminal suspect, and she's going to be treated that way."

Kelly moved closer. "What happens now?"

"Now we try to find her."

CHAPTER 18

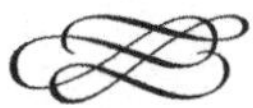

Kelly

I WOKE ONCE AGAIN TO THE SOUND OF THE SHOWER, BUT IT STOPPED BEFORE I rolled out of bed, so I waited for Adam to finish before venturing in. The thought of repeating the previous shower challenge terrified me. Baby steps on the road to more adventure.

He came out before long, fully dressed. "Morning, Sugarbear. Sleep okay?"

"Yeah. How about you?" I regretted the question as soon as it escaped my mouth.

He stretched. "I'm acclimating."

How one acclimated to sleeping on the floor escaped me. "We could switch?"

He laughed. "That'll be the day."

There was another challenge for me, but not one I had to decide on this morning. Did I have to prove a Benson was as tough as a Cartwright?

I climbed out of bed and didn't miss the way he looked at me as I walked by. My boobs bouncing under my thin nightshirt drew his eyes.

He went downstairs to make breakfast while I got ready. After the shower, I dressed in non-office attire, which meant jeans, sneakers, and an extra long-sleeve shirt in case they had the air turned up too high. Good thing my purse was stocked with caffeine pills because watching guys use an x-ray scanner sounded about as exciting as watching a Senate filibuster on C-SPAN.

~

Adam

I'd had to go home to trade out my car for the stakeout junker after I dropped Kelly off. My Lexus would stick out like a sore thumb in this neighborhood.

Harper's expression said it all when I arrived a few minutes later than normal at our perch overlooking the trafficker's house. "I have a family to get back to, you know."

"Couldn't be helped, Sal. I'll be early tomorrow."

"Still nothing going on down there. I sure hope the intelligence wasn't buggered up." He shook his head and left.

It had been a long time, and his concern was warranted.

I made a mental note that tomorrow I was going to arrange to have the city maintenance guys trim one of the branches on the nearest tree, which was partially obstructing our view. It was something we should have done the first day here.

I opened my computer and went back to the BENSNAP file. A little while later, I got a text.

> KELLY: Thanks for trusting me

She could wait. I went back to the file. It was the shooting review board report.

> Special Agent J. Cartwright's statement that he believed the suspect fired a weapon at him is not corroborated by the evidence at the scene. Special Agent A. Spencer stated that at no time did he observe a weapon. No weapon was

> recovered at the scene. All bullets and cartridge casings located at the scene were matched with Special Agent J. Cartwright's service weapon. Lighting at the scene was determined to be suboptimal. However, Special Agent J. Cartwright's statement regarding a muzzle flash from the suspect was not corroborated by Special Agent A. Spencer, the only other person at the scene in a position to witness said muzzle flash. It is therefore the determination of the board that in the shooting of 12 July, Special Agent J. Cartwright did not follow proper procedure, and that the use of excessive lethal force led directly to the death of the suspect and failure to recover the victim in this case. Appropriate disciplinary action is left to the discretion of the local SAC. It is not in this board's purview to review actions that led to the confrontation with the suspect prior to recovery of the victim in this case. Agent J. Cartwright's statements regarding the victim in this case also bear further investigation.

It took a few minutes of searching the file to find the statement they were referring to in a separate interview with Uncle Jack, and it was horrible:

> SAC Donnelly: Why didn't you consider removing yourself from the investigation?
>
> SA Cartwright: Why? Because she was a stuck-up little Benson girl?
>
> SAC Donnelly: Based on your history with the victim's family.
>
> SA Cartwright: I don't have to like them to do my job.
>
> SAC Donnelly: You know how this looks, right?
>
> SA Cartwright: I don't give a fuck how it looks. The guidelines are I shouldn't be on the case if I'm related to them. I'm not. End of story.

These days, answers like that certainly wouldn't fly. Uncle Jack definitely shouldn't have been on the Benson case with that attitude. He couldn't even hide his disdain for the family when talking to the SAC. He'd been an idiot about it.

The verdict was pretty clear. Uncle Jack shouldn't have been on the case in the first place, and then he screwed the pooch by shooting the kidnapper. The SAC had been right about the optics—they sucked, and so had Uncle Jack's judgment.

The separate review of the conduct of the case had also made it clear that Uncle Jack should never have confronted the kidnapper at the ransom pickup. Standard protocol was to follow, or to track the money, but never to confront the suspect. Even rookie agents knew that.

I rechecked the street before dialing the person I had to have a very hard conversation with.

~

Kelly

After Adam dropped me off at the Natural History building, I found out Hal and Len were the two guards manning the x-ray. Hal introduced me to the other two handling the metal detector and hand wand. I took my station behind them and settled in the chair for a very long and boring day. The air conditioning blowing down on us made me glad I'd brought the extra shirt, but I hadn't anticipated the hard plastic chair and regretted not bringing a pillow to sit on.

Almost everybody coming in to perform the inventory failed on their first pass through the metal detector, and they weren't happy about being told to remove belts, jewelry, watches, and the like to get through the device. It was one of those TSA microwave scanners where you held your arms up and the radar or whatever it was looked through your clothes.

"Why do you guys have to set this thing even higher than they do at the airport?" the tenth unhappy camper asked.

"Just doing what they tell us," was the answer, same as the previous nine times. Security had been given a script, and they were following it.

"Why such a tough screening on the way in?" I asked Hal softly.

"To get them used to it, so they don't bitch on the way out."

I shrugged. My only job was to see that they didn't skip anyone.

Anything that looked odd in the x-ray caused them to use a plastic stick to move things around in the bag to see the offending item. Both guards had to tell me what they found, and they had to agree.

Whoever had come up with these procedures after losing the moon rock last year had done a thorough job. Nothing was getting out past us.

One of the metal detector guards logged the digital cameras he passed out to everyone for the pictures they were to take during the inventory.

Yolanda arrived shortly after we opened the doors, still hard at work on the display for her new exhibit.

"Will you be ready?" I asked.

"Have to be. It opens Tuesday morning."

She disappeared inside, and I settled back into the monotony of watching the guys. I should have brought an energy drink or two.

Adam

Dad answered on the second ring. "Hi, Adam, your mother tells me you have a girl for us to meet."

This wasn't the conversation I wanted. "She's mistaken. I have something else to ask you."

"Sure. Shoot."

I took out my keyring with the big silver C attached and laid it on the table. "I want you to tell me about the origin of your problems with Lloyd Benson."

There was a palpable silence on the other end.

"Dad? You said it had to do with Uncle Jack."

"This is a conversation for another time."

"No, Dad. You're not putting this off."

He sighed. "Okay, here it is. Lloyd Benson never liked me. He got the idea in his head that when his brother's child was kidnapped—Debbie, I think her name was—well, he thought Jack got the child killed on purpose."

I sucked in a deep breath. Finally some of this made sense, but Dad didn't know the girl hadn't actually died back then.

"Now, my brother would never do anything like that. He was trying to get her back when things went wrong. He told me he did everything by the book, but it just didn't work out."

I now knew that was plain bull on my uncle's part, but I let Dad continue.

"Like I told you, the Bensons wouldn't let it go. They got Jack kicked out of the Phoenix office, and that's what got him killed in the end. So I blame them, and so help me, I'm going to bring them down if it's the last thing I do."

I needed to tell him the hard truth. "Uncle Jack was at fault."

"Bullshit, that's a Benson lie."

"I've seen the file."

"It doesn't matter."

I sucked in a breath. "Uncle Jack screwed up."

"Bullshit. You don't know everything, and I'm not discussing this for one more damned second."

Pushing him now wasn't going to get me anywhere. "Okay, Dad. Maybe we can talk about this later."

He grunted and hung up.

I rechecked the street.

Dad thought I didn't know everything, so I went to the Bureau online directory to find the number for my next call.

He answered quickly. "Donnelly here." Donnelly had moved up to an Assistant Director position here in DC after being the SAC of the Phoenix Field Office while Uncle Jack was there.

"This is Cartwright in the DC Field Office. Do you have a minute?"

"Cartwright, you said?"

"Yes, sir. Adam Cartwright, and I have a few questions about the BENSNAP case."

"That case is restricted access," the AD snarled.

I checked the street again. All was quiet. "I know. I've got access."

"That was a long time ago. Everything's in the file. I don't know what else I can tell you."

"We have new evidence on the victim. She's alive."

An audible gasp came across the line. "Does the family know?"

"They've been notified."

"I sure didn't expect to hear that after all these years."

I waded right into the deep water, the actual reason for my call. "Sir, is it true that the Benson family pushed to get my Uncle Jack out of the Phoenix office?"

"Who the hell told you that?"

I didn't answer.

"Nobody pressured me to get rid of him. Exactly the opposite. I was ordered not to discipline him, and that could only have come from your father's friends, not the Bensons. I hate to break this to you, but your uncle was a fuck-up, a loose cannon, and I didn't want him screwing up another one of my cases."

I waited for him to go on.

"He got that little girl killed—at least we thought so at the time. He was so far off the reservation, he might as well have been in fucking Poland. I did the only thing I could do. I chained him to a desk until he found a place in another FO. I wasn't letting him out in the field again on my watch to fuck up any more lives."

"And the Benson family didn't have anything to do with it?"

"Listen here, Cartwright. If you want to insult me by asking the same fucking question twice, come over here and do it to my face, man to man." He hung up.

I hadn't scored any points with HQ today. But I'd listened to his words, and judging by the tone, I had no reason to doubt them.

Uncle Jack had lied to Dad about the transfer, as well as the case.

Up had become down, and down had become up.

My family had wronged the Bensons, not the other way around.

The street was still empty, which was good. I needed time to get my head around this. Dad had always insisted DNA was destiny, and all the Bensons were a bad lot.

But that had been based on backwards information from Uncle Jack. I mean, Dennis was still a jerk, but maybe the rest of the family wasn't. Turns out my name had a bad rap in the Bureau for good reason, and it had nothing to do with the Bensons. If DNA really did determine fate, I wasn't cut out for the Bureau. And I wouldn't accept that.

I checked the street again before heading to the tiny bathroom. Several splashes of cold water on my face focused my thoughts.

The man who looked back at me from the mirror. Who was he?

If I was being honest with myself, redeeming my family name at the Bureau had been the reason I'd joined. Learning the truth had turned out not to help at all. Everything Dad had told me had been a lie.

Until today, the Cartwright name had always been one I wore proudly. The truth of Uncle Jack's past undid that.

How many lives had Uncle Jack upended? And what did Dad really know? What was he hiding?

After wiping my face dry, I returned to my lookout position, determined to forge a better path forward—one I could be proud of.

Not all the Bensons were model citizens, but Kelly was certainly blameless, and she deserved better than the way I'd treated her.

I couldn't bear to look at the keyring anymore, and put it back in my pocket.

The past couldn't be repaired, but the trajectory of the future could be changed, and I intended to start tonight.

CHAPTER 19

Kelly

WE LOCKED THE DOORS AND SHUT DOWN THE EXIT STATION FOR OUR SCHEDULED quick lunch in the cafeteria with the entire inventory crew.

I was following Hal when I scraped my arm on the corner of a counter while entering the cafeteria, and I surprised us both by crying out. I didn't do that normally.

Hal looked at my forearm. "You're bleeding."

I put pressure on the scrape. It wasn't deep, but it stung like the devil.

He grabbed napkins from a nearby table. "I've got something for that." He pulled a carton of Band-Aids from the pocket of his cargo pants.

I dabbed at the cut with the napkins. The bleeding had pretty quickly stopped, but the pain hadn't.

He deftly applied two Band-Aids over the cut. "That should do you for now. I guess you can file for worker's comp tomorrow." He laughed.

"And admit how this happened? Not on your life."

We continued to the food line, and I chose the ham and cheese and a bottle of iced tea.

I made a detour after eating to the employee locker room where I'd stashed my purse, and changed the Band-Aids after adding Neosporin to the cut. I also popped two Advil for the sting—well-stocked purse to the rescue again.

The afternoon was exceedingly slow, and I found myself wondering about Adam. I pulled out my phone to send a message.

ME: How's work?

The return message didn't take long.

ADAM: Boring

ME: Same here

ADAM: What do you need?

ME: Just checking in

ADAM: Let me know a little before you're done

That said it all. Don't bother me until I have to be on duty protecting your sorry ass. Nonetheless, a minute later I was mentally replaying our shower scene in my head. My skin prickled as I visualized myself naked in front of him. His words said one thing, but his body had conveyed another.

The sound of an x-ray customer walking our way brought me back to the present. This was the first person to return his camera and hand me the serialized SIM card with his pictures.

After the employee exited the building, I went back to my daydream. What did Adam really think of me?

Len interrupted with another of his rants about the evil of insurance companies. He'd lost his wife to breast cancer, and he blamed the insurance. It was sad, but he obviously needed something or somebody to focus his grief and anger on.

Hal obliged him with the occasional agreement.

I kept on my feet to walk a bit between stints on the unforgiving chair. As the end of the day neared, one by one, the departing employees were cross-checked against the entry log on their way out.

Every single person leaving was subjected to the same extensive metal detector and x-ray protocol as coming in. My additional task was collecting all the SIM cards from the cameras.

The director of paleontology tried to get his bag through without an x-ray, but six-foot-six Len wasn't having it. The big guard seemed to enjoy telling him off, and the director backed down.

A little after six we'd crossed off almost all the regular employees and were down to the two dozen guards and about six others, including Yolanda.

I texted Adam.

ME: Almost done

Mark, Evelyn, and Kirby were among the last out. They were all haggard, but Evelyn looked the worst. Kirby grumbled about how Mr. Heiden had skipped out after lunch, leaving the rest of the day to us peons.

Yolanda came down from upstairs at the last minute. "I'm still going to need all of tomorrow," she lamented. "I was going to make chili for us, if that sounds okay?"

I waved. "Sounds terrific."

After the last employee was done, we handled the guard staff. It was funny to hear them voicing the same complaints about having to remove belts, rings, and watches as the others had in the morning.

After they were all through, Len shut down the machine. "That's it. Time to lock up for the night. Now on to the Gallery on Wednesday, I guess."

"Something like that," Hal said.

I sealed the envelope I'd been collecting the camera SIM cards in.

Len smiled as he picked up his backpack. "Kelly, I can give you a lift home. It's on the way for me."

It bothered me that he knew I lived on the way, but I guessed the security guys had access to that kind of information. "No thanks. I've got a ride coming to pick me up."

Len nodded dejectedly and waited by the door.

I hurried to the employee locker room to get my stuff and put the SIM cards safely in my purse. I'd seen the movie *Night at the Museum*, and I had no intention of being locked in here after dark. Kirby was convinced it was based on a true story, and I wasn't ready to check it out for her.

"Sure you don't want a ride?" Len asked again when I returned.

I could see Adam's car waiting by the curb.

"My ride's here," I told him, pointing toward the street.

Len left quickly, not looking any happier than the first time I'd turned down his offer.

The door closed behind Len before Hal spoke. "You know, he's just trying to be helpful."

"I know."

It took Hal a minute to place his carefully folded OPS jacket into his backpack. He held the door open. "Let's get outta here; my dinner's getting cold."

I slipped by. As I did, the shoulder strap to my purse caught on the door handle. My bag hit the ground with a thud. The strap had broken loose where it attached—again. I picked up the heavy bag and cradled it on my hip.

"You sure are accident prone today," Hal noted as he locked the door after us.

"Ain't that the truth." I was a walking disaster.

Hal radioed the central OPS office. "We're out and locked for the night at Natural History. You're a go for the alarms."

"Thanks for the first aid," I called as I turned to meet my ride.

"Anytime." He waved and headed east.

CHAPTER 20

Adam

After her text, I waited at the curb for Kelly outside the Natural History Museum.

She finally came out with a guard, who locked the door behind them. The kiss she gave me was worth the wait. I couldn't get enough of her, and she didn't pull away.

The feel of her taut nipple under my thumb as I copped a feel told me she was as excited as I was. I breathed in her scent and wished I hadn't left the shower the other morning.

She clawed at my back, and I wished we weren't on the street so I could find out how her bare tits would feel against me. She looked up at me breathlessly when I broke the kiss. She smirked.

I opened the door for her. "What's so funny?"

"Oh, nothing."

"Remember the honesty rule."

She put a hand on my chest. "I was thinking I like the kissing practice."

"For no extra charge, I can include lessons."

"Is that allowed?"

I pulled her in and nuzzled her ear. "There aren't any firm rules against it." I'd double checked the Justice Department rules and ethics guidelines.

She shifted to rub her hip against my crotch. "Are you offering any other lessons?"

She was hot as a pistol tonight.

"It depends."

She stretched up to whisper, "Are you propositioning me, Mr. Cartwright?"

But her mention of my family name killed the vibe completely. She'd managed to remind me how foolish this was.

I let go of her. "Get in."

Her lips tilted down. "What?"

"Time to go."

She slid into the seat.

I didn't notice her bandage until I started the car. "What happened to the arm?"

"Scraped against a sharp corner in the cafeteria at lunch."

"Was anybody near you when it happened?"

"No. Why?"

Her answer calmed my nerves. She probably wasn't aware of the half dozen ways SMK could attack her with a compound introduced through a wound like that. But this sounded like an accident.

"Just curious."

She shifted in her seat.

"You okay?"

She stretched her shoulders. "Tired and sore is all."

"Long day?"

"I can tell you I would never make it as a TSA screener, and the chair they gave me was hard as a rock." She shifted in her seat. "My butt is sore. Good thing the next one isn't tomorrow. I couldn't take two days in a row of this."

I held back a chuckle. The princess clearly wouldn't be able to handle the kind of stakeouts I got assigned. "Not much you can do about that, unless you want to go for a walk."

"I feel more like vegging out in front of the TV."

"A walk is better for you."

"And maybe a backrub," she added a block later.

The mental image of my hands on her had blood flow moving south in a hurry. I kept my eyes on the traffic, not hazarding a glance in her direction that would telegraph my desire.

"Please?" she asked. It was clear she was looking for an answer more definitive than my silence. "I can give you one too."

My engorged cock strained against my pants, and my skin tingled from just the thought of her hands on my body. "That won't be necessary." I glanced over and gave her the briefest of smiles.

"Whatever." She looked out her window, her expression hidden from me.

I turned onto her street a minute later.

"Thank you," she said, catching my eye.

"For what?"

"For caring."

"Just looking out for my career," I said before realizing I should have held my tongue. I pulled to the curb at the first available space a few houses beyond hers.

She didn't wait for me to get out and instead, like a petulant child, opened her door.

I stopped the engine and set the brake. "Wait."

She ignored me and climbed out. "Wouldn't want to inconvenience you."

My mouth had clearly gotten me in trouble again. I climbed out to find a man approaching on the sidewalk from the direction of her house.

She'd started down the street and was almost to him.

I ran. "Wait, Sugarbear."

She stopped and turned. "Why?"

The man continued walking in her direction.

"I need to kiss you," I yelled as I raced up.

Her mouth dropped open.

I reached her just before the man did and pulled her to the street side. I turned her and shielded her from the stranger with my body.

The man walked by.

I lifted her off her feet and turned us so I could see the man as he walked off. "Don't do that again," I whispered into her ear.

"What?"

"We have no idea what SMK looks like. That could have been him. I told you to wait for me."

"Don't be silly. That was Mr. Ornacost from down the street."

I let her go, took her hand, and we walked toward her house. "Still, don't do that again."

She stopped. "You forgot something."

I looked back toward the car. "No I didn't."

She smiled with a slight tilt of her head. "Yes, you did."

I couldn't get enough of that smile.

She set her purse down on the ground. "Now think hard." She moved closer and looked up, seemingly daring me to back away.

My brain fog cleared, and I encircled her with my arms. "Is this what you had in mind?"

"Almost." She snaked a hand behind my neck and pulled herself up.

My lips met hers, and the kiss became intense. Her hunger met my desire in a more passionate embrace than earlier. My hands roamed her back to find the ass I wanted to grab—the ass I wanted to lift onto my aching cock.

She smashed herself against me as our tongues began the dance of lovers.

The feel of her tits against me had me wishing there wasn't all this clothing in the way. At the slight scent of strawberry in her hair, I envisioned what she would taste like, and the sounds she'd make with my tongue making her come.

This girl was a temptress. I cut the kiss short before I tried to sneak a hand under her shirt out here in public.

"Is the offer of lessons still open?" she asked as I broke my hold on her.

"Maybe later." I leaned over to get her purse. The shoulder strap was broken on one end. "What happened here?"

"Snagged on the door handle. It's happened before. I've got a guy who can fix it. I'll take it in on Monday."

I continued toward her front door. "This thing weighs a ton. What do you have in here?"

She followed. "Pretty much anything I might need."

I held the purse while she rummaged through it to find her keys.

~

Kelly

. . .

An hour or so later, the three of us sat down to a late dinner of chili with cornbread that Yolanda had prepared.

Yolanda dipped her spoon in. "I hope it's not too hot for you."

Adam blew on his spoonful of chili before taking it into his mouth. "I haven't had chili this good since leaving California," he said after a moment.

Yolanda beamed.

I looked over at Adam appreciatively. He had a knack for playing the attentive fake boyfriend much better than I would've guessed. Yolanda certainly had fallen for his act.

"What country or area do you cover at State?" Yolanda asked.

"How are the preparations for your exhibit coming?" I asked.

Yolanda put her water glass down. "I still have more to do tomorrow, but I'll be ready on time for the Tuesday opening."

Adam lifted his spoon. "These traveling exhibits come around very often?"

She shook her head. "Not in my area. They get a lot more traveling exhibits in American History."

Adam swallowed. "And you said this was Hollywood stuff?"

She swallowed before answering. "Jewelry, actually. The movies use props, so these are reproductions of the movie pieces, but with real stones. Expensive stuff."

"Anything we would recognize?" I asked.

She wasn't getting much of a chance to eat with our questions. "Thirteen in all. Remember the necklace from *Titanic*? That's one, and the ruby-and-diamond necklace Julia Roberts wore in *Pretty Woman*? That's another."

Adam nodded. "Sounds pretty cool." He lifted his beer. "To a successful exhibit."

After dinner, Yolanda came down from her room with a backpack. "I'll be over at Bogdan's." She winked at me on the way out the door.

"What kind of name is Bogdan?" Adam asked while he did the dishes.

"Ukrainian." I logged on for another check on email from the Ghost.

There it was, in black and white.

Specific instructions will follow next week. Remember Brooks.

"Adam, you need to see this," I called.

He sauntered over, wiping his hands with a dish towel, and leaned down to read the message. "Well, now we wait." He scratched the top of my back between the shoulder blades.

I scrunched my shoulders and leaned into his scratching. "Keep that up," I purred.

He stopped too soon.

I closed the computer and moved to the couch.

Scrolling through the TV listings, I didn't find much I wanted to watch, so I chose another *Friends* rerun. As the episode ended and the next began, I was still waiting for Adam to join me.

I lay down on the couch. "Hey, what happened to the backrub you promised me?"

He appeared at the door a moment later.

I gave him my warmest smile. "I thought we were going to exchange backrubs."

"That's not the way I remember it."

My smile melted into my best pouty face. I wasn't above a little emotional blackmail at this point. "I thought you were a man of your word."

He walked over with a sigh that signified defeat. "Scoot up."

I did.

He pulled the back cushions off the couch before settling on my thighs.

I rested my hands above my head.

He began with a hard, deep massage of my shoulders. "You're tight. Loosen up."

I groaned a mixture of pain and relief as his powerful hands worked my shoulders and out along my arms. "You can do this every night."

"Not part of my duties." He worked his way down my back. "Lift up," he said as he pulled the hem of my shirt up to my armpits. Just as quickly, he unhooked my bra and pulled my shirt back down.

"You can leave it up."

He pressed extra hard down either side of my backbone. "This is better. I don't want to rub your skin raw."

I hadn't considered that in my desire to feel his hands on me. I moaned as he ran the heels of his hands up and down my back with heavy pressure, alternating with occasional kneading, using his knuckles.

His roughness gave way to more gentle pressure, and quickly, the relief outweighed the pain.

Knots loosened, and I relaxed into the cushions with simple grunts each time he pressed down on me.

He shifted down farther. "Unbutton your pants."

I lifted up, undid the button, and pushed the zipper down a bit.

Cool air hit my ass as he pulled my pants down to almost the bottom of my butt cheeks—farther than I'd expected. His knuckles worked on my lower back, hard at first, then more moderately.

I relaxed into the cushions, very glad to have asked for this.

He moved lower to massage my butt as well, and things were definitely moving into the risky zone. Then, just as suddenly, he pulled up the waist of my pants and took his hands off me. "Did that help?"

Help was too mild a word. "A ton. Your turn." I tried, but I couldn't roll over with him straddling my legs.

"I said no need." He pulled up the hem of my shirt and re-hooked my bra —completely too proper.

"Come on. Let me do you." Once again, my mouth ran ahead of my brain filter. I didn't intend the innuendo—or did I?

He climbed off me and stood. "Not tonight." He walked back to the kitchen to resume his work without another word.

"Want to join me and relax a while?"

He turned at the door. "Not tonight." A moment later, he was gone again.

I hadn't won, but I'd survived my brief foray into risky, and it had felt exhilarating, even if it had ended too soon.

A bit later, I got up to try again.

Adam was hunched over the laptop, staring at the screen and scrolling with the touchpad.

I came up behind him and started to knead his shoulders, not as hard as he had me, but in the same manner. "Does this help?"

He had a report on the screen instead of the bank video. He slammed the laptop lid closed. "Not tonight, I said."

I worked his muscles harder. "What's the problem?"

He scooted the chair back and stood. Turning to me, he grasped my shoulders and spun me toward the door. "Not tonight. I have to concentrate."

I took one step toward the door and pivoted back to him. "And you find me distracting?" I should have taken a moment to think up a better line, but it expressed how I felt.

He scowled. "Can't you do what I ask for a change?"

"What do you mean *for a change*? Kelly, do this. Kelly, don't do that. You're always giving me orders."

He turned away, sat, and opened his laptop again. Then he looked over at me with an unspoken command to get lost.

I stood my ground.

His phone rang, and he picked it up.

"I'll leave you alone." I reached behind and unhooked my bra.

"Hi, Mom," he said into the phone.

Wiggling out of the straps, I pulled it out from under my shirt and threw it on the table.

His eyes bugged out.

After retreating to my couch, I restarted the TV and turned up the volume to keep from eavesdropping on his family call.

~

Adam

"What's her name?" Mom asked.

I waited until Kelly was farther away. "Who?"

"The woman I heard talking to you."

"Nobody. Just work." I removed my eyes from the lacy bra she'd thrown on the table.

"Your father told me he thought there might be a woman in your life now. When do I get to meet her?"

"Mom, it's work. I told you."

"This late at night? What's her name?"

If I didn't give her at least a small nugget of information to chew on, she'd be calling me three times a day until I cracked. "Her name is Kelly."

"Is she an agent? You know seeing someone you work with can be problematic."

She would know. She'd been working for Dad when they'd started dating. It had taken a fair bit of digging on my part to find that out because neither wanted to admit it.

"She's not an agent."

"So it's not work-related after all?"

"She's someone we're protecting."

"You shouldn't be protecting a criminal. I think that's just plain wrong."

I let her go on as I salivated over the bra in front of me.

"They should all be sent to prison and hung after what they did to your Uncle Jack."

"Don't worry, Mom. She's not associated with the mob."

"She's a good person, then?"

A month ago I wouldn't have said this about a Benson. "Yes, she's a good person."

"Oh, is she a singer? Like Whitney Houston in that movie—*The Bodyguard*? Kevin Costner was so yummy in that, but singers are a fickle lot, I think."

"It's not like that." I sighed. "Mom, I have to go. I still have work to do tonight."

"Sure. I wouldn't want you to keep Whitney waiting."

"Some other work."

"You know, I'm due out in New York in a few weeks. I could stop off in Washington to see you two."

"That would break protocol, Mom. You know we have rules."

It wouldn't actually break a rule, but it was the only thing likely to get her to drop the idea.

"It would just be for dinner."

Dinner with a side of interrogation was more like it. "Do you want me to get in trouble?"

"Another time then. Is she cute?"

I sighed. There was no denying Kelly's beauty. I brought the bra to my face. "It doesn't matter." Twenty questions was turning into two hundred questions.

"I heard that tone. You think she's cute. I look forward to meeting her."

I put the bra down. "Bye, Mom. I really have to go."

We hung up.

I'd dodged that bullet, and hopefully this assignment with Kelly would be over before they ever found out I was protecting a Benson. My dad would croak if I told him.

It struck me how natural it had become to think of her as *Kelly* without attaching the *Benson*.

CHAPTER 21

Adam

After Mom's call, I downed half a glass of wine and refilled it, then filled another glass before joining Kelly on the couch.

The thought of her braless tits had tormented me during Mom's call. The way they'd jiggled when she'd walked by had almost sent me through the roof. But then, any guy would have reacted that way, wouldn't he? Problem was, I wasn't any guy. I was the guy who'd seen her naked in the shower mere inches from me.

And Kelly's line, "*And what if that's what I want?*" had been an eleven on the seductiveness scale. I'd resisted her—I deserved a fucking medal for that, or the stupidest-fucker-in-town badge, maybe. The girl was one-hundred-percent female temptation.

I sat next to her and pulled her close. I stroked her side and accidentally caught a bit of side-boob while I was at it. Since she didn't react, I didn't stop. A light purr from her was my first clear indication that her teasing came from mutual attraction.

The wine gave me the confidence to speak. "We need to talk."

She placed a hand on my thigh, *my freaking thigh*. "You've said that before."

It was a shitty start, but I sucked it up and went on. "You know our families haven't liked each other for a while."

She snorted. "More like outright war."

"I like you, Sugarbear." There, I'd said it. If I'd misread her, I'd hear about it soon enough.

Her hand stroked my thigh, getting my cock's attention—more than I wanted at this point. "And I hope you know I like you too, Mr. Cartwright." The name grated on me like fingernails on a chalkboard.

"That's what I want to get past. I want you to think of me as Adam, and leave the Cartwright off."

"Sorry, I didn't mean it that way." Her finger drew little figure-eights on my thigh.

I drained most of my wine glass. "And I want to start by apologizing for my family, my dad and my uncle in particular."

"We shouldn't focus on the older generation. Let's get to you and Dennis."

Fuck it, I'm not going there. "There's a history between our fathers you don't know, and frankly, it's one I don't think my family acknowledges either."

"I don't even know how it started, do you?"

I had to tiptoe around this and still get the thrust of it out. "Now I do."

She waited for more of an explanation than that.

I gulped more of my wine. "It's my uncle's fault."

"The FBI uncle?"

"Yeah, Uncle Jack did something that hurt your whole family, and that started this mess. My uncle screwed up your cousin's kidnapping case. Your father blamed my uncle, thinking Uncle Jack had caused her death."

"But now we know she's not dead."

"He still screwed up, though. If he hadn't, she probably would have been back with her family."

"Oh. I never heard Daddy talk about your uncle, just your father."

"I think that's because my father took my uncle's side on it, and the back and forth just got worse. My dad didn't understand the truth, at least I don't think he did. I think now is the time to put it all behind us and move forward, with my family admitting our part in this."

Her eyes held mine. "I don't see how you're to blame for anything just because you have an awful last name."

I had to chuckle. "Only half as bad as yours. All kidding aside, when I heard my assignment would be to protect you, my first reaction was to pull out and hand it to someone else."

She took my hand. "I'm glad you didn't, and I had the same trepidation."

"As far as the two of us go, I apologize for my family's part in the past, and I hope we can drop the animosity that's eaten away at our parents all this time."

"Me too." Her smile conveyed an honesty I couldn't doubt.

Here I was, breaking with my father and taking the Bensons' side in this. I'd expected it to be hard, but now that I'd learned the truth about Uncle Jack, I felt relieved to be able to get it out in the open.

I'd stressed about this conversation ever since learning the truth hidden in the BENSNAP file. I took the next leap. "Can we just be Adam and Kelly, and forget the last names for good?"

She moved over to snuggle with me again—a good sign.

I draped an arm behind her. With the guilt I'd felt since reading the BENSNAP file finally unloaded, I relaxed into the sofa. Worrying about the talk, followed by actually getting it out in the open had drained me. It could have gone wrong in so many ways.

This time, she was the one to move my hand up to the side of her boob. "Hi, Adam. I'm Kelly." Her other hand returned to my thigh, and my cock took notice once again. "Your kissing student, remember?"

I kissed the top of her head. "I remember. Want to watch a movie?" The feel of her against me was electric, and the fact that we'd gotten past Benson and Cartwright made it feel even better.

Her soft eyes connected with me. "If you do."

I raised my glass for another sip. I needed decompression time.

"Maybe you've had enough?"

Normally I would have taken offense at someone commenting on my drinking, but her tone had been kind.

"Maybe so." I'd needed it to calm me earlier, but having her warm form against me was better medicine.

Her finger tapped my thigh. "Thank you."

"For what?"

"For talking to me." Her hand shifted higher on my thigh. "Like a boyfriend."

The twitch in my cock shifted to my heart as I understood the words. She wanted to take things further.

~

Kelly

It hadn't been the talk I'd expected, it had been better. Putting the family feud aside and not letting it affect us the way it did our parents seemed overdue.

The man next to me wasn't the ogre I'd been taught any Cartwright would be. He had integrity, and an honesty that put him far ahead of any of the men I'd met since coming to this town.

My reaction upon learning he'd be my protector now seemed so alien to me. I'd recoiled at the idea of spending any time with him, and I'd been so horribly wrong.

"You're not saying anything," he said after a while.

"Just thinking."

"Me too."

His opening up to me about his uncle's past made his evasive behavior understandable in retrospect. It had been a hard set of things to admit—betraying his family almost.

As I snuggled up against Adam, I closed my eyes and ignored the movie. I could feel the beat of his heart, a true heart, a kind heart, the heart of a brave man to have admitted what he had tonight.

He'd been open with me, and I could only hope I hadn't gone too far with those words I wanted to be true.

His thumb continued to stroke the side of my breast through my shirt as the movie played.

I'd been groped before—what girl hadn't? But this wasn't that at all.

He didn't go any further, although I wouldn't have minded. Each gentle touch sent a tingle of hope—a hope that Kelly and Adam had a chance free of family complications. The contact was his unspoken question as to whether I was comfortable with him, and my answer to him was a clear yes.

I put it out there in plain English. "I'm glad I met you."

He gave me a gentle squeeze. "Me too. No, scratch that. *Glad* isn't a strong enough word."

"Really?"

"Yes, really."

Being up against his side with his gentle touches told me what he didn't need to verbalize, and the bulge in his pants completed the story. I was attracted to him, and he to me, although something still held him back.

I'd thought my kissing-student comment had been pretty obvious, but he'd limited things to holding me and cuddling. Had I been too forward?

Now it was me and him, Kelly and Adam, suddenly without the complication of family history. The chance to turn fake to real loomed. There was only one way to find out.

My inhibitions took a backseat, and I remembered my sister's advice. A hand on the thigh that moves up tells more than a dozen words.

My insides crackled with anticipation of knowing what "more than glad to have met you" really meant. But as I contemplated making the first move, fear took over, and I froze in place.

Was this the trepidation guys felt when they considered asking a girl on a date?

CHAPTER 22

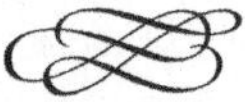

ADAM

HER HAND MOVED TO MY THIGH, AND MY COCK STRAINED EVEN HARDER AGAINST my zipper. Then her hand started up my leg. Her eyes stayed glued on the television, but the nonverbal implication was obvious. She was a red-hot tease.

Generally, I could take some teasing, but not tonight. "Careful, Sugarbear."

She feigned innocence. "What?"

"If you start something, I won't be held responsible for where it ends up."

Her hand shifted farther, just short of my aching cock. "Start what?"

I pulled her hand away.

Was I going nuts? This girl was offering the release I craved, and I was the one pulling back? Since when? It wasn't against the rules, that much was clear, but it didn't need to be rushed either.

I captured her gaze. I knew exactly how to scare her off for tonight. "I'm not your type. I don't do nice. I don't do gentle." The words had worked before, and I'd just sentenced myself to only hand action tonight. I was nuts.

Her hand moved back to my thigh. "I thought I proved you wrong about my risk aversion with our discussion in the shower. You know, where you got scared and ran away?"

I got up. "Want anything to drink?"

"You can't just leave."

I shook my head and continued to the fridge. "I asked if you wanted something to drink."

She followed me into the kitchen. "Why do I scare you?"

I ignored the question and pulled open the refrigerator door. "Wine or beer?"

She pushed the door closed. "Answer me, goddammit."

"Nothing scares me, princess."

She wrapped her hands behind my neck and pulled herself close. "And you don't scare me."

The feel of her warm tits up against me threatened my concentration. "I told you—"

She cut off my statement by pulling herself up to mash her mouth against mine. A second later, she jumped up and wrapped her legs around me.

My hands cradled her ass to hold her up. I'd warned her, and now all bets were off.

Our tongues dueled for position. She'd shifted from demure, to teasing, to banshee. Her hands threaded through my hair, keeping us close.

Hardly able to see, I carried her to the counter and set her ass down to free my hands. I pulled away enough to make quick work of her top while she fumbled with the buttons of my shirt.

I lifted her marvelous boobs and fondled their soft warmth.

"Baby, you have great tits."

~

Kelly

Adam's compliment was crude, but hot as hell with his hands on me. Taking Serena's challenge to let my inner cavewoman loose was already paying off.

"I warned you," he growled, pulling my pants off.

I'd lit the fuse and was about to feel the explosion of the beast. I poked the tiger again. "You don't scare me." I finally got his belt loose.

He yanked at my panties.

I lifted up.

He pulled them down, and the cold granite against my ass was a contrast to the heat racing through me.

"You look like a cock teaser that hasn't been properly fucked."

Just his words sent tingles everywhere, and my core clenched.

I was in an unknown new dimension of risk with this man, but was determined to not show it. "And you think you're the one to show me?"

He growled. "Careful what you wish for, Sugarbear." He traced fingers under my breasts and over, circling my pebbled nipples.

Hot prickles under my skin followed his light touch. I had to be making a wet spot on the counter.

I grabbed for the button of his jeans, but he swiped my hands away.

His fingers moved down my sides and traced a slow, hot journey over my thighs. "How long has it been?"

I gasped as he pulled my legs farther apart. "Too long." The slow, light finger movements were torture.

He swiped my hands away again after another attempt at his pants.

His gaze on my boobs was a heated stare.

I squeezed them together and up.

He moved in to lick one nipple, followed by the other.

My ass was freezing on the stone counter. But the cold air he blew on my nipples made me shiver with delight. If this was his idea of *not gentle*, he was full of shit.

No guy had taken this kind of time to tease me. No guy had built anticipation in me like this.

He moved back and pulled me off the counter. "Go to the couch." His tone was firm, commanding. "Please."

Was that what this had been leading up to? I'd done it on the couch once before. I went over and laid down.

He yanked off his pants and boxer briefs, releasing the cock I'd seen in the shower. Tonight it looked even thicker.

Instead of telegraphing my concern that I might have trouble taking him in, I licked my lips when he looked over.

I didn't see where he pulled the condom from, but he quickly sheathed himself and came over.

He offered his hand.

I took it.

He pulled me up and into an embrace, another hot kiss. His mouth devoured mine. I gripped his hair and pulled myself up on my toes to give him back the same passion.

A hand around my back squished my breasts to him, and his other hand grabbed my ass and pulled me hard against the rod of his erection. The strength of his grip almost took me off my feet. The skin-to-skin contact intensified as our tongues sparred and we traded hot breath, and hotter desires.

All I could hear were our traded moans. He tasted like raw desire and smelled like pine. The room fell away as I melted in his arms.

He squeezed my butt so hard, I was sure I'd have a mark tomorrow.

He broke the kiss, leaned over to grab a throw pillow from the couch and led me to the table. Without words, he put the pillow against the edge of the table, spun me around, and had me spread my legs.

My apprehension grew as he bent me over and positioned himself behind me.

His tip found my soaked entrance, and he entered.

I winced at the size of him but held my yelp.

He grabbed my hips and pushed all the way in with a groan. He pulled back and pushed again and again. With each thrust, the pain of his size receded, replaced with the pleasure of being filled more fully than ever before. His hand on my back clamped me against the table.

I spread my arms out to brace myself. The wood was cold and tugged against my breasts every time I got shoved forward. The sensations built as he pounded against me with the primal energy of the leader of the pack. Every plunge into my heat seemed to take me higher and send my nerves closer to overload.

His grunts grew louder. My eyes squeezed shut, and the next thrust did it. My hands clenched into fists, and my core clamped down around him as I shook and my orgasm let loose.

He slowed to a steady rhythm as the waves of pleasure rolled over me. The long, slow strokes extended the experience.

For another minute, slow, full strokes melted me into the table.

Without notice, he pulled me back, and his hand came between me and the pillow at the edge. "Come for me, baby. Come again for me."

Each time he drove into me, he pushed my clit up against his fingers.

The electric jolts his fingers forced quickly sent my blood boiling out of control again. He thrust harder and faster, sending me over the edge. My walls spasmed around him as my climax overtook me again.

He pulled his hand from under me and grabbed my hips. The sound of flesh slapping against flesh filled the house as he pounded into me. His release came with a loud groan, and he kept himself buried deep inside me as his cocked jerked.

The pulsing of his cock slowly died down, and he lay heavily on top of me. "You feel so fucking good, Sugarbear."

I smiled. "You too."

"Did I hurt you?"

I laughed. "I'll let you know when you start fucking me hard."

He swatted my butt. "Wise ass. Next time you're getting the wall, or maybe the counter."

"I told you I wouldn't break." I relished the feeling of fullness from him being inside me.

He lay on top of me for another minute, his breath hot against my neck, his weight plastering me into the table. I savored the warmth of him against me in the afterglow of my first time to have multiple orgasms.

He'd said he didn't do gentle, and now I understood what he meant. He was Serena's leader of the pack. He didn't put a leash on his passion.

Eventually, he pulled out and carried me to the shower.

When he set me down, I was so relaxed I had to brace myself against the wall for a moment.

Washing each other under the hot water after our session was half relaxing, and half titillating. His hands glided over my tingly skin. As he washed my back and playfully worked his hands around to soap my boobs, I couldn't think of an experience with another man that came anywhere near the pleasure he gave me.

I squeezed my thighs together. I could still feel my pulse tingling between my legs.

He urged me to turn around. "What are you thinking, Sugarbear?"

I grabbed his cock and tugged. Gathering up my courage, I put it out there. "I'm thinking I like you as a real boyfriend."

"You just like my big dick."

I let go and looked down to hide my disappointment. I shook my chest. "And you just like my boobs." Making fun of it was my only defense after his non-answer.

He pulled me back to him. "Not just. I told you once I thought you were an amazing woman. I mean that."

Warmth welled up inside me. "Thank you." I still couldn't tell where that put us, though, and I was scared of what the answer might be. "What do we do now?"

"A little sleep would be nice."

"That's not what I mean."

He pushed me back and lifted my face with both hands. "I'm thinking I'd like to date you for real." His eyes held mine with a warmth that was undeniable. "What do you say to that?"

"Aren't you supposed to ask a girl that before you get her in bed?"

His smile grew. "Technically we haven't been in bed yet, so you still owe me an answer."

I lifted up on my toes for the kiss that would seal it. "I'd like that."

Our lips met, and his grip on me tightened, melding my body to his, bringing us together as the couple we were now committing to be.

When he finally let me go, I had my answer. He wanted me as much as I wanted him.

As we kissed and hugged and turned under the warm water, I marveled at how in a matter of days I'd gone from blind dates with the likes of Harold and debating kissing the frog, to having the most unlikely prince show up at my doorstep and now in my shower.

He adjusted the water temperature up a little. "What are you thinking, Sugarbear?"

"Just thinking I like it here."

"In the shower?"

I considered a wiseass answer but held it back. "No. With you."

That earned me a kiss on the head. "Me too."

I stroked his back. "Are you sure this isn't going to get you in trouble?"

He took a moment to answer. "I'm sure, but it's still best if we keep it to ourselves. Because…"

"Appearances?"

"Yeah."

I had to ask the hard question. "What happens when you catch him?"

He pulled me closer and rested his chin on my head. "You couldn't get rid of me now if you tried, Sugarbear." He stroked my back with a tenderness I relished.

As I closed my eyes and listened, the thump of his strong heart serenaded me. Serena had been right. The leader of the pack beat Milton Milquetoast by a mile. I'd found a high-testosterone man for a change, and I wasn't letting him get away—even if I had trouble getting him to talk to me.

CHAPTER 23

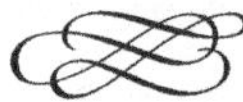

Adam

I blinked the sleep out of my eyes on Sunday morning. Kelly's open eyes were easy to make out in the light peeking past the shades.

A smile broadened on her face. "You were out like a light. How do you feel this morning?"

"How long have you been awake?"

She placed a hand on my chest, and her finger started to draw circles. "I dunno, maybe a half hour? Why do you always answer a question with another question?"

I stretched my shoulders before rolling toward her. "This bed is comfortable. You should have woken me up." I placed a kiss on her nose.

The cute crease in her brow appeared. Not cute because it meant something good was coming my way, but just cute because so much about her was adorable.

"You know it's okay to kiss me, like, for real," she said.

I rolled over and my feet met the floor. "Morning breath."

She had a retort before I reached the door. "Self conscious much, or is it because I had my lips wrapped around your dick last night?"

Letting that go by and discouraging her wasn't going to happen. I returned to her side, wrapped her up tight, brought her over on top of me, and kissed the living daylights out of her. Our mouths crashing together like we'd missed each other brought it all back. Last night had been unforgettable—starting with the table, but not ending there.

The strawberry scent in her hair was faint but still reminded me of our first real kiss. The sensation of her all over me had my dick voting for a day in bed. Nothing compared to the soft pressure of her tits on my chest, and her stomach over my swollen cock.

She was the one to break the kiss. "That's more like it."

"Do you have any idea how cute you are?"

"No, why don't you tell me?"

I rolled her off of me. "Cute enough to take on an all-day date. Now get up. We have a lot to see."

"You just can't stand to wait another minute to get to your toothbrush. That's it, isn't it?"

"On second thought." I rolled over on top of her, an arm on either side. "Maybe I should fuck you so hard you have to call in sick tomorrow because you can't walk."

She kissed a finger and brought it to my lips. "Promises, promises."

I kissed the finger and got up. "Shower time. Like I said, we have a lot to do today."

Now I was turning down sex to spend a day walking around with this girl? *Earth to Adam, what the hell are you thinking?*

She was up off the bed before I could reconsider my mistake. "Where are we going?"

I followed her toward the bathroom. "Surprise."

She stopped. "What if I don't like surprises?"

"What if you don't argue about every little thing?"

That cute little brow crease appeared again, but only for a second before a giggle overtook her. "Sorry…conditioning. I still don't want to go out." She turned and continued into the bathroom.

After quickly brushing my teeth, I joined her in the shower.

She handed me the soap and turned away. "Now who's taking risks?"

I started to soap her back. "What risk?"

"That getting us all wet and slippery, I might jump your bones and make us stay here." She turned to face me. An evil grin overtook her face.

I started to soap her front. "You wouldn't dare." Her boobs got my extra-special treatment.

"Why not?"

I gave her tits another good massage. "Simple. You need this too much."

She cocked her head. "A boob wash?"

I handed her the soap. "You need a day of relaxation more than anything. When was the last time you had lunch outside in the sunshine and ignored work, ignored the clock, and just watched the people go by? Have you ever?"

She started to lather my arms.

"Since you moved here?" I added.

She soaped my shoulders and chest. "It's too hot in the sun."

"Now who's not answering the question, Sugarbear."

She moved lower to soap my engorged dick, which hadn't been able to shut out how beautiful she looked, and how wonderful she felt under my fingers.

"Somebody wants to stay in and play."

"Deflecting isn't going to get you anywhere." Her continued slippery stroking of my dick made it difficult to get the words out.

She finally took her hands off me, set the soap on the shelf, and rinsed in the stream of water. "You're right. I haven't."

I took her in my arms, urging her soft form against mine, which didn't do anything to lessen my raging hard-on.

She laid her head against my chest. "Can't we stay in?"

I squeezed her tighter. "I'll keep you safe. You need this." I rubbed her back. "Please trust me."

She pulled back to look up. "Promise?"

I'd guessed right that she was scared about being out in the open. I kissed my finger. "Absolutely." I moved the finger to her lips.

She kissed it. "I'll make breakfast." She pushed away to get out.

"No. We'll have breakfast out."

She turned back. "But I always have pigs in a blanket on Sunday."

I pulled the door closed behind her to keep the cold air out. "What happened to not arguing about every little thing?"

She shook her head and grabbed a towel, without responding for once.

"Oh, and wear shorts."

She spun around. "Is that an order, DA?"

I rolled my eyes. "A request. Please. I want to be able to watch your lovely legs all day."

She smiled. "A leg man?"

"When it comes to you, Sugarbear, I'm an everything man."

~

Kelly

I TURNED AWAY TO HIDE MY BLUSH. "BECAUSE YOU ASKED NICELY." I WAS completely naked, but that didn't embarrass me one tenth as much as when he said something insanely nice.

Adam dried off while I was blowing my hair out. Guys had it so easy. He dressed in a loose fitting T-shirt that hid his muscular chest and cargo shorts before heading downstairs.

I chose a scoopneck top to go with the shortest pair of running shorts I owned. The man had demanded a show, and that's what he was going to get. I added more mascara. Checking out my legs in the mirror, I decided they weren't bad, but having him say he wanted to watch them all day sent an odd tingle up my back. I was dressing for him, and instead of feeling put out, I felt good. Turning both ways in front of the mirror, I smiled.

He likes my legs. Who woulda thunk?

Downstairs, I found Adam in the kitchen. I twirled around once for him. "Okay?"

He nodded. "Perfect, but then you'd make a burlap sack look sexy."

I grabbed my tea mug. "Stop trying to embarrass me."

He sipped his coffee. "Okay. You look terrible."

He put down his cup and rubbed his hands together. "We need to get going, Sugarbear."

"But I haven't had my tea yet," I complained.

"We'll get it on the way."

"But I want *my* tea."

"Sure." He walked to the tin where I kept my teabags, grabbed several, and stuffed them in one of his pockets. "Let's get going."

That wasn't what I meant, but it was better than nothing. I followed him to the door, picking my purse up off the table.

"You're not taking that."

He was right, with a broken strap I needed to swap.

I ignored his rudeness. "I'll just be a minute moving things over to my other purse."

"Not today. We're traveling light."

"I don't ever go out without my purse. Where will I put my keys?"

He pulled the house key I'd given him out of his pocket. "Got us covered. Traveling light means no purse. Bring your phone along, if you want."

I tried to stare him down, but gave that up after a few seconds. His eyes carried a steely determination I wasn't going to overcome.

I stated the obvious. "I don't have any pockets in this."

He held his hand out. "I'll carry it for you then."

I handed him the phone. "And a few more things."

He opened the Velcro on one of his pockets to deposit the phone.

"Sunscreen," I said, handing him the tube. "Mascara," I added as I searched for it in my purse and handed it over.

"You call this going light?"

"I don't go anywhere without my mascara."

He nodded toward the door. "Ready now?"

I exited first and headed for his car.

Someone I didn't recognize walked toward me on the sidewalk, and I retreated to be beside Adam while he locked up, looping my arm with his.

I grabbed tighter as the stranger came closer, then walked past without a glance in our direction or a greeting.

Adam leaned into my ear and whispered. "You're safe with me."

I let go of his arm, suddenly ashamed at how skittish I'd become, and ambled to his car by the curb.

Adam walked past. "We're hoofing it today."

I caught up and took the hand he offered. The warmth of his touch as his fingers interlaced with mine reminded me we were no longer in fake-boyfriend territory—another reason to feel good about this morning. "Where are we going?"

"You really don't like surprises, do you?"

Appropriately chastised, I walked beside him in silence for half a block.

When we reached Dupont Circle, we crossed through the middle to 19th.

I asked how much farther and got nothing, so I tried a different question. "What does your family know about us?"

"Nada, zilch, nothing so far. What are you going to tell yours?"

"I don't know yet. All I know is I'm not ashamed to be with you."

He stopped us and moved in close. His eyes softened. "Me neither, Sugarbear."

I held his gaze and tried to control my smirk. "You just like getting off the floor."

He started us walking again. "Side benefit," he said after a few steps.

This FBI special agent didn't have as thick a skin as he pretended. He turned us right down a side street.

I regretted breaking the mood with my smart-ass comment.

A few steps later he mumbled, "I meant it."

Before I could come up with an un-snarky reply, he stopped and held a door open. "We're here."

"McDonald's? That's the big surprise?"

"Just the first stop."

"I get it that you think I'm a cheap date, but isn't this a bit much?" I regretted the rude words as soon as they escaped.

The face on the lady at the register said she'd heard me and didn't appreciate my attitude.

"We're playing tourist today, and this is our first stop."

"But they don't have pigs in a blanket."

He chuckled. "Sugarbear, today is not about your normal routine. Go off script and be daring."

I could feel my face scrunch up at his suggestion. I'd been quite daring lately, if you asked me. I needed some semblance of my routine to keep me grounded and comfortable.

"I'll make it easy and order for you." He moved up to the register.

Adam ordered us both Egg McMuffins and hash browns. "And a cup of hot water for the lady's tea. She brought her own teabag."

The mention of me wanting to use my own tea instead of theirs earned me the you-must-be-a-stuck-up-bitch sideways glance from the cashier.

"Will there be anything else?" she asked.

I slunk off toward the tables with my hot water. Usually I was nice to everyone, and I'd really put my foot in it this morning. There wasn't anything wrong with McDonalds. Hell, I'd been here before. Trying to come up with the last time, though, meant I had to rewind to being in California, which sort of made Adam's point for him. I took a booth and prepared my tea while he waited for our order.

He brought the tray and sat across from me. "Can we talk about our families for a moment?"

I tried not to seem surprised. "Sure."

"I think my dad is going to have a fit when he finds out."

I unwrapped the nearest breakfast sandwich. "Maybe you should tell him, rather than have him find out?"

"I didn't mean it that way. Sure, I'll tell him, but I'm worried about how. It's not like I have the words figured out. 'Hey, Dad, you know this Benson family you hate? Well, I'm going out with one of them.'" He took a bite.

I finished chewing. "Have you told him what you told me about your uncle? That might be the way to start."

He shook his head, swallowing. "I did, but bringing it up again implies he was wrong—and he either knew it, or should have known."

I took a bite of hash brown. "You should expect the best from your dad, not the worst, and lay it all on your uncle… Just a thought."

He nodded. "Maybe."

"Doesn't he deserve the benefit of the doubt?"

"Got me there." He sipped his drink. "You sure are smart."

"I'm a Benson. What'd you expect?"

We laughed together at what would have been fighting words a week ago.

"What about your family?" he asked.

I shrugged. "What they don't know can't hurt them. I won't see Daddy till the holidays, so it won't come up for a while."

He lifted his cup again. "So you *are* ashamed to tell them you're seeing me."

I reached across. "I told you, no, that's not it. It's just that I don't want to upset Daddy, and I have to figure out the words. I haven't been super open with him in the past, so it's not like delaying telling him is out of character for me."

"Don't you talk on the phone?"

"Not often. Daddy prefers face to face." And I was hoping it wouldn't come up, because I had the same wording problem Adam did, and no idea how to handle it. "I guess it's us against the two families."

He took my hand while he finished chewing. "I'll bet on us any day."

His confidence was contagious. We could handle this.

My phone chose that moment to ring.

Adam produced it from his pocket and looked at the screen. "So much for *it won't come up for a while.*"

It was Daddy.

CHAPTER 24

Kelly

"Hi, Daddy," I said into the phone. "Isn't it sort of early out there?"

Adam smirked at my predicament.

"It probably is, but I was in New York yesterday, and I decided to stop by before heading home to see my favorite youngest daughter. The benefit of a company plane is I get to go where I want."

I needed time to think. "What were you doing in New York, Daddy?"

"Let's meet for breakfast, and you can ask me all you want about my boring customer meetings."

My delaying question had failed at its job. "I can't. I just ate." At least it was a partial truth.

"Well, you can watch me eat then, while I quiz you."

What did *quiz me* mean? "Daddy, I wish I could, but I'm on my way somewhere. Maybe next time you swing by."

"Sounds like you're out somewhere already. Where are you? Maybe we could meet in between."

I could withhold things, but one thing I couldn't do was lie to Daddy. "I'm in McDonald's."

Adam started to shake his head slowly, obviously not approving of me giving out details.

The door to the street slammed, and I jerked in my seat to look over. A gun-toting federal agent was with me, and I still felt paranoid. The thought made me cringe.

"McDonald's?" Daddy's voice carried his characteristic curiosity. He was about to pull on the string to unravel a secret. "I thought you swore off McDonald's after that salad-contamination scare?"

"Yeah, well, it's on the way, and I needed to get something for a friend." Technically that was also the truth. We'd had to get Adam his breakfast.

"*A friend* sounds interesting. Dennis told me he suspected you were hiding a boyfriend from us. I'd like to meet this friend."

I'd lost control of the conversation. "I don't know what Dennis is talking about."

"I can stick around as long as needed. The three of us can meet for lunch."

"I can't."

"Dinner, then."

I pulled out the only trump card I could think of. "I promised to spend the day alone with him." Promises were sacrosanct to Daddy, and this would back him off—I hoped.

He was quiet for a second.

Adam had his chin on his hand, watching me squirm, and the raised corners of his mouth said I entertained him.

"A promise is a promise, so I won't ask you to break that. Are you going to at least tell me his name?"

"His name? Nope."

Adam jerked back and shook his head vigorously.

"It's just a casual date."

"If you say so. I'll tell Dennis his hunch was right."

"No way. I mean…please don't. He wouldn't tell me his new girlfriend's name."

Daddy didn't answer right away. With a little luck, I'd just shifted the target of his curiosity. It would serve Dennis right.

"Would I be correct in guessing that your new man is there with you now?"

I didn't answer.

"I'll take that as a yes. Tell him I expect him to treat you right."

I moved the phone away from my face. "Daddy says if you don't treat me right, he'll kick your ass all the way to Cleveland."

Adam couldn't contain a laugh. "Sugarbear, tell him that won't be necessary."

"I heard that," Daddy said in my ear. "Sugarbear, huh? I like him already. And I'll look forward to meeting him next time."

"Maybe," I told him before we said our goodbyes.

I'd gotten by the first hurdle without a lie, but the cat was definitely out of the bag, and I was not going to hear the end of it.

The more I thought about it, the more Daddy's previous statements about the Cartwrights came to mind. He wasn't going to accept this. There was no way he'd approach it rationally.

Adam finished the last of his hash brown. "That was fun."

"Fun?" I shot back. "I'd like to watch you try to explain it to your father." *Fun* was not in the same universe as where this was heading.

"Sorry, I was just trying to lighten the mood. Looks like we need a script."

I really was not ready for this. This was going to be what my brother would call a *clusterfuckus gigantus*, and I would be in the center of it.

Adam

She'd gone white when her father called, and I'd laughed right up until she reminded me my turn in the hot seat was coming as well.

My dad might not be so easy to put off.

She nibbled at her hash brown. "I don't know if he's going to want to kill me or you when he finds out."

I reached across to take her hand. "Hey, forget about it for now. Today is about decompression."

"How? All I can think about is how Daddy's going to react when I tell him your name."

"Simple. Today is about us, not them." I crumpled my empty wrapper and stood. "Let's get going."

She added her wrapper to the pile and followed me as I carried the tray to the trash. Outside, her arm came around my waist and welded her hip to mine as we walked. "Us."

"You and me, Sugarbear. That's all that matters."

The soft eyes of my new girlfriend looked up at me. "Us sounds good."

The warmth in her gaze said all I needed to know about how today would go.

Putting the phone back in my pocket, I felt the pouch with the Secret Service necklace in it. For a moment I considered giving it to her. I removed my hand and refastened the Velcro on the pocket.

Today was about being carefree, and the necklace would only be a constant reminder around her neck of the danger lurking out there. The time wasn't right, and what was the point if she wasn't going to be out of my sight anyway?

"Are you going to tell me yet?" she asked.

I turned us south on 19th again toward our first destination. "You told me you've lived here a year already, right?"

"Give or take."

"Anybody who comes to this city should take a day to see the sights, and that's what we're doing today."

Instead of arguing, this time she pulled herself closer to my side for a few steps. "What sights are on our tour today?"

"The usual: the White House, the Capitol Building, the monuments—a nice hike around the Mall."

"You've been here four times as long. In that time, how many of the Smithsonian museums have you visited?"

I was stuck for an answer to that one. "None yet, but I've had a lot of weekend work."

She stopped with me to wait for the walk light at the next intersection. "It's only fair that I give you, I mean us, the museum tour, then."

"Fair enough. Another day."

~

KELLY

THE SUN WAS HIGH, AND WE'D JUST FINISHED THE LINCOLN MEMORIAL AFTER visiting the Washington, Jefferson, FDR, Korean War, and several other memorials I was already forgetting the names of.

Adam led the way out, stopping at the steps leading down. "Sit right over here, against the column."

I had no idea what we were doing, but I settled down where he told me to.

He also sat on the marble step and put a strong arm around me. "See how everything lines up?" He pointed out toward the reflecting pond, the Washington Monument, and the Capitol beyond.

It was cute, but his arm around me reminded me the real reason we were here, and it wasn't marble buildings with solemn engravings. This was about spending time together, us time, and I was grateful for it.

"Do you see it?"

I nodded, but where he saw an alignment of structures, I saw an alignment of paths. His path and mine had crossed, and come into an unlikely alignment—one that felt very right.

"Did you know the Washington Monument is still the tallest stone structure in the world?"

"I didn't know that." I also didn't particularly care at this moment. "You're talking too much." What mattered to me was that we'd been able to bridge the family issues that had kept us apart. Now that I got to spend time with him, the setting didn't matter, just the company.

He was quiet for a few seconds. "Sorry, I do that when I'm nervous."

"Nervous? Why?"

His face came to mine, a mere inch away. "Because I don't want to blow it with you." The words roared over me like a tidal wave. He cared about me, us.

I closed the distance to initiate the kiss.

The people around us disappeared in a fog, and nothing mattered except the hold he had on me and his admission that he cared. The pine scent of his hair and the taste of his lips had me wishing we weren't in public.

In what was becoming a signature move for him, his thumb traced the side of my boob. The sparks hadn't subsided, and instead they intensified as each kiss had me yearning for more of his touch.

Eventually, I broke the kiss, fearing I might rip his clothes off. "You'll only blow it if you don't feed me."

"We can't have that." He rose and pulled me up.

After a stop at the refreshment building south of the Memorial, I followed him and the food I needed to a spot on the grass north of the reflecting pool. We didn't have a blanket to lie on, but otherwise this was the perfect picnic lunch.

We fed each other in the shade of a tree as we watched the tourists wander by. We guessed at where the groups came from and made bets on which way they'd look next.

He pulled the hot dog away from my mouth. "Hey, smaller bites. You need to drag it out and make it last."

"But you're teasing me."

His eyes fell to my chest in a stare. "I'd say you're the tease today."

I smiled at the compliment and tugged down on the hem of my shirt, exposing even more cleavage. "This little thing?"

His eyes bulged, then slammed shut for a second. "Here, have my hot dog." He shoved the remainder of his dog at me. "I've got an appetite to eat something else." His eyes fell to my shorts, and his smirk grew.

I squeezed my thighs together. "Oh, no you're not." My one and only time, Danny Delaney had puked his drunken guts out ten seconds after burying his face in my crotch. He'd said I smelled. That experience had ruined it for me, and I'd refused to try again.

"Oh, yes I am." He pointed. "Washington DC." He took us back to the guessing game. The group he'd pointed out were two Park Police officers on horseback.

"Could be Maryland or Virginia."

He nodded.

We finished our food, and after another half hour of people watching resumed walking.

He pulled out his phone and mumbled softly to whoever was on the other end. "When is stagecoach due at the castle?" was all I could make out.

"Where to next?" I asked when he'd hung up.

He checked his watch. "You'll see. We need to get moving if we want to make it on time."

When we made the turn north on 17th, the destination became obvious. We hadn't walked by the White House yet.

He turned us at the corner, and we walked down the blocked section of Pennsylvania in front of the White House. They made everyone stay on the north side of the road, behind barricades and tape. Uniformed officers were spaced about every ten feet—overkill for this motley throng of sightseers. By the time we made it partway down, the rumble of motorcycles came in the distance.

Adam pushed me toward the front of the crowd. "The motorcade's almost here."

"You mean the president?"

Adam pulled me to his side. "Yup."

Moments later, a dozen motorcycle cops turned the corner, followed by a half dozen black SUVs and three of those presidential limos you see on TV. The Suburbans and limos passed through a gate onto the White House grounds. The motorcycles stayed on the street in front of us, rumbling loudly.

All we could see from this distance was a man and a woman getting out of the limo that pulled up to the front door of the White House. It had to be the president and first lady, and the man waved in our direction.

The uniformed cop in front of me pulled his weapon and leveled it at me. "Gun!" he yelled.

I froze.

Three other Secret Service officers rushed over, guns drawn.

Adam

The officer pointed his Glock at us with a jittery hand.

"Hands up," Mr. Jitters yelled.

Several other officers had drawn their weapons and converged on us as the sea of onlookers pulled away.

I raised my hands and moved away from Kelly.

Abject fear wrote itself on her face as she raised her hands.

"FBI," I told the skittish officer.

"On the ground, face down, hands behind your head. Interlock your fingers," he screamed.

I put my hands behind my head and lowered to my knees. "ID, right back pocket."

"Face down," he yelled again. His voice cracked in fear.

He'd probably never executed a takedown in the real world before, which was scary, given that he was holding a Glock and had his finger on the trigger. With no safety, it was no gun for an amateur—accidental discharges were all too common.

I went to the ground.

One of the other officers put a knee on my back. He had to be way north of two hundred pounds. He pulled my Kel-Tec PF-9 out and threw it to the side before frisking me for more.

"FBI. ID, back right pocket," I repeated slowly.

The second officer had a cuff on one wrist before I felt the third pull out my creds.

"FBI," I said again.

A sergeant arrived, huddled with Mr. Jitters, and studied my identification while they kept me pinned. "Let him up."

"But he had a gun," Mr. Jitters complained.

The sergeant took Mr. Jitters to the side, patted him on the back, complimented him, and sent him off.

The other officer wrestled with his handcuff key before finally getting the metal bracelet off me.

I rubbed my wrist as the sergeant took my weapon from the uniform who'd picked it up.

"This isn't standard Bureau issue," he said as he released the clip and cleared the chamber.

"Undercover," I told him. My PF-9 was a lot smaller and easier to conceal than our standard service weapon.

He handed me back my unloaded weapon and clip. "Don't you ever come armed and unannounced on my street again, or I'll shoot you myself."

"Yes, sir," I told him, eager to get as far away from here as possible, as quickly as possible.

I gathered up Kelly, and we retreated north toward her house.

She shivered against me. "That was scary."

What I'd planned as a special sight had ended up endangering her.

"Sorry," was the only word I had as we walked.

Kelly

• • •

ADAM WAS SILENT AS WE WALKED BACK.

I couldn't have asked for a nicer way to spend the day. I gripped his hand. "Thank you." Up until the gun incident, this had been a wonderful, relaxing gift.

"For what? Almost getting you shot? I should have known better."

He was still focused on the negative instead of the positive the entire rest of the day had been.

"For taking me around. It's something I never would have done on my own."

"I should have known better."

I pulled him to a stop. "Stop that."

His brows drew together. "Stop what?"

"You told me to accept a compliment from you. The least you could do is reciprocate."

"You don't get it. That was a dangerous situation back there, and it was all my fault. What if—"

"What if nothing," I said. "How come you can't listen to me for a change?" I let go of his hand and started walking home. The man was impossible.

Adam quickly caught up to me, and this time he pulled me to a stop, with hands on each of my shoulders. "Sugarbear, I'm listening to you now."

I drew in a breath. "I know you would never do anything to hurt me."

He pulled me into a hug. "Of course not."

"I was trying to say thank you for forcing me to try a new experience. I had a great time today."

He rubbed my back. "But—"

I pushed away enough to give him my meanest scowl. "Stop with the buts," I insisted.

He squeezed my ass. "But I like your butt."

"You keep it up, mister, and you can sleep on the floor tonight."

His smile grew. "I apologize if I'm being a butthead. I accept your compliment, and your thanks, and I had a great time with you as well. How's that, Sugarbear?"

CHAPTER 25

Kelly

On Monday morning, Adam started his shower late, and I ended up running late as well. Naturally, it had nothing to do with me changing my mind about what I was going to wear today, or my hair dryer deciding to die. It was all Adam's fault.

He was the reason I hadn't gotten to sleep on time.

When I got downstairs, Adam tapped his watch as a nonverbal reminder that I was late.

I passed him on the way to the kitchen. "I know."

"You're the one who told me you couldn't be late on a Monday."

The kitchen was empty, save the plate of scrambled eggs waiting for me.

"Where's Yolanda?" I grabbed my phone off the charger.

He followed me into the kitchen. "She had to leave early to set up her exhibit."

"Right." I forked as much scrambled egg into my mouth as I could, while Adam tapped his foot. The time on the microwave put me closer to thirty minutes late. I swallowed and gobbled another monster bite before heading for the door. "Let's go," I mumbled.

Grabbing my purse, I realized another mistake. I'd forgotten to change to my second purse. Pulling open the coat closet, I located it on the shelf and pulled it down to start transferring contents.

Adam pulled my wallet from the broken purse and stuffed it in the other. "We don't have time for that. Phone and wallet, everything else can wait."

I'd already put the phone in, but searched the bottom for my hair brush and keys. I found the keys.

He grabbed both bags off the table. "We're leaving." He pushed me toward the door.

"I need my brush."

He exited with both purses while I locked the door. "I'm not letting you be late."

We speed-walked to his car. He popped the trunk with the key fob, tossed the full purse in and closed it, handing me the incredibly light, empty one.

After two blocks of him driving like a maniac, I commented on the obvious. "I could have moved things from one to the other on the drive."

He gunned it around a taxi without comment.

I shut up, deciding that surviving the trip was more important than pointing out how right I was. With three brothers, I knew all too well how guys didn't like to be told they were wrong.

Adam accelerated through the yellow of the next light.

I pulled my leather repair guy's card from my wallet and placed it on the console. "If you have a chance, drop the purse off for repair."

He grunted and nodded. A few minutes later he pulled to the curb in front of my building in record time. "Have a great day."

"You too." I climbed out and rushed to the building. At the door I turned.

Adam was watching and waved as I entered the building.

If he hadn't rushed me, for sure I would have ended up on the naughty list of late entrants today.

Adam

After dropping Kelly off, my desk upstairs in the field office seemed a little alien. Having spent Sunday with her, just walking and talking, instead of being a Bureau guy twenty-four-seven, meant it took a few minutes to get back into special agent mode and get my head straight.

To be honest, it hadn't really been the day out in the sun that slowed down my thought processes this morning. It was more that I couldn't get her out of my head. Kelly was becoming an obsession with me.

"Nice day walking around yesterday?" Neil asked when he returned with a coffee mug he'd most likely already refilled for the second time.

I'd forgotten that tracking my cell phone location was one of his duties as my backup, even when I didn't need him physically following. "Yeah. If the cover is boyfriend, we have to do some typical couple kinds of things, like a day on the Mall."

He didn't look convinced. "Right. Tough job having to hang out with a looker like her all day."

"Maybe we should ask your wife if we can switch places."

That shut him up.

"I still haven't seen anything good on the bank video," he said after a moment. "How much farther back you want to go?"

"I say we keep going, unless you have something better to run down."

"Nah. I went back over the interviews and didn't find anything useful." He turned to his computer.

I did the same and checked my email.

"Cartwright." It was Dempsey calling from his office door—never a good sign.

I raised my hand, stood, and started his direction without having to be told. These were always a call to meet behind closed doors.

He sat on the edge of his desk, instead of in his chair.

I closed the door behind me and waited to hear the latest complaint.

"I got a call from Secret Service this morning. Want to guess what it was about?"

I knew instantly. One of the uniformed Secret Service douches had run our altercation up the flagpole. "It probably has to do with me being armed on Pennsylvania Avenue on my undercover."

"You should know better. They don't want anybody with a weapon anywhere near their motorcade that isn't cleared, and all you had to do was have your fucking badge around your neck to have avoided it. But what's got them really steamed is the press coverage."

That was bad news I hadn't expected. "What press coverage?"

"Somebody sent a cell phone video of it to the news guys, and it was on TV last night."

"I didn't know."

"Neither did I. I reviewed it this morning, and since your face was in the dirt you're not blown, but the video sure makes them look like idiots."

"Sorry. I didn't expect a problem."

"Tell me, Cartwright, why are you the only one in the office I have to keep cleaning up after?"

I didn't dare answer.

"Keep this up, and you'll find yourself in the basement for the rest of your career. Got it?"

"Yes, sir."

Kelly

Kirby was already outside my cube when I made it upstairs after Krause's meeting. "Where's Evelyn?" she asked.

"I'm not her keeper. I just got in."

"Coffee run time." She started off.

I followed.

"How that man can talk for twenty minutes every Monday and say absolutely nothing is some kind of weird."

I nodded. "Privilege of rank. He gets to do what he wants."

She punched in her coffee selection while I added hot water to my cup.

Len the guard was in Kirby's cubicle when we got back, and two other women from our office were with him. He pulled open one of Kirby's drawers.

"Hey, what are you doing?" Kirby asked in a not-so-calm voice.

"Is this where you keep your purse?" Len asked her.

"Yes, and I'll thank you to stay out of it."

"My purse was taken too, for the second time," Laurie from an aisle over said.

Zenia echoed her. "Mine too."

"Did you take it?" Kirby asked Len. "It was locked in there before the meeting."

Len raised his hands. "No way. The lock's been forced."

I rushed to my cube. My purse drawer, which had been locked, now pulled open easily.

Fuck. It was empty. These locks were easy to break.

"They got mine too," I announced. At least I'd carried my phone with me to the meeting.

"We need to check everyone's for my report," Len told us.

As if that would do any good. The previous reports hadn't resulted in anything being returned.

Mark stood above the walls another row over. "I'm fine."

The guys had it easy in this. They carried their wallets in their pockets.

A few minutes later, the theft statistics stood at six purses. Whoever it was had to work here. Only the women's cubes had been targeted.

"The thief is one of us if he or she knows the layout," Len said, ignoring the obvious. We had name plates on our cubes. Even an idiot wouldn't force Mark's drawers open, looking for a purse.

"Another reason Krause's meetings suck," Kirby lamented as Len filled out his useless paperwork. "Put down that I had three hundred dollars in mine."

Len nodded. "And yours?" he asked me.

"I don't know exactly, but I probably had eighty dollars in my wallet."

The bigger hassle than the money was that I'd have to cancel and replace my credit cards and get a new license and insurance card. I was totally behind Kirby's sentiment—Krause should have to personally reimburse us.

I sat down and opened the password manager on my phone, to pull out the credit card details I'd stored there.

An hour later, new credit cards were on the way, the old ones canceled, and I was still on hold with the health insurance company to get a new card. That left just my lost keys to deal with. I had spares at the house, but I'd need Adam or Yolanda to let me in.

A text arrived.

ADAM: How are you doing?

ME: Not so good – six purses stolen including mine – again – maybe we should call the FBI

ADAM: I think they have more important things to do

A minute later another message arrived.

ADAM: Wish I could help

"Your boyfriend?" Kirby asked as I checked the message.

"Yeah, he's sweet." A week ago, calling a Cartwright sweet would have been cause for me to have a brain scan. This morning, however, the words fit.

"It's good to see you finally happy."

As her words rattled around in my head, I realized Adam did make me happy.

"Are you making good progress with this one?" she asked.

"You could call it that."

Her smile grew. "Good for you. You deserve a break on the dating front. We'll go to lunch, and you can tell me all about him."

I was still confined to the building without Adam as an escort. "Sorry, I can't do lunch. Maybe later."

She shook her head, and her smile turned down. "You look great. What do you need that stupid diet for?"

I shrugged. "I'm not quitting early just because you tempt me with tasty Indian."

"Or sushi, or Thai, or Greek, or Italian—"

"Get outta here," I cut her off before she drove me nuts.

She left and was replaced a minute later by Mr. Heiden, with his usual lack of greeting. "I need to visit my mother this afternoon," he said.

"Give her my regards."

He smiled. "Thanks, I will. Please give Nancy the SIM cards from Saturday, so she can start on them."

My jaw dropped. By rushing me to change my purse, Adam had kept me from bringing in the SIM card envelope. Which luckily had also kept me from losing it to the purse thief. "Sorry, I left them at home."

"Why'd you do that? Nancy needs to start transferring them today if we're going to keep on schedule."

My heart thumped loud enough to be heard across the room. "I meant to, but—"

"I don't want to hear it." His mood always deteriorated on days he went to visit his mom.

Silence on my part seemed like the best course.

His cell rang, distracting him from chopping off my head, or whatever he had in mind for me. "I have to take this. Just don't forget them tomorrow." He scurried off with the phone to his ear.

I sat down and took a few slow, deep breaths to calm my racing heart. His visit gave me a newfound appreciation for karma. Adam's rushing me had possibly just saved my job. As mad as my boss was about me not having the cards this morning, that was nothing compared to how he'd likely react to having to repeat the entire Saturday inventory because they'd been in the purse that was stolen.

CHAPTER 26

KELLY

BECAUSE OF A SEVERE THUNDERSTORM WARNING, WE WERE TOLD TO LEAVE EARLY on Monday afternoon, or risk being locked in the building until the storms passed. So at four o'clock, I waited downstairs for Adam to arrive as the rain began.

Great. No purse meant no umbrella, among other things. My stomach felt as sour as my mood, and the rain outside only compounded it.

Out of nowhere, a soaked Adam came through the door.

"I didn't see you pull up."

"You called early, so I'm driving a different ride."

"You have an umbrella?" I asked.

He held up his hands. "No such luck."

I followed him outside as he jogged to the street through the downpour.

He stopped beside an old blue Chevy and pulled open the door with a loud squeak. He hadn't been kidding when he said *different ride*. This prehistoric beast was half rust.

I slid in onto the vinyl bench seat, which was wet.

He closed the door and raced around to the other side.

The rain leaked in around the window of the convertible top on my side, so I scooted over to the center to avoid it. "This is your other car?"

"A Bureau undercover car."

I searched for the other end of the lap belt and clicked it in place. It didn't have shoulder belts. "You guys need a serious budget increase if this is the best you can afford. Are you sure it's safe?"

"Mechanically it's fine. It just looks like shit."

I tried to ignore the moldy smell. "I beg to differ. Fine would include keeping the rain out and not smelling like a garbage can."

"Well, there is that."

The engine surprised me by starting right up. The windshield wipers were another matter. They squeaked and pushed the haze around without making the view any clearer.

He pulled into traffic, and before long we turned onto Massachusetts Avenue.

The light turned yellow, and Adam stopped behind an Audi.

I didn't hear a screech, but I definitely felt the collision as we were hit from behind and pushed into the car in front of us.

"Fucking asshole," Adam yelled.

I stayed in the car while Adam jumped out to berate the idiot behind us.

Steam rose from the hood of Adam's car—not a good sign.

Adam yelled at the lady behind us, and was joined by the driver of the Audi.

A few seconds later, Adam was at the door. "Get out. The gas tank is leaking."

With visions of becoming chargrilled in an explosion, I raced out my side of the car and sloshed through the deep water at the curb to reach the safety of the sidewalk.

With no umbrella, and no bus stop, storefront, or other shelter, I was soaked to the bone in minutes.

I shivered on the cement while a cop car with flashing lights parked behind the mess and got involved in the drivers' verbal altercation.

After what seemed like an eternity in the rain—but was probably only ten minutes—Adam stomped over to me. He was on the phone telling someone where we were. "That's right. It needs a tow, and I need another vehicle delivered for tomorrow… No, we'll get ourselves out of here."

I shivered. "What's the deal?"

"The fucking deal is…" He pointed to the lady who'd started the chain reaction. "That lady needs to have her fucking driver's license revoked." On the zero-to-ten anger scale, he was nearing an eleven right now.

I shifted side to side, trying to warm up.

"You're cold," he said, finally noticing. "Let's go." His volcano of anger had probably kept him warm.

"Don't you have to stay for the tow truck?"

"It's handled." He tried to flag down the next several taxis, but they all had fares.

The phone in my hand rang. It was Yolanda.

"We've been robbed," she sobbed. "They broke in. The house is a mess."

"Robbed?" I asked. The news made me even colder than I was.

That got Adam's attention, and he came close. "What happened?"

Yolanda was going a mile a minute. "The cops are here. Please come home. I don't know what to do."

"We're on the way," I assured her. "Be there as soon as we can." I got off the line.

Adam

"What happened?" I asked Kelly as she hung up.

She was shivering uncontrollably now. "Yolanda said someone broke into my house."

"Stay right here."

A second MPD car had arrived on scene.

I hustled over to the cop waving traffic around our collision and pulled out my credentials. "We need immediate transport to a crime scene."

He looked at me like I was crazy. "I ain't a fucking taxi service."

I shoved my creds in his face. "If you don't want to drive, give me the keys. We have an active kidnapping and homicide investigation. Trust me, you don't want me to kick this upstairs."

He pointed to the nearest car. "Okay, already. Get in." He put up a hand to stop the traffic. "Jimmy, take over for me here," he yelled to another uniform.

I waved Kelly over. We piled into the car, and with lights and siren, we were at her place quickly.

She was still shivering when we exited the patrol car.

I flashed my creds at the cop guarding the door. "This is her house."

I didn't see any sign of forced entry at the front door.

Kelly gasped as she took in the sight. Each of the rooms downstairs had been thoroughly tossed in an apparent search.

Yolanda took Kelly into a hug as they consoled each other.

"I'm going to talk to whoever is in charge," I told them as I headed upstairs.

A guy in a suit, obviously a detective, was surveying the damage in the bedrooms.

I introduced myself, and we traded cards.

"What's the Bureau's interest in this?" Detective Capra asked.

"We're providing protection for the lady that owns this place."

"Kelly Benson?"

"Yeah?"

"If this is federal protection, you guys suck at it."

I held my anger in check. "I'm protecting her, not her stuff. And she's safe."

"Well, her stuff took one hell of a beating. I've only seen three others like this in the last year."

I understood exactly where he was going with this. "Yeah?"

"Does she have a load of jewelry or something, 'cuz this ain't local kids. I can tell you that. They were after somethin' specific."

My interpretation matched his. "I don't know." Everything was tossed around, all the drawers emptied. It was a search for specific valuables.

"The last two I saw like this, the crew—and based on video, there's three of them—got away with real hauls. A ton of jewelry, expensive watches and shit on one, and the other family had fucking gold bars hidden in the house. On the third one, the victim clammed up, and we never found out what they took. Your lady had something they wanted."

"Any idea how they target the places?"

"Not yet. I'll need to talk to your lady to see if we can find overlap—the same hairdresser, you know the drill."

I knew it well. We often had to go into excruciating detail to find the links between the victims. "She's pretty shook up. Tomorrow okay?"

He huffed. "Sure. And call me when she tells you what she was hiding."

I ignored the sarcasm. "How'd they get in?"

"Back door. Broke the door jamb."

"Thanks." I grabbed the comforter I'd been sleeping on from under the bed and took it downstairs.

Kelly was where I'd left her.

I wrapped the comforter around her and gave her a quick hug.

Yolanda spoke up. "I'm not staying here. I'll be at Bogdan's place." She headed for the stairs.

"You should get together some clothes. You're coming to my place," I told Kelly.

She pulled away. "But this is my home."

"The back door is broken. It's not safe."

She waved her arm around. "Why would anybody do this?"

"Thieves. But we need to get you dried off and warmed up, and now." I urged her toward the stairs. "What valuables did you have in the house?"

"I don't buy anything expensive. I've got a Coach purse I don't use, I guess." She climbed the stairs, and her tears began in earnest as she saw the destruction of her bedroom.

A single Coach purse made no sense at all for something like this.

I didn't push her. "Do you have any garbage bags?" I asked, seeing only one suitcase in her closet.

"Under the sink in the kitchen."

Detective Capra handed Kelly his card. "Ms. Benson, is that right?"

She nodded.

"What do you think they were looking for?" Capra asked.

I held back to let Kelly answer.

She sniffed. "I don't have anything worth taking except my car."

"I'll need to talk to you tomorrow," Capra told her.

I retrieved several plastic bags from downstairs, and returned to find Capra interrogating Kelly again.

"What about your roommate? What kind of valuables did she keep in the house?"

Kelly shrugged. "You'd have to ask her. I never saw anything particularly expensive."

Seeing me, Capra backed off. "Tomorrow then."

"Who would do something like this?" she asked, the question directed to the detective.

I answered before he could. "Local kids have been pulling jobs like this around here."

The answer seemed to mollify Kelly. "I hope you catch the little bastards."

Capra shot me a sideways what-the-hell? glance. "We're doing what we can, as fast as we can."

Kelly entered the closet and returned with a purse in hand. "It wasn't my Coach purse they wanted after all." The bag was sized for a child instead of an adult, and she'd said it was valuable. Women's fashion never made any sense to me. Why pay extra for jeans with rips in them when a pair of scissors could get you to the same place?

We loaded her suitcase and several bags with clothes she'd picked up from the mess on the floor.

"That's enough for now," I told her when she'd filled the third garbage bag.

"But—"

A raised finger stopped her before the argument began. She wrapped her arms around herself, with a slight shiver.

CHAPTER 27

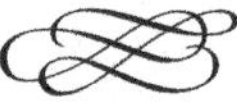

Kelly

We reached Adam's place quickly. With the blanket he'd given me, I was cold during the drive, but no longer frozen to the bone.

The officer who drove us helped get the bags of clothes inside.

Then the door closed behind him, and we were alone in a small one-bedroom, more modest than I would have expected, but it was cozy.

All I wanted to do was cry about how awful today had become.

Adam quickly shuttled me into the master bathroom and turned on the shower. "First order of business is getting you warmed up." It wasn't a request.

I released the hair clip I'd picked up on the way out of the house and dropped the comforter.

He helped me out of my clothes. His firm actions got me down to my bra and panties before he shoved me under the water.

I had to adjust the temperature. Even the lukewarm water felt boiling hot to my frigid skin.

He stood outside, arms folded.

I turned in the warm spray, and cold rivulets ran down my legs, as the water gave up its warmth to me. For the first time, I realized he was shivering as well. "You're cold too." I nodded, urging him to come in. Hogging the hot water while my savior froze to death was selfish, and that was one thing I wasn't.

He stayed leaned against the counter, ignoring the implied invitation.

I made it clearer. "Please come in."

After a moment, he started shucking his wet clothes.

I undid my bra and tossed it over the glass onto the pile.

He joined me, still visibly shaking, in just his boxer briefs and that silver ring he never took off.

Not clear why we were still partially clothed after the other night, I moved over to give him access to the spray.

Instead, he took me in a hug and rotated us under it, so we both got the benefit of the water.

I looked up at him. "Can you help me out of my panties?"

"Keep them on."

My heart fell. What was it about me in the shower that turned him off?

He turned us so my back was under the shower and adjusted the temperature up a bit.

I planted my head against him, closed my eyes, and let him guide us. For minutes, I rocked back and forth in his arms, slowly turning in the water—getting warmer every minute and not wanting to stop.

He rubbed my back.

I could feel the scratch of the ring he wore. "Why don't you ever take that ring off?"

He changed to a fingertip massage of my back. "I'm sorry. Did it scratch you?"

"Just a little."

He turned us so the water was running down my back.

"Well?" I asked.

Adam kissed my forehead. "We'll talk later."

I laid my head against his chest. "You know I'm going to hold you to that."

"I know."

As we moved, his arousal began to press against me. What had at first been shriveled from the cold had come to life under the warm water and our contact.

He pulled away. "I have to get out and make you something to eat."

I pulled at him. "Don't go yet."

"If I stay, I'll have to fuck you against the wall." It was the same comment as the first time he'd abandoned me in the shower.

"What if I—"

He put a finger to my lips, keeping me from finishing the sentence. "I'll make us something to eat. We have things to talk about."

He left the shower, and I didn't get to finish my naughty line, or ask what things we needed to talk about.

The warm water from the showerhead didn't make up for the warmth I'd lost when he pulled away. I watched him towel himself dry as I had at my house, but he seemed different in a way I couldn't put my finger on. Maybe it was just the distortion of the water droplets on the glass, but then again...

After he left, I stripped out of my underwear, draped them over the top of the glass, and turned the water up as hot as I could stand.

He reappeared briefly, tossing clothes on the counter. "These should help you warm up."

Normally being alone under the hot shower would have felt luxurious, but tonight it felt lonely. I twisted off the water. After drying, I slipped into the panties on top of the pile he'd brought, followed by USC sweatpants that were way too big. The drawstring fixed that, and the elastic at the ankles would keep me from tripping. I skipped the bra and added the oversize sweatshirt.

After wrapping my hair in a towel, I ventured out to find him in the kitchen.

"Feeling better?" Adam asked.

I went to where he stood at the microwave and wrapped my arms around him. "Much better, thank you."

He nodded to the right. "Plates are up there."

I let go to help with dinner.

"Sorry, all I have is microwave. I thought mac and cheese would hit the spot."

I pulled down two plates. "Sounds perfect." Hot and gooey would be a great way to relax after all that had happened today, and relaxation was what I needed. "Anything with you would be perfect tonight." That was how I felt, and it was time I was honest about it.

A smile grew on his face, and he blew me a kiss.

My heart melted at the simple gesture as I walked the plates over.

He opened the microwave and pulled down the mac and cheese dinners, which he stirred and scooped out onto plates. "Wine is in the fridge, or beer if you prefer."

I located a bottle of merlot in the door. The shelves of the fridge were almost bare, save some beer, apples, cheese, and a package of hot dogs that had seen better days. I carried the wine to the small nook table where he'd set the plates and glasses.

Screwing off the cap, I started to pour. "Say when."

"I need a full one or two tonight," he said with a laugh.

I didn't stop until we both had full glasses. I couldn't fathom what *he* needed the extra wine for.

As traumatizing as my home's burglary had been for me, it had to be on the mundane side for a hardened FBI dude.

I raised my glass. "To talking," I offered.

He sucked in a breath, hesitating long enough for me to wish I hadn't said anything. "To understanding each other."

I could handle that. I took a bigger-than-normal gulp of wine.

"Sorry I don't have anything better," he said.

"This is great. Just what I need."

He took a swallow of wine. "My schedule has been kind of unpredictable, and I keep having to throw fresh food out."

"This is fine, really. I like simple food." I'd meant to say something else; *simple food* sounded like a put down. "The kind Momma used to make," I added to soften the blow.

He shrugged. "Dig in."

We ate for a while in silence, neither of us willing to be the first to bring up the talk we needed to have.

I hadn't exaggerated about liking the simple pleasures, and the hot, cheesy concoction hit the spot. As Momma would have said, it coated my ribs. It had been a long time since I'd thought to add this to my menu at home. "This is great."

"That's because I added my own special touch."

Looking at it, I didn't see anything that hadn't come out of the package.

"Three extra seconds in the microwave."

I chuckled. "You have talent."

When I looked up after my next bite, I caught a smile on his face as his eyes averted from my chest. I sat up straighter to make my boobs more prominent under this baggy attire. If he liked it, I didn't mind.

He finished his glass, picked up the bottle, and offered me more.

"Sure."

He topped off my wine before refilling his and taking a big gulp. A bit of the wine escaped onto his shirt.

I pointed. "You should slow down."

He glanced down and held his shirt out, appraising the small stain. "Maybe, maybe not."

I pulled the bottle to my side of the table. "Maybe yes."

"What are you, my babysitter? I've only had one glass." He finished the one in front of him, and as full as he'd filled it, he was now closer to three. There wasn't much left in the bottle.

"Maybe you should drink slower is all," I said, trying to ratchet this back from becoming an argument.

He stood, went to the refrigerator, and came back with another bottle, which he used to refill his glass. "I need this," he half yelled.

I stood and took my plate to the sink. "You don't need me to get drunk."

"I'm not getting drunk; I'm getting ready."

Was there something horrible he needed to reveal?

He brought his plate over, and I rinsed it off for him. Settling in behind me, he encircled my waist with his hands—not grabbing, but holding. He pressed me against the counter, and his mouth came to my ear, hot breath sending tingles through me.

"I'm sorry I yelled, Sugarbear. Please join me on the couch."

I nodded. "No worries."

Releasing me, he took both our glasses and the bottle to the couch.

I loaded the few dirty things in his dishwasher, dried my hands, and joined him.

The pleasant surprise came when he pulled me over to him. "We should talk."

I'd wanted those words desperately, and I snuggled up against his muscular frame. All the places we touched warmed me with a feeling I hadn't felt in way too long.

I purred and snuggled closer. Tonight was about closeness and talking.

Adam

Her finger paused its circuits of my thigh.

"He may be your brother, but Dennis is an asshole with zero morals," I began.

Her hand left my leg. "He is not. You just have to give him a chance, and you'd see he's a principled guy."

I held out my right hand with the silver ring. "You asked about this ring. It's a reminder of what that fucker took from me."

Her hand came back to my leg as she snuggled toward me. "I'm listening."

"A scout for the Cowboys gave me this ring junior year." I stopped to gather the strength to recount the story. "I'd had a really good game at the Rose Bowl. All the scouts were there." I smiled, recalling how wonderful that day had been.

She pulled closer.

"I was pretty sure I'd get drafted after my senior year if my stats stayed as good as they had been. I was going to have a shot at the NFL—a real shot."

Kelly didn't say a word.

"And your fucking brother ruined it." I tensed as my anger boiled up. "At the beginning of senior year, he jumped me, and that's when I got injured. Torn ACL. No games senior year, no NFL. It was all over."

After a few seconds of silence she asked, "What was the fight about?"

"It wasn't a fight. It was an ambush."

"But why?"

"Complete bullshit. He thought I'd raped my girlfriend."

The word triggered her to jerk up. "Rape?"

"He had it all wrong. Celeste, that was my girlfriend, had told me a week earlier that another guy, Alex, had forced himself on her—sort of. She didn't use the word *rape*, but what she meant was pretty clear. So, me and my roommate chased Alex half way across campus before we lost him. He was going to get a beatdown he wouldn't forget. He left school right after that. All I could ever figure was that your brother heard the wrong name and decided to come after me. Asshole. Cost me my shot at the pros."

She went back to hugging me. "I'm so sorry."

I blew out a breath. "So now you know."

"Did you ever confront Dennis about it—the mix up I mean?"

"What would be the point?"

She didn't answer, because there was no answer to that question.

CHAPTER 28

Kelly

I listened to Adam's heartbeat after his explanation of the history between him and Dennis. The story had been disturbing, but it was a relief to have Adam finally open up to me.

I didn't see a way forward yet, but it sounded like I had to find a way to get Dennis to come forward and deal with what he'd done.

I got up and pulled the towel off my hair, shaking it out. "I think we've had enough soul baring for tonight." I got back on the couch, straddling him this time. "I know. Right now I have a request."

His hands came up to my waist. "What's that, Sugarbear?"

I leaned forward, with my hands on either side of his head and my breasts inches from him. "I need you to make me forget my shitty day."

"That's the alcohol talking."

I brought my mouth an inch from his. The electricity between us almost crackled in the air. "No, this is your girlfriend talking, and you promised me something about a counter or a wall."

~

Adam

My hands slid up her sides. Resisting her was torture. "I think you should relax."

She leaned back, put her hands over mine, and brought them up to caress her chest. "Help me relax, then."

I let her hands guide mine to squeeze her tits. "I meant sleep, Sugarbear. You've been through a lot today." Her warm breasts felt wonderful in my grasp, just begging to be uncovered, licked, sucked, bitten.

She ground her crotch over my straining dick. "We can sleep after." She pulled at the hem of her sweatshirt and lifted it off. She leaned forward again, and because she was braless, nothing separated me from my treat. "Are you sure I can't convince you?"

I gave in when she brought a nipple to my mouth. I licked and sucked the pink bud while thumbing the other.

Her eyes closed and a soft moan escaped her lips. She'd asked for the counter, but I had a different plan for tonight.

I licked a circle around her nipple and blew on the taut little bud. "I think I have just the thing to relax you."

She rubbed her crotch over my cock. "I can tell."

I ran a hand down between us to rub her through the sweatpants. I licked my lips. "You need a proper tongue lashing."

"No. You promised the wall."

I rubbed her some more in between licks of the nipple in front of me. "I said we'd get to that, and we will. First, I'm going to feast on you."

She shook her head.

I pushed her back enough to look her squarely in the eye. "What's the problem, Sugarbear?"

"I'm not sure I can…" her voice trailed off.

Her spunk had disappeared into fear of something.

I lifted her off and shifted her to the couch beside me. "Then let's relax with a little TV instead." I picked up her sweatshirt from the floor and handed it to her.

She hesitated before pulling it back on.

"We won't do anything you're not comfortable trying."

"I'm up to try the wall."

I picked up the DVR remote and shook my head. "Not on the menu tonight." Tonight's menu was going to start with her, or nothing.

"But—" she complained.

I turned to her and put a finger to her lips. "Doing you in the butt is also not on the menu tonight."

That finally got a shake of the head and a giggle.

Clicking through the channels, I found *Bonanza* on a western channel and started that.

"The Cartwrights? Really?"

I recognized the episode. "You'll like it. In this one Adam saves the girl."

Her hand moved back to my leg and up toward my crotch. "And does she throw herself at him?"

I pulled her hand away and laughed. "No. She rides out of town on the stage, and he's heartbroken."

"She probably knew he was overbearing and controlling."

I wrapped an arm behind her and pulled her over to me. "You'll have to watch and judge for yourself." My cock protested the lack of her touch, but that was the price I'd have to pay.

With only a few grumbles about fairness, she settled in against me to watch.

"Is it just a coincidence that your name is the same as the oldest son on the show?" she asked.

"All Mom told me is that if they'd had a girl, she would have gotten to pick the name, but I wasn't, and Dad picked Adam."

KELLY

BONANZA HAD BEEN A SERIES DADDY WOULDN'T LET US WATCH AS KIDS. BUT Serena and I could get in one or two episodes on cable after school, when he wasn't home. Looking back now, it had been a pretty childish rule that we couldn't watch the show because it portrayed a fictional Cartwright family as heroes instead of villains, but that's just how Daddy was.

Adam had suggested for the second time that he wanted to go down on me. He certainly hadn't gotten the hint that I wasn't interested.

Because what if I grossed him out? I'd never seen Danny Delaney again after that disastrous first try, and it had hurt, because I'd liked him a lot. What if I drove Adam away as well?

I'd always nodded knowingly when my college roommate had said you had to give a little to get a little. She'd clearly enjoyed it. And none of the few hundred sex articles I'd consumed in women's magazines had been negative about the experience, yet I'd never gotten up the courage after my first failed attempt. Maybe if my boyfriends hadn't all been scared of my brothers, one of them would've pushed me harder, and I'd have gotten past my hang-up by now.

The woman in this installment of *Bonanza* was stuck in a cabin with Adam. He'd caught and cooked a rattlesnake for them to eat. She turned her nose up at it, and I didn't blame her. *Yuck*. Eating a snake? How gross could you get?

"Suit yourself. It's this or go hungry," onscreen Adam told her. "Try it. I guarantee you'll like it."

In the end, she gave in, tried it, and declared they could serve it in restaurants in New York City if they gave it a French name.

Gathering up my nerve, I decided it was time to try the snake. I leaned over to lick my Adam's ear. "Will you stop if I can't take it?"

He turned to me. "If you give it a chance, you won't want me to stop."

After a minute of sensuous kissing, he carried me to the bedroom. My insides churned as he laid me down and pulled off my panties. Clamping my legs together, I wasn't sure I was ready for this. The actress on the TV show had probably actually eaten chicken instead of snake.

Adam shucked off his clothes and pulled a tie from the closet.

"Do I have to be tied up?" I asked, cringing. I'd read fifty shades, but I doubted I was ready for anything like that yet. I was back to juggling fear and titillation.

"Blindfold," he explained. "Just lie back and concentrate on the experience."

"Maybe later."

He shrugged, dropped the tie on the bureau, and settled in next to me. "Relax, Sugarbear." His lips found mine, and his hands started the roaming of my body that sent tingles everywhere.

My butterflies slowly settled as he deepened our kiss, and I let myself fall under his spell. Being in his arms was better every time.

His hand slid down through my curls and a finger parted my folds, sliding up and down my slippery slit.

Willing myself to relax, I spread my legs to give him access and found his cock with my hand. Taking his advice, I kept my eyes closed and concentrated on the feel of his member in my hand and his touch.

His fingers circled and stroked my clit, before moving down to enter me and returning again to my sensitive little nub. More nerves fired every time he returned to my clit, drawing moans out of me that I couldn't control.

"Relax, baby, and give in to it." His mouth moved to my breast, and his licks and cool breaths made me shiver. But they didn't chill my desire for him.

He kissed up my neck and bit my earlobe lightly. "Tell me what you want."

"I want you inside me."

"Later." His fingers moved side to side over my little bud. "Side to side?" The fingers circled my clit. "Round and round?" The jolts of pleasure shot through my body with each touch.

"Yeah… Like that… Faster… Oh my God…" I arched into him, looking for more pressure, more of everything he did to me.

He worked me like a musical instrument as his mouth moved from my neck to my breast, and his fingers kept up their attack.

My breath caught, and all I could get out between the moans were single words. "Adam… Fuck… Yeah… Christ." Without warning, my climax rolled over me in quick waves. I shook and pulled him to me, finally relaxing into the bed as a pile of mush in his arms.

His cock throbbed in my hand as his lips found my ear again. "Is this helping relax you?"

"Oh, yeah. I'm…" I searched for a better word, but settled on *super relaxed*.

I lost my grip on his cock when he moved down and was suddenly between my legs.

I opened my eyes—a bad idea, as Adam's face was replaced by Danny Delaney's. I tried to close my legs, but Adam didn't let me.

"Close your eyes, lie back, and relax."

Hyperventilating, I could only say, "But…"

"Relax." His hands ran up to my breasts, down to my hips, and up again in a soothing motion.

Slamming my eyes shut, I slowly wiped the movie screen behind my eyelids clear of Danny puking all over me. Adam hadn't done anything I hadn't liked so far. "Okay." I braced myself and dreaded what would come next.

I didn't need to open my eyes to recognize the feel of his fingers entering me, sliding up to and circling my swollen clit.

His breath on my pussy was hot, and his stubble scratchy as his fingers worked me again, relaxing me as he had minutes ago.

I let my legs go wider and sunk into the bed with the building pleasure of his attention.

"Now, tell me again what you like."

"Yeah… Like that…"

A moment later, his tongue replaced his fingers. His hands held me as I pulled away.

But slowly, my trepidation was replaced with desire as the sensations rolled through me even more powerfully than before.

His tongue darted over me, flicking and licking, adding pressure and sucking lightly. He lifted up. "Talk to me."

I didn't have the words. "Just keep it up." I threaded my fingers in his hair and pulled him against me, widening my legs and giving in to the pleasure.

He kept at me, bringing my blood to a boil as each dart of his tongue sent shockwaves through me. In no time, he'd pushed me up the mountain of pleasure and over the edge into bliss with a second orgasm that shook me to my core. When he'd wrung the last spasm out of me, he finally slid up my body to give me a kiss.

"Relaxed yet?"

"Like you wouldn't believe." The simple kiss, with his mouth wet from me, was my reward for pushing my boundaries in ways I couldn't have imagined a few weeks ago. "I only need one more thing."

His hand lay on my breast, his finger circling my nipple. "What's that, Sugarbear?"

I squeezed his cock again, now that he was close enough. "I need you to mount me." I rolled over and got up on all fours. "And don't hold back."

CHAPTER 29

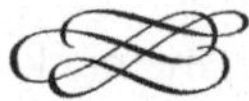

Kelly

I ROLLED OVER THE NEXT MORNING AND BLINKED AWAY THE SLEEP TO FIND ADAM already awake, staring at me. I hadn't been dreaming. Last night had really happened—the bad and the good.

The situation with my stolen purse and my poor house had been offset by the way Adam had opened up to me and then forced me to forget my inhibitions. This morning I was mad at myself for letting my experience with Danny Delaney set a boundary for me.

We still hadn't gotten to the counter or the wall, but what Adam had given me was better—confidence to push myself.

He leaned over to place a playful kiss on my nose. "Morning, Sugarbear."

I circled my hand behind his neck and pulled him back for the real thing. "Is that all I get?"

He pulled away. "Just a sec." He went to the bathroom, and the sound of running water and a toothbrush started.

I didn't understand his hesitation with a little morning mouth. Hell, he'd kissed me last night after having his mouth all over my lady parts. A smile curled my lips as I remembered the experience. It wasn't going to be my last.

After returning from the sink, he landed on top of me, placing one arm on either side of my head, his lips mere inches from mine. "I wanted to brush first."

I lifted up closer to him, his breath hot on me. "It doesn't bother me."

In a split second, his mouth claimed mine, and he rolled, pulling me over on top of him. His hand found my ass.

I gave him the kiss back with the same intensity. Memories of last night flooded through me, heating my core again as the connection with him sent tingles racing all the way to my toes.

He ended it too quickly, rolling me back off him. "We've gotta go, and I have to get your house fixed." He rose and headed to the bathroom again.

Locating the clock on his side of the bed, the answer wasn't good. It was much later than I usually woke. Mind-blowing sex was obviously a good sleep aid.

The day was not going to be a good one. And his reminder that I was only here because my house was a disaster zone threw a pall over the morning.

I put my hair up with the clip I'd brought last night and joined him in the shower without any of my previous trepidation. His gentle soaping of my body was just what I needed to lift my spirits. With a man like him beside me, there wasn't anything I couldn't tackle.

I was his Sugarbear. Make way: I am woman, hear me roar.

He was the first out to dry off.

I rinsed quickly and followed him out, doing my best to keep from getting my hair wet.

I located a suitable ensemble of work clothes from the garbage bags and joined him downstairs.

The microwave was running. The empty box on the counter was breakfast burritos. After the ding, he set one on a plate for each of us with a fork. "We have to be quick. Sorry I couldn't make your over-easy eggs."

I cut into my burrito. "This is fine. It's good to mix it up a little, right?"

He snorted. "Yeah, big step into the danger zone."

I was tempted to fling a piece of burrito at him, but thought better of it. This was the first Tuesday in a long time without my over-easy eggs. Just thinking that made me seem like a cardboard cutout instead of a living, breathing person.

My phone came to life on the counter with Yolanda's ringtone.

"I won't be home for a while," she told me, her voice cracking. "It's a disaster." She'd seemed pretty steady when she left for Bogdan's last night, but that wasn't the case this morning.

"Adam is going to work on getting the door fixed today," I told her.

"It's not that. Some of the jewels were stolen last night, and the exhibit's being canceled." She talked almost too fast for me to understand. "I have to fly out today and escort what's left back to LA."

"Your Hollywood exhibit?"

Adam looked up at the note of alarm in my voice.

"Yes."

"How?"

"I don't know. This morning they're just missing from the receiving cage. The owners are blaming the Institute, and my boss is blaming me."

Things were bad when Yolanda referred to the Smithsonian as the *Institute*, even if that was the official name.

"How long?" I asked.

"No idea. How long does keel-hauling take? Or fingernail pulling? That is *if* I come back alive."

She hung up after agreeing to keep in touch.

Adam forked the last piece of his burrito. "What's up?"

"Yolanda has to leave town. She said some of her exhibit was stolen from the museum last night."

"Could that…"

"What?"

"Never mind." He stood and took his plate to the sink. "Let's go."

The time on my phone agreed with him. I was already late. I scarfed down another forkful and joined him at the sink with my plate.

I loaded my phone, some spare cash, and mascara—always my mascara—into the tiny Coach purse I'd brought, which was about all that would fit. Hopefully the leather guy could fix my black beauty quickly.

Adam opened the door to a different car than last night, but just as ugly.

"What's this?"

"Replacement Bureau car."

"Can't we take your real car?"

"Sorry if this isn't up to your standards. Half the country would be happy to have this car, and I need it for work today."

I slid into the stained seat. The number of people who'd want this piece of junk was more like half a small town than half the country. It smelled just as bad as last night's leaky bucket, but at least it had a real roof and the seat wasn't wet.

He drove aggressively on the way.

As I watched the blocks fly by, my thoughts returned to last night.

Why hadn't I ever had a guy like Adam before?

The simple answer was, I hadn't looked for one, and the ones who'd found me were all intimidated by my family. In California, they'd all met one or more of my brothers, or my father, or all of the above. The threat that they'd better not upset me had always been clear.

Only Adam had been self-confident enough to push me beyond my comfort zone. I called it risky—he called it living. He was right. For the longest time, I'd thought my vibrator was a good-enough stand-in for a man. But Adam had proven me wrong—oh, so wrong.

We passed a phone store.

Fuck me, I'd screwed up again. "I forgot the SIM cards. We have to go back."

He didn't slow down. "What SIM cards?"

"From the inventory on Saturday. They're in my purse with the broken strap, the one in your trunk. I was supposed to bring them in yesterday."

"We don't have time right now. You're already late—we're both late. How about I get them and drop them by this afternoon?"

"But I got in trouble for not bringing them yesterday."

"I can't help that. I'm getting you to work safely. It's your responsibility to pack the right shit." Tough love was coming my way.

I deserved it for being a dumbass. "That will have to be good enough, I guess."

Two days, two fuck-ups at work, and two sets of thieves. I could only hope these things didn't come in threes.

~

ADAM

AFTER DROPPING KELLY OFF, I WENT STRAIGHT TO THE FIELD OFFICE. HARPER had been assigned to the stakeout this morning so Neil and I could work on the Fawkes Crew robberies.

The call from Yolanda still bugged me. Jewelry stolen from the museum the same night the place Kelly and she lived was burglarized was too big a coincidence. Could Yolanda have had a key, a pass, or something else that enabled the theft? SMK's email was on a Ukrainian site, and her boyfriend was Ukrainian. Something didn't smell right…

The top thing on my agenda was to get Kelly's door fixed so at least the house could be locked up. That became my first call when I reached my desk.

The contractor I'd used to work on my back steps agreed to get to the door as soon as he could.

A few minutes later, Dempsey laid eyes on me. "Cartwright," he yelled. "Now."

I didn't dawdle, but he tapped his foot nonetheless. The door slammed behind me, and the eruption began immediately. "What the hell do you think you're doing calling Donnelly?" He had one hell of a red-hot poker up his ass.

I hadn't expected that calling the AD to ask about Uncle Jack would become a problem. "I didn't think—"

"You sure *didn't* fucking think." He took his seat. "There is no fucking *I* in team. How could you go over my head like that? That's not the way it works on my team. You should fucking well know that, you fucking dipshit. Do you have any idea how badly he reamed me because I can't control you? Crap like that reflects on me, and I won't fucking tolerate it. One more asinine move and you'll be downstairs alphabetizing records for the rest of your very short career."

I got a word in edgewise when he stopped to think of the next thing to yell at me. "The Benson kidnapping is related to the Guy Fawkes Crew robberies, and he had personal knowledge I had to ask about."

"What you should have done is asked me to ask him what you wanted to know. What possessed you to insult an AD? That is the most boneheaded move ever. You have to learn your place."

Donnelly had obviously taken my asking about Uncle Jack worse than I'd thought. "Do you want me to call and apologize?"

"No fucking way. I don't want you to ever talk to him again—not ever."

I nodded. "I won't. Promise." Pissing in his coffee wouldn't have bothered him as much as having his ass chewed out by Donnelly.

"Get out of my sight, and go relieve Harper on the stakeout."

"Yes, sir." I escaped the ASAC's office as quickly as I could.

~

Kelly

Kirby found me as soon as I got situated upstairs. "Where's Evelyn? I didn't see her at all yesterday."

I locked up my purse. "No idea. I just got in."

"I'm not waiting for her. Coffee run time." She started off.

I followed her to get my morning tea.

I pulled the lever for hot water while she punched in her coffee selection.

"Benson." It was Mr. Heiden from behind me. "My office. Now." He glared at me while I removed the teabag from my cup and gathered it up.

Kirby avoided eye contact.

"Yes, sir." I followed him, preparing to get reamed again about forgetting the SIM cards this morning.

Through the glass, I could see Krause when we reached his office.

Fuck.

Either the SIM cards were a bigger deal than I thought, or Krause had noticed me come in late after all, and now I had to pay the price.

I followed my boss in and tried to get ahead of the problem. "I didn't mean to be late."

Krause shook his head. "Sit down."

Heiden moved to his chair behind the desk, and I took the chair farthest from Krause.

"Benson, isn't it?" Krause asked.

He probably remembered me from the time I'd been late to his meeting, the only time we'd ever met.

I nodded.

The cleft between Krause's bushy eyebrows narrowed. "You're going with Paul here down to OPS. But before that, I want to know who you let get by security." Apparently Krause was allowed to use Mr. Heiden's first name. Rank had its privileges.

His question didn't make any sense. "I don't understand."

"Paul tells me you were auditing the exit procedures on Saturday."

"She's our best. Meticulous attention to detail," Heiden offered.

Krause looked ready to blow a gasket. "Then how did we let several million dollars worth of objects walk right out the door?"

My mouth dropped. "What went missing?"

"Never mind that. Answer my question. Who did you let bypass the procedures?"

"Not a soul," I answered firmly. I wracked my brain for any time Saturday when I'd paid less than complete attention and came up empty. "We shut down the exit for lunch, and that was all."

Krause turned his venom on my boss. "You and OPS told me the procedures were foolproof."

"They absolutely are," Heiden started.

"The results say otherwise," Krause shot back. "OPS is reviewing the tapes now. You will escort this young lady down there, and by the end of the day, I expect to know what happened." He rose, and a second later the door slammed behind him.

"What happened?" I asked.

"Jewelry that was supposed to go on exhibit this week was found missing this morning."

Yolanda's call came back to me. "The Hollywood exhibit?"

"I don't have the details. Anyway, like he said, we're going down to OPS to get this straightened out."

"You don't think I—"

"Of course not, but it seems you let the guards slack off."

CHAPTER 30

Adam

My cell rang. It was Kelly, but way earlier than normal. It wasn't even near lunchtime yet.

"Hey, Sugarbear, what's up?"

"I need to be picked up…now." Her tone was off, pleading more than anything, which wasn't like her.

"What's the problem?"

"Please."

It obviously wasn't something she wanted to talk about right now.

"Give me a few minutes. I'll be there as soon as I can."

"Thank you," she managed before hanging up.

It probably wouldn't have helped if I had tried probing any deeper, not that I got the chance.

I dialed Dempsey and told him I needed a relief agent over here for the rest of the day.

He wasn't happy about it, but we didn't have much choice. Letting Kelly leave work unprotected wasn't an option, and neither was a gap in surveillance here. It was up to the ASAC to figure out the manpower problem.

~

I PULLED UP AND PARKED IN THE RED ZONE IN FRONT OF KELLY'S BUILDING.

A DC cop on foot patrol walked up as I got out. "Can't park there."

I stood by the car, not seeing Kelly anywhere yet, and ignored the uniform while I typed my text.

ME: Here

"You understand English?" the cop asked, pulling the ticket pad from his pocket.

I walked around him to put my back to the Smithsonian building and pulled out my creds, holding them close enough to my chest that no one but the officer would be able to see. "Won't be long."

He shook his head, pocketed the pad, and walked off with a mumble about "feebs." It was never appreciated when we pulled rank.

I turned back toward the building.

Kelly walked my way, without her usual smile.

A uniformed Smithsonian guard watched from the doorway with an equally sour look.

I opened the car door.

Despair screwed up her countenance, and she buried her face against my shoulder. "It's not fair." She wrapped her arms around me, and the sobbing started.

I'd had the warning of her tone on the phone earlier, but was unprepared for the waterworks. I rubbed her back. "It'll be okay. Tell me about it, Sugar-bear." I kissed the top of her head.

She continued to sob and shook in my arms. "I didn't do it."

"Do what?"

"I can't do this here. Can we go home?"

I rubbed her back and pulled her chin up to look into her teary eyes. "I'm here for you. You know that, right?"

She nodded and glanced up at the building. "Can we go?"

"Sure." I released her and helped her to the car, shutting her in firmly. As I walked around the car, I looked up at her building for what scared her. All I saw was eight floors of impenetrable blue glass.

After we were safely away from her building, I asked, "Want to tell me about it?"

"No." In spite of the warmth in the car, she shivered in the seat with her arms wrapped around herself.

"A smart girl I know once told me it helps to talk."

She repeated the one-word answer. "No."

I gave up on questions and placed a hand on her thigh instead.

A block later she said. "Not in the car."

It used to be I couldn't get her to shut up, and now she refused to talk.

Women.

Kelly

It felt so good, so safe to be with Adam after that terrible experience. I hadn't wanted to let go of him outside, but I could feel the evil heat of dozens of eyeballs staring out the windows of the Smithsonian, looking down on the traitor, me. What had been a welcoming place this morning was no longer that.

I hadn't done anything wrong, and I'd been summarily convicted and publicly humiliated as if I were guilty. I had to get away from the judging eyes.

Now I needed a glass of wine—no, a bottle—and another hug, neither of which I could get until we reached his place. I couldn't even go to my own house. Everything sucked.

The car was traveling damnably slow, and the irony of the situation almost, but not quite, brought a smile to my lips.

I'd asked to talk about him and Dennis, and he'd shut me down cold. Now here I was, the supposedly open, oversharing one, clammed up and refusing to speak. The difference was, my self-imposed silence was only going to be a few minutes.

"I got suspended," I blurted out, unable to obey my own rule and hold it in.

He pulled the car to the curb and stopped.

Exactly what I didn't want. "Please keep going. We need to get home."

His eyes held mine with a steely resolve. "If you agree to talk to me."

"Not here, please."

He pulled into traffic and sped up.

"They think I stole from them."

"That's ridiculous."

I didn't dare say more until safely ensconced in his place. I wrapped my arms tighter around myself, wishing they were his. "I need a drink."

He sped through a yellow light.

I closed my eyes and counted silently. I needed something, anything to calm me.

He pulled up and parked. Rushing around, he opened the door for me.

I was so weak he had to help me out. I collapsed into him. "Don't let me go." I lost control of my tear ducts again.

He held me tight. "I've got you." Ten seconds later, he swept me up and carried me to the front door, setting me down only long enough to unlock, before carrying me the rest of the way to his couch. "I'll be right back with your drink." He returned in record time with glasses and a bottle of Black Label.

I'd been picturing wine, but this was better. I took the glass he poured and chugged half of it immediately. The burn didn't bother me. It was just a signal that relaxation was on the way.

"Slow down there, Sugarbear." His arm snaked fondly around my shoulder.

I shook my head and held out my glass for more. "They think I stole the jewels."

"What are you talking about?"

I appreciated the warmth of being against him. It wasn't as good as a hug, but I was getting the booze down, and that was priority one. "Or that I helped Evelyn steal the jewels—Yolanda's exhibit jewels."

He didn't catch up with me, but he did sip his drink. "That's ridiculous. You've been with me the whole time."

"Saturday during the inventory shutdown." I downed the rest of my glass, and the liquid warmed my belly.

His grip on me tightened as he pulled me closer. "It doesn't make any sense. SMK's last email said nothing was happening until next week, right?"

Was he questioning my honesty? I pushed away. "How can you ask that? I told you everything I've gotten from him."

He put a hand on my thigh. "Sugarbear, that didn't come out right. I'm just talking through the problem."

I relaxed back into him. "I know."

After having learned the real Adam, I should have known better than to jump to a stupid conclusion. He was the one person right now I could count on, the one solid rock in my world.

He planted another of his sweet kisses on my head. "It'll be okay."

From my vantage point, the future didn't look so sure. "It doesn't make sense. They have to have the timeline wrong. Nobody left the building Saturday with anything. It has to have happened either before or after."

ADAM

IF KELLY SAID NOTHING LEFT THE BUILDING WHILE SHE WAS THERE SATURDAY, that would be the one truth we had to start with.

"The fucking SIM cards," I blurted. It was so obvious I'd missed it.

Kelly sniffled. "Another reason I am *so* fired. They were due in the office yesterday."

I rose and pulled her up.

"What?"

I pulled her along behind me, toward the door. "What's on them?"

"Slow down." She hobbled along behind me with only one shoe on. "Pictures of everything in the inventory."

I extracted my car key while opening the front door. Two presses of the button, and the trunk clicked open before we got there. "Show me?" I lifted the trunk lid.

She unzipped and rummaged around in her purse, extracting a sealed envelope, which she handed me.

I took the envelope and tore it open. It contained a zillion SIM cards, each one numbered. Two of the cards escaped into the bottomless mess of her purse.

"Hey, don't do that out here. I can't lose any. I'm responsible for them."

"Inside, then. Let's see what's so valuable."

I hefted the purse before closing the trunk and ushering her back inside.

"Why are you interested in these?" she asked.

"They're probably evidence someone wants to destroy. It's so obvious now. Your purse was stolen to get these, and your house was searched when they weren't in the purse you took to work."

Her hand went to her mouth. "My God. But the detective said it was kids who broke into my house."

"It wasn't kids. I just didn't want you to worry."

Her eyes turned cold. "How can I trust anything you say? You wanted me to be honest with you, but it doesn't go both ways?"

She was pissed for good reason. I moved to take her shoulder.

She backed away.

"I was trying to protect you, and I'm sorry."

"So you blow up at me if I'm not as open as you want, but when you lie to me, you just say you're sorry and that fixes it?"

"What else can I do to make it up to you? I knew you wouldn't be able to sleep if we told you how professional the job looked."

Her stance hadn't softened one bit. "You owe me a favor, I'd say." The girl was a stickup artist, quid pro quo for letting me off the hook I'd hung myself on.

I sighed. "Name it." There was no other good way out of this.

She came to me and kissed my cheek. "I'll save it for later." In a second flat her demeanor had shifted to amused satisfaction. "Let's figure this out." She set the purse down on the table.

I'd been played. That was something about her I'd have to remember for next time. The girl could shift on a dime into actress mode, and I'd fallen for it. But I did deserve it.

Spilling the contents of the envelope onto the table, I sifted through them to see if I could find anything out of the ordinary.

She pointed at the little pieces of plastic. "What are you looking for?"

"Anything besides SIM cards that might have been slipped into the envelope."

"I'm the one who filled the envelope. You won't find anything else."

With this many cards, there had to be tens of thousands of images, and even if I could look through all of them, how would I know what I was looking for? It could be something as ordinary as the wrong person in the background of a shot.

"If this is what he wants, we should get another message. Check the email. Use my laptop on the counter."

Her face scrunched up in disapproval.

"Please," I added.

She trundled off to check. "You need to find the two you lost. I'm still responsible for those."

I started pulling items out of the bottomless pit: hair brushes, curling iron, makeup, eyelash curler, first aid kit, and a million other things. Eventually the table was full and the purse was empty. The two offending SIM cards had slid into a corner.

The bottom of the bag was oddly lumpy.

"Found a message," she called out from the counter. "He wants them."

I located a tear in the lining and pulled out what had gotten lost between the lining and the bottom. "Hey, Kells, come over here."

"No, you come over here to read it."

"Sugarbear, stop arguing and get your butt over here."

CHAPTER 31

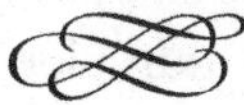

Kelly

To assert my independence, I stopped by the fridge and pulled a Diet Pepsi out before returning to the table.

His two big hands hid something. "Sit down."

I took a chair even though I didn't feel like it.

"Look what I found." His hands lifted to show the most gigantic yellow diamond.

If I hadn't been sitting, I would have fallen over at the sight. "Where?" I squeaked.

His hand went into my purse and extracted a ruby-and-diamond necklace. "Under the lining of your purse."

"No way. I didn't put those there."

He let out an exasperated sigh. "I know that. Are these the ones that went missing?"

"Yolanda said five in total." I pointed at the large yellow stone. "That has to be the Isadora Diamond, and that one the *Pretty Woman* necklace."

He fished into the bottom of my purse, coming out with another necklace.

When I picked it up, I was certain the Heart of the Ocean necklace from *Titanic* was the most beautiful thing I'd ever seen. Of course it wasn't the one

Kate Winslet had worn in the movie. That had been costume jewelry. According to Yolanda, this was the real thing, a monster sapphire surrounded by real diamonds, and worth a literal fortune.

Adam pulled another out. "These are what he was after, not the SIM cards."

I still had a burning question. "How'd they end up in there?"

He pulled out the fifth. "That's the last of them. Pretty ingenious, I think. You said your job was to watch the exit guards?"

"Audit. Yes, and I'm sure they didn't let anything get by."

"The question is, who audits the auditor? You'd be the last person anyone would check for contraband."

"And these have been in there since Saturday?"

"It's brilliant, actually. You carry them out without a clue you're doing it, so you won't be acting nervous. SMK steals the purse Monday morning and nobody's the wiser as to how these left the building, not even you. But switching purses screwed him up, so he ransacked your house looking for them. He's probably getting pretty desperate. Let's see that message now."

He followed me to the laptop.

The message was still on the screen.

> Remember Brooks.
> I want them.
> Tomorrow night 7PM Dupont Circle with your phone.
> Bring them in a Whole Foods grocery bag.
> No cops. No tricks.
> Remember Brooks.
> We are watching.

This message creeped me out as much as the first one. The repetitive reminders of the grisly fate that had befallen Melinda Brooks was worse than having a gun pointed at me. A gun would be mercifully swift. I couldn't hold back the chill that wracked me.

Adam finished reading and put his arm around me.

I huddled close to him. "I have to call my boss and tell him I found these."

He turned me to face him with a frown. "No way."

I pulled back.

Adam had no concept of how much trouble I was in between Heiden and Krause. I could lose my job. I couldn't keep these hidden.

"Call Yolanda right now, and let me talk to her."

"But they think I helped steal these."

"Who gives a shit what your boss thinks. Focus. Call Yolanda… Now."

"But—" I stopped mid-sentence, realizing I'd gotten myself into another no-win argument with DA-mode Adam, and it was time to try it his way.

I pulled out my phone and dialed Yolanda, who would be somewhere on the west coast now.

The call went to voicemail.

"She's not picking up," I told Adam.

"Try a text and tell her to call you right now. You have information about the jewels. I need to talk to her."

I typed a semblance of the message he wanted.

ME: Call me ASAP, found where exhibit jewels are

Adam leaned against the table. "SMK works in your building. If you call in to tell them about these, he'll probably find out. We can't risk that."

It took less than twenty seconds for my phone to ring with Yolanda's name on the screen.

Adam held his hand out.

~

Adam

KELLY HANDED ME THE PHONE. "YOLANDA, THANKS FOR CALLING. THIS IS Adam."

"What do you know about the jewelry?" she asked.

"Are you where you can talk?"

"I just stepped out of a meeting with the owners. What can you tell me about them?"

"Good. We've found the pieces—"

"Where?"

To slow this down, I took time for a breath. "Never mind about that. I need to talk to you and them together."

"I can tell them they've been found, right? All of them?"

"Slow down. I need to talk to all of you together."

"But we found them, right?"

"Let's talk to the owners, and I'll explain the situation."

"Okay."

I heard the sound of a door, and then Yolanda said, "They have all been located," before it went to speaker mode and a jumble of people all talking over one another came over the line. "I have someone who'd like to explain," she said over the group.

"You're on speaker, Adam," she said.

"And who is this?" a gruff male voice asked.

"FBI," I said. The room quieted.

"I want my necklace back. I should never have agreed to this," Mr. Gruff said.

"What happened to them?" a scratchy woman's voice asked. She was followed by a few more similar questions, everyone speaking over each other.

I waited a few seconds for the ruckus to die down. "If you will all be quiet for a moment, I'll explain the situation."

"I want my necklace," Mr. Gruff repeated.

"And your name is?" I asked.

"Sparks. Jeffrey Sparks. And what is your name, young man?"

I ignored the question about my name, and the implication that I was too young to be taken seriously. "Mr. Sparks, this will go much faster if you let me explain the situation first." If I'd been physically in the room with him, I would have throttled the guy. Well, probably not, but I would have given him a threatening look to shut him up.

"You can't talk to me like that," Mr. Gruff shot back. "And you didn't tell us your name."

"I'm the one with the authority to determine when your property is released to you." A few mumbles came across the line, but thankfully nothing from Mr. Gruff. "And whether that happens soon, or in a few years."

Mr. Gruff rose to the bait, as I'd expected. "You can't do that."

This is where it got tricky. "Your belongings are evidence in an ongoing kidnapping and murder investigation." That much would have been true if I'd logged the items as evidence already.

Miss Scratchy Voice was the first one to speak up. "That doesn't have anything to do with us."

"The way the legal system works in this country, the defense has a right to examine the evidence ahead of the trial, which means we can't release your items until they have had a chance to do so."

Mumbled concerns were all that came from them after that.

"If you would like to get them back earlier, I do have an alternative."

"What's that?" Yolanda asked before Mr. Gruff could get involved.

"To catch the culprit, I need replicas of the jewelry."

"What difference will that make?" Miss Scratchy Voice asked.

"And I need them tomorrow—all of them—for a ransom drop where we expect to catch the kidnapper. Then your jewelry will no longer be needed as evidence." I'd voiced more of a hope than a fact.

The other room erupted with multiple voices saying, "That can't be done," and "That's impossible," and a single "Why?"

"You must have contacts at the studios. Jewelers? Other collectors? Either I get them tomorrow for this exchange and we catch the killer with your help, or our hunt goes on for another year or more, and we'll need to hold on to your items."

Their arguments came through the phone, but I ignored them again. "Your choice. Replicas tomorrow, or wait a few years. And one more thing. Nobody can discuss this outside of this group. No wives, no husbands, nobody. If it leaks, it could endanger people on this end, and I will put the full weight of the FBI behind punishing the culprit."

The room on the other end went quiet, a good sign.

"I'm not doing it. I'm getting my lawyer involved," Mr. Gruff said.

He wanted to call my bluff.

"Nonsense, Jeffrey," Miss Scratchy said. "You heard the man. The set needs to be complete. I know you know George at the studio. Just call him and get the movie prop. Do you really want to bugger this up and make enemies of us all?"

"Yeah, Jeffrey," another said. Two more piled on after that.

Mr. Gruff gave in, and the group started to plot how they could get the replicas we needed.

CHAPTER 32

Adam

By late Wednesday, the entire team was at my house, preparing for the drop. I'd called in half a dozen extra agents, and I was going over assignments with them while Kelly was getting wired in the bedroom.

My phone rang with Dad's name on the screen. I stepped out the front door to take it.

"Adam, have you sent that whistleblower information to the SEC?" Yesterday, he'd emailed what he wanted me to send on about Dennis Benson.

"I took care of it this morning." I'd attached an affidavit saying I'd gotten it from a confidential informant and forwarded it on.

"Great. I'm going to be out in DC in the next day or two, and we'll do dinner."

"Dad, I might not be able to make dinner, but lunch might work." There was no way I could make a dinner with my responsibilities with Kelly, but that was too complicated to go into now.

"I'll call and let you know."

Nothing ever changed. He meant he would dictate the terms of our meal.

We hung up, and I went back to the group inside.

Playing hardball with the jewelry owners yesterday had paid off. Yolanda had arrived this afternoon with convincing replicas for all the stolen items. She believed what I had in the backpack I'd prepared would pass inspection by anybody except an experienced jeweler.

I'd added the tracking necklace the Secret Service had given me to the bottom of the pile. It wasn't as upscale as these other pieces, but it didn't stand out when they were all thrown together.

My phone rang, and it was our boss, Dempsey, no doubt triple-checking to see that we were ready for this evening's operation.

"We're ready," I said before he had a chance to ask the question.

"That's not why I'm calling."

Waiting for the punchline, I stayed quiet.

"Our Guy Fawkes group hit another bank. I'm pulling Jenkins and Harper to check it out. You and Neil stay."

"But we need them here to cover the SMK meet."

"It's not your call, Cartwright. Montgomery County isn't going to hold the scene forever for us. Figure out how to make your operation work with fewer assets. If he's smart, SMK won't be personally at the meet anyway."

I'd had the same concern myself. "That would be the smart play, but he has ten million reasons to want to handle it himself."

Kelly

Rylie, one of the extra FBI agents Adam had called in for this, was with me in the bedroom. She was fitting me with my wire.

The FD-473 form I'd just completed lay on top of the bureau. I'd gladly signed away my privacy rights for them to record me at this meeting, or drop off, or whatever it was.

Adam was in with the guys, figuring out how to stake out the location.

I hadn't gone in to the office today. I was on suspension, and everybody at work seemed to have heard about it. Kirby had called with her message of sympathy this morning, and we'd commiserated about how awful Krause was for blaming me. Another two friends from the office had also called in the afternoon.

I didn't trust either of them to keep their mouths shut as much as I did

Kirby, so I avoided badmouthing Krause on those calls. The last thing I needed right now was to let my personal opinion of Helmut Krause get me fired before I even got back to work.

All I'd managed for lunch had been crackers and cheese. Even that little bit had come up this afternoon after the FBI crowd had arrived and I realized how dangerous this could be. If this was the minimum-risk outing that Adam had said it was, why did he need a dozen agents to help him? Not letting him see me shake had been my top goal today. If there was a chance I could help to catch Melinda's killer, I owed it to her and the rest of the Smithsonian crew to give it my best.

"Arms up," Rylie said. She snaked the wire from the tiny microphone at the center of my bra under my boob and around to the side where the tiny transmitter disk sat under the sideband. "How's that?"

It wasn't comfortable, but I had no idea how bad it had to be to complain. "I can deal with it." The shakiness of my voice probably gave me away.

She rechecked the microphone placement. "You can put your shirts on now."

I donned the loose T-shirt followed by the button up she'd helped me select. Two layers, she said, were best to keep the listening device hidden.

After I adjusted my clothes, she pulled out several long, thin gadgets of different colors, each with a clear plastic tube at one end. She held the first one up to my hair. "This is your receiver, so you can hear us. I just have to match your hair color." She held them up to my hair one by one.

I stood still. "I thought you had little earplug thingies."

"Only in the movies. Those are too easy to spot." She held up the tiny thing. "I glue this to your hair, and this end…" She flexed the long, skinny end. "Goes in your ear. If someone is going to check you, you just swipe your hair away from your ear, and they'll never see it. The problem with these is they don't have much volume and don't work well in a noisy environment. And, if you do swipe the end out of your ear, it's not easy to get it back in place properly."

I could remember that. "So the hair swipe is a last resort."

"That's right, and if you have a nervous habit of tucking your hair behind your ear, you have to control that too. That's really important. Do you think you can do that?"

Another thing I had to remember. "I think so."

Act casual, don't be obviously talking to myself, no hair tucking behind the ear. It sounded easy enough, except that I'd also be scared shitless about meeting the Ghost.

She parted my hair above my ear and fiddled with the thin little thing and the glue.

"Where will you be?" I asked while she fussed with my hair.

"Oscar and I get to play a couple by the fountain."

I noticed the wedding ring on her finger. "Is that a little awkward?"

"It goes with the territory. I might have to remind him to pop a Tic-Tac, though."

I giggled.

"It's like being in the movies," she said. "If kissing is in the script, you have to get into character and do it, until the director calls cut."

"And your husband?"

"He's an air marshal; he'd understand."

"So you won't tell him."

"I won't lie about it, but it's easier if it doesn't come up."

I contemplated her answer for a moment. She thought some things were better not discussed. Would it have been better for Adam and me if I'd left his history with my brother alone?

She arranged the hair around my ear. "Now check yourself in the mirror and tell me if you can see it."

Even though I knew where to look, the device was invisible to me. "Can't see a thing."

"That's the idea. Now walk to the far end of the bathroom."

"Can you hear me?" she asked into a small radio after I was far enough away.

I heard it, but she'd been right about the volume being low. I nodded.

"Say something."

"I hear it, but it's faint."

"Try yes followed by no," she said.

I tapped my chest where the microphone lay the way she'd taught me. One tap for yes and two for no if I wasn't able to speak.

"I can hear you fine. We're good to go."

I followed her into the other room where the guys were congregated and almost tucked my hair behind my ear by accident. That was going to be difficult to control.

"How do you feel?" Adam asked when I reached him.

"Nervous."

He smiled and squeezed my shoulder. "You can do this. We have your back, Miss Benson. Everybody here will have eyes on you." With the other FBI guys here, he hadn't called me Sugarbear once, or Kells either.

Somehow reassurance flowed through his touch, and my doubts lessened. "It's the only way, right?"

"It's the best way… Now, tell me what you're supposed to do."

I felt the eyes of the entire group on me. "Answer the phone when it rings. Repeat anything important, if I can. Cough twice if the caller is a voice I recognize from work. If somebody comes up to me and I recognize him from work, also cough twice. Follow instructions, but refuse to get in a car with him and go anywhere."

"And if he asks you to change locations and go somewhere we can't see you?"

"I refuse, because I'm in charge. I've got what he wants, and he doesn't have anything I want."

"Very good."

Looking around the room, I felt better as the other agents nodded at me. I could do this. I had to do this.

One foot in front of the other, follow the steps. Take the call, turn over the bag of fake jewelry, stand back, and wait for Adam and his crew of armed agents to take him down when he reached wherever his lair was.

I shivered at the word *lair*. It was such an appropriate word for the animal who'd killed those women. I shivered, trying not to imagine how long Melinda and Daya Patel had endured the horror of being assaulted by him, tortured and killed. He was lower than an animal. Animals killed to eat. He'd killed for who knows what reason, certainly not to survive.

Adam's glance broke me out of my temporary trance—the look that said he understood how scary this was. I wanted to find the strength in his arms to carry this out, but couldn't with the other agents around.

He followed it with a simple nod that told me he cared, told me he understood. My man had my back.

After we caught the Ghost, I planned to have Adam escort me back into work. If Krause had a problem with being kept out of the loop, it was a sure thing that a talk with my FBI boyfriend would get it all straightened out. At this moment, there wasn't any problem Adam couldn't fix, anything we couldn't tackle.

Krause was a pompous ass, and Adam was ten times the man he was. Krause would fold like a cheap suit.

"Okay, let's get set up ahead of time. I'll bring Miss Benson over a few minutes ahead of schedule," Adam announced to the group.

With that, they started to file out. In a moment we were alone.

Adam took me in his arms. "I know you're scared, and that's okay."

I tightened my hold on him. "I don't know if I can do this."

"Follow the script, and you'll be okay. I'll be just across the street. Rylie and Oscar will be by the fountain. We have people in each direction. Just say the safe word, and we'll all be there in a flash." He'd chosen the safe word, *yesterday,* because it was easy to weave into normal conversation without standing out.

I pretended I'd gotten enough strength from our short hug. "Let's do this."

CHAPTER 33

Kelly

Rylie and Oscar had their arms around each other by the fountain as I crossed the street to the center of Dupont Circle.

The giddy smiles on their faces were making their boyfriend-girlfriend act look pretty convincing. But what would her husband think if he saw them? After another kiss, I decided she might be right that the details were better left untold.

It went both ways, didn't it? Did Oscar also have a wife who'd be jealous? I hadn't bothered to ask.

Adam's reassuring voice sounded weakly in my ear. "When you get to the outer circular walk, turn right, and sit where we can see you well."

I nodded, remembering the admonition to not talk to myself. Reaching the outer walkway, I took a seat on the bench and checked my phone. It was charged, and I was five minutes early.

"That's a good place to wait," he said.

I nodded. Nobody caught my attention as I looked around.

My phone rang, and I jumped. My heart raced as I squeaked out my answer. "Hello?"

The voice was mechanical, disguised. "Did you bring the merchandise?"

"Yes."

"Good. Now listen very carefully. You are not to say a word, not a single solitary word. Nod, if you understand."

I nodded and looked around.

Clearly, he could see me.

Nobody in my field of view was holding a phone, but then, he could have been in one of the many building windows overlooking the circle.

"Get up and walk right on the circle toward the CVS and P Street. Do not talk. Nod if you understand." The distorted mechanical voice was disturbing in its own right.

I stood, nodded, and started that way, checking both directions and still not seeing anyone I recognized from work. I'd woken this morning in Adam's arms, snuggled against the warmth of my own personal protective special agent, and I wanted him next to me now. Oh, how I needed him next to me.

Adam's voice was hard to hear over the traffic. "You're doing fine." His voice in my ear was all I was going to get until this was over.

I hit the mute button on the phone and did my best ventriloquist imitation of talking without moving my lips. "Thanks."

"I told you no talking," the creepy voice said. "You think I can't tell from the lack of street noise when you put it on mute?"

"It was a mistake," I blurted out.

"One more mistake and she dies. Nod if you understand me."

Who dies? I thought I was the one with a target on my back.

I nodded, afraid to ask who he threatened now.

"Stop there," he said. "And sit on the bench closest to the garbage can. There is a phone taped under the seat. Hold it up when you find it."

I pulled it out and held it up. It immediately started to ring.

"Answer it, and toss your phone in the trash."

I dropped my phone in the trash can and took the call on the phone he'd left.

"That's very good my dear. Her fate is now in your hands. Nod if you understand." The wickedness coming from this phone was unmistakable. He was pure evil, enjoying this.

My nod was halfhearted—I swallowed back the bile that rose in my throat. I hadn't planned on being responsible for someone else's destiny.

"Stand up and keep walking the same direction. No words."

"What is he saying?" Adam asked.

Walking again, it only took a few steps before the urge overwhelmed me and I lurched forward in a dry heave. If I'd had anything left in my stomach, it would have painted the sidewalk. Recovering, I started walking again.

"Tell me what he's saying," Adam insisted.

I kept quiet.

Rylie and Oscar had started a dance on the concrete in front of the fountain and ended up shifting around in the direction I was walking.

"Do you see the seat with the Whole Foods bag under it? Sit down there, with your bag on the ground."

The bench was just ahead.

My knees were weak, so sitting down was a relief.

"Stay there, and don't move until I tell you."

Did that mean he was coming to me? The thought was chilling.

"What the hell is he telling you?" Adam yelled in my ear. "Tell me or I'm pulling you out."

I tapped my chest twice, then twice again.

"Not good enough."

Ignoring him, I brushed my hair behind my ear, exactly as Rylie had warned me not to and tapped my chest two more times.

Adam could be stubborn, but I could be more stubborn, and I couldn't do the right thing with him yelling at me.

Rylie and Oscar were stealing glances in my direction.

As I looked both ways, I still didn't recognize anyone from work. He had to be someone I worked with, but who? The voice was disguised, and the speech pattern didn't bring a face to the fore either.

When Rylie next looked my way, I gave her the smallest shake of my head I could manage.

Her head bobbed in an equally subtle way and her lips moved. She'd gotten the message and was relaying it to Adam, I hoped.

The Ghost finally spoke again. "When the man with the dog passes you, take the bag from under the bench, and leave the one you brought in its place. Follow the man with the dog and sit down again when you reach the other side of the circle. Nod if you understand."

I looked right. No man, no dog.

The left was a different story. A dachshund strained against his leash, pulling an older gentleman along.

"I said nod if you understand."

I nodded vigorously.

"Follow my directions exactly, or your friend Evelyn dies."

My mouth dropped open. Now I had a name.

Evelyn hadn't come to work yesterday or the day before. The Ghost had taken her—two days of hell on Earth. And now her future was in my hands.

Adam

Kelly stood and started walking toward P Street again.

"I don't like the direction this is going," I said. "We need to pull her."

"Let it play out," Neil said. "There's nobody near her."

Two taps came to my headset, followed by two more.

Kelly was objecting—to me?

"She says no," Rylie said. "And I agree."

Was I the only one concerned about the turn this had taken?

"Don't jump the gun," Neil urged me.

I took several deep breaths and decided to let it continue a little longer.

"There's a guy with a dog approaching," Rylie said. "And you should know, she swiped the earpiece out."

Damn her. That was not her call.

"Kelly, tap if you can hear me."

No taps came back, so I repeated the question with the same result. Rylie was right. Kelly had stopped listening.

"He can't be our guy," Neil told me after a quick glance through the field glasses. "He's the far side of seventy at least."

With the current state of disguises, his assessment didn't make me feel any better.

The man passed her, and Kelly followed.

"She's coming your way, Doug," Neil radioed before we lost sight of her.

"Got her. She's following the old man with the dog," Doug said.

"We need to reposition," I told Neil.

He shook his head. "Too early."

I hated her being out of sight. "Rylie, talk to me. Should we reposition?"

"She's still listening to the new phone. It looks like this is a move to check for tails. I'd say we stay put."

It was a minute before Doug gave another update. "She's sitting on a bench again, roughly P Street eastbound. Still nobody approaching her."

I turned to Neil. "Now we reposition." I keyed the mic. "Reposition to a closer circle toward the east end."

Neil started the car.

Once on the other side, facing the Circle again, my heart rate calmed with Kelly safely in sight.

Ten minutes passed with nothing of note except our dog walker making multiple laps around the Circle. My headset was filled with normal street noises, still not a single word from my woman.

"Rylie," I said into the mic. "Let's have you and Oscar do a walk by."

It took them another minute to reach Kelly in a roundabout way and pass by. Ten yards later, her report came. "There's been a switch. That's not the bag she started with."

What the hell? "Explain," I said as I pulled out the phone.

"The bag from her house had a small stain. This one's clean."

I unlocked the Secret Service phone and swiped to the location app. Sure enough, when I zoomed in, the locator dot was on the far side of the Circle. "Fuck. It's where she first sat down. Doug, do you have eyes on that location?"

"No. I moved closer to the east exit," he said.

"I've got eyes on it," Joe radioed. "A guy just sat down. No, now he's up, and he has the bag."

The locator dot on the phone started to move north. "That's our guy. Take him down. Rylie you stay with Benson. Oscar, cut through the center."

Neil screeched into traffic and around the Circle.

Doug was running in from the south, and Joe from the north.

SMK halted, then took off toward the fountain.

Neil hit the brakes, and we screeched to a halt on the west side of the Circle.

Ron came toward the fountain with his weapon drawn.

SMK turned tail and started running straight toward the two of us.

Neil leaped out of the car. "FBI. Stop right there."

SMK halted and looked rapidly in each of his possible directions. We'd cut them all off.

I made it around the car and drew my weapon as well.

The man's eyes darted from one side to the other, like a scared animal.

"Hands behind your head. Interlock your fingers," Neil commanded.

He didn't comply. "It doesn't matter anymore."

The tone and the words were ominous. The situation could easily spiral out of control.

"We just want to talk," I told him.

Ron moved off to the side, out of our line of fire.

SMK closed his eyes and put a hand in his coat pocket.

"Hands where I can see them," Neil yelled. "Now."

SMK opened his eyes and fixed me with a blank stare. "I'm not going in." He pulled out a gun.

"Gun," Doug yelled.

SMK slowly raised his piece in my direction.

We'd trained on this, but training was nothing like the chill that ran through me as he raised the Glock. His eyes were lifeless, blank, and suddenly all I could see was the ugly end of the barrel as it arced toward me.

I fired. Two slugs forced him back, and he collapsed onto the path.

Joe reached him first, kicked away his gun, and checked for a pulse.

SMK stared up into the sky. This killer hadn't wanted a trial. His words and actions were textbook suicide by cop. He'd decided getting shot was better than getting arrested. A quick end to an ugly life.

Kelly was safe, and nothing else mattered.

"He's gone," Joe announced.

I holstered my weapon as Doug ran up.

Neil holstered his weapon as well. "You know this could have been avoided if we hadn't repositioned on the other side."

He might have been right, but I didn't give him the pleasure of agreeing with him. "I made the right call." I knew keeping a close cordon around Kelly was the most important thing.

He didn't drop it. "If we'd stayed put, we could have gotten the drop on him when he picked up the package instead of running at him like mad men."

"We needed to keep it tight around Kelly."

His raised eyebrow indicated that he'd caught that I'd switched from Benson to Kelly. "That's not good procedure, and you know it."

His critique was damning.

"Her safety had to be the primary objective."

"And if one of your rounds had missed him and hit a bystander on the street behind him?"

I stated the obvious. "I didn't miss. Two shots, two hits. It's a righteous shoot."

"I didn't say it wasn't, but it wasn't necessary. You let your emotions influence your call, and that's a mistake you don't want to repeat." He turned away.

Doug held up the dead man's wallet. "Leonard Sanderson, address in Chevy Chase. And a Smithsonian ID."

I photographed both IDs with my phone.

The Metropolitan Police arrived, and Neil held up his creds as he approached them to explain.

At the same time, Doug phoned the incident in to the field office.

Rylie was holding a frantic Kelly by the fountain.

I walked their direction and was immediately assaulted by a crying Kelly. "He has Evelyn, and you killed him. We have to find Evelyn. We have to find Evelyn."

Rylie let her go, and I took her in my arms.

She sobbed. "He said he has Evelyn."

Fuck. This changed everything.

I grabbed her shoulders. "Who's Evelyn?"

Neil left the body to come over.

She sniffed. "Evelyn Gossen works with me. She has the desk next to mine, and she hasn't been in this week."

Neil held up the car keys. "We need to get over there now, then."

"We'll find her," I told Kelly.

Her crying only increased.

"Neil and I have to go now. Rylie will take you to my place and stay with you till I get back." I pulled Kelly off of me.

Rylie took her hand and accepted the house keys I pulled out.

"Who was it?" Kelly asked.

"Leonard Sanderson."

"Len? He's one of the OPS guards," Kelly told us.

I backed away from her. "We have to check his house. I'll be back as soon as I can." The one thing I wanted most to do was hold her and comfort her, but I couldn't now. The job demanded it wait until later.

As soon as we pulled into traffic and headed north, with full lights and siren, Neil decided to lecture me. "This is now officially FUBAR."

"I know." I'd been running this, and he'd just reminded me whose ass was on the line. I'd just shot our best lead at finding the Evelyn lady. Not my finest hour.

"And you can't promise we'll find her friend."

"I know," I repeated. I hadn't been able to give Kelly the standard bullshit FBI line; she deserved more than that.

The Bureau had lots of procedures and protocols, and overpromising and underdelivering wasn't one of them—another thing I could look forward to getting reamed on.

As the scenery rolled by, the shooting replayed in my head. Each time the loop ended with that look on SMK's face. He'd forced it, and yet the bullets surprised him, or so it seemed.

There hadn't been a way to avoid it. Firing before he did had been my only option.

CHAPTER 34

Kelly

I RODE WITH RYLIE BACK TO ADAM'S PLACE.

"You shouldn't have pulled the earpiece out," she said as soon as the car door closed.

"What?"

She shot me a you've-got-to-be-kidding glance. "Don't try that on me."

"But he said he had Evelyn, and I had to do the right thing for her. Adam was talking too much in my ear."

"And you decided to trust a murderer instead of the team."

"I was trying to save Evelyn."

"You don't get it," she sneered. "We all stay safe by trusting one another and doing what we're supposed to, not by making it up as we go along."

Soft, supportive Rylie had morphed into a jerk.

"Because of you, Adam changed the plan, and we ended up with a shooting situation that could have gone horribly wrong. Adam or Neil could have ended up on the pavement instead of that dirtbag."

I shrank in my seat.

"That man is most probably dead because you didn't trust us." Her tone seemed to indicate that I might as well have pulled the trigger. "And that makes it infinitely more difficult to find your friend. If you'd spoken up about her, so we knew about it, instead of going rogue, that would have changed everything about how Adam handled the situation."

A chill came over me as her words sunk in. I wrapped my arms around myself. If they couldn't find Evelyn, it might be my fault.

She drove in silence for several blocks. "And after we either do or don't find your friend, there's another problem."

I wasn't sure I could handle another problem after the guilt trip she'd laid on me.

"Your boyfriend's going to need your support," she said as we neared our destination.

"What boyfriend?"

"Give me a break." Her gaze locked with mine for a second. "You do realize I'm paid to notice things?"

I shrugged.

"Adam just shot a man. If he tells you it doesn't bother him, he's lying. It bothers everyone it happens to."

I didn't respond for a moment. I couldn't catch my breath. "What can I do?"

"Be there for him. I don't know if he'll want to punch the wall, cry, go silent, or what. Just know that he's dealing with the hardest part of the job, and he needs you more than he'll be willing to admit."

She pulled to a stop outside Adam's place, turned off the car, and looked over. "He's a good man. He doesn't deserve the shit they put him through, and you just made it worse."

I followed her to the door as new questions swirled in my head.

She opened the door and locked it again behind us. "I'll fix some coffee."

"None for me, thanks. I don't drink the stuff."

She located the pods under Adam's coffee maker and started one.

I started my tea before turning to her. "What shit is he going through at work?"

"It's not for me to say. You should ask him."

That was a bullshit answer. "Hey, you want me to help him, then tell me what I need to know."

Her coffee finished before she relented. "His uncle was in the Bureau."

I located a teabag and started dunking it. "He told me."

"The short of it is, his uncle fucked up big time. So Adam is constantly fighting against that legacy. It eats at him."

Something like that would be difficult for anybody. I lost count of my teabag dunks and kept going. "What can I do to help that?"

She narrowed her eyes. "He obsesses about it, and he shouldn't. I tried talking to him, but he shut me down. He needs to let go. Maybe he'll listen to you."

"I can try." I'd had pretty much the same shutdown experience trying to get him to talk about the incident with Dennis. But if Rylie thought it was important, I'd do what I could.

We didn't speak for a moment.

She reached over to touch my shoulder. "Sorry about jumping down your throat earlier. Let's set."

I followed her to the couch.

She picked up the remote and clicked on the TV. "What do you feel like?"

"You don't have to stay."

A game show started on the TV. She muted it before turning to me. "I'm staying."

"Really. I'm fine now."

"You need to listen better. I told you we work as a team and all do our part."

"But I'll be fine."

She gritted her teeth. "Adam told me to stay until he got back, so that's what I'm doing. I told you the team succeeds by everyone doing what's expected of them."

"Is he your boss?"

She snorted like it was funny. "No. That would be Dempsey, but Adam was given lead on this op, and that makes him the onsite boss until we wrap it up."

I slumped back into the couch, realizing the woman I'd thought I'd bonded with was only here because it was her job.

"And," she added, "Adam is like a brother to me. You're important to him, and that makes you important to me, so I'm not leaving until we know you're safe."

"Of course I'm safe. The Ghost is dead."

She shook her head and snorted again, like I was a child who didn't get it. "And what makes you so sure that guy wasn't just an errand boy for the real

SMK? Until we have evidence one way or the other, I don't know that, and neither do you."

Her words erased the certainty I'd had a moment ago that my nightmare was over. Now I desperately wanted Adam to come through the door and hold me.

CHAPTER 35

Adam

With the news that another woman's life was in play, we had to hustle. Before leaving the Circle, I pocketed the Secret Service tracker and gave the bag of fake jewels to Doug to log.

I sent Doug and Oscar to check out Evelyn Gossen's apartment and get the search for her underway, and Rylie to take Kelly back to my place.

Neil and I reached Len Sanderson's house in record time. The office had called while we were driving to give us his particulars.

He lived alone—nearest relative was a sister in Seattle. He worked as a guard at the Smithsonian, and his record was clean, not even a speeding ticket. He'd been married, but his wife was deceased.

I cleared the downstairs and came up empty checking for the abducted girl.

Neil holstered his gun as he returned from upstairs. "No sign of our lady."

We donned gloves and started a simple search before the forensic techs arrived.

Downstairs was neatly kept and pretty plain, save multiple photos of a woman, who—based on the ring on her finger in the pictures—had to be his wife. Searching his desk went quickly. The guy had been neat and organized. His files didn't show any evidence of a secondary location—no bills or papers of any kind on another property, a storage location, or anything beyond this house.

"Cleaner than my place," I told Neil. "You sure this guy was single?"

"Easiest way to tell is the bathroom upstairs."

Neil's phone rang. "Yeah, we're there now. Okay, I'll tell him. Thanks." He hung up. "Dempsey wants us to confirm if we're sure this is our guy before he talks to HQ."

I checked my phone. It wasn't dead. Dempsey should have called me, but chose Neil instead.

Neil led the way into the master bedroom. "This guy seriously missed his wife." Even more photos lined the walls. In serial killer cases, the victims were often similar to someone in the killer's prior life, but not here. Neither of the two previous victims, or Kelly, resembled the wife, or even each other.

The upstairs drawers all contained what we would expect, and the bathroom had not a single item to suggest a woman in the house.

I opened a small wooden case on the nightstand. "Bingo." I held up my find. "This pretty much nails it. Souvenirs: four drivers licenses and four rings."

"Names?" he asked.

I nodded as I fanned through them. I saw our two vics, plus Evelyn Gossen, and a new name we hadn't run across.

Neil came over to my side of the bed to examine them. "Who's Ruth Picard?"

I shook my head. "No idea." I got on the phone to the office to have them run it down after bagging what I'd found.

The forensic team arrived and started downstairs, and we'd finished upstairs when the answer to our question arrived. This time I got the call.

"Ruth Picard was a missing person case a year and a half ago, handled by Montgomery County Police. No resolution," the support tech said.

"Why didn't she come up on our radar? We have a Smithsonian badge here."

"She'd left that job and was working at a hospital when she disappeared."

I thanked him, and filled Neil in.

"So he might have had a previous victim, and we didn't even know it," he said.

"Looks that way."

I was walking the hallway, checking the baseboards with a flashlight when I bumped into a bookcase.

It moved.

"What do you want to bet?" I asked rhetorically as I rocked it slightly by leaning into it.

Companies sold things like this on the Internet as hidden doorways. Neil joined my search for the latch mechanism along the inside surfaces.

A half minute later, I'd found the lever, and the case swung inward, books and all. It opened to a landing and stairs going down.

We drew our weapons as we reached the bottom.

Neil opened the door, and I was the first through, with Neil right behind me.

The lights were on, and a woman lay on the disheveled bed in the far corner.

When I reached her, the bad news was evident. She matched her license from upstairs. Evelyn Gossen's lifeless eyes stared up at the ceiling.

I reached down to check her for a pulse, even though I knew the answer. Her skin was cold to the touch. "Cold. Dead half a day at least."

We'd leave the specifics to the scientists.

Neil looked around. "Well, this is going to keep forensics busy for a while."

While Sanderson kept the upstairs neat and clean, the basement was the opposite. Aside from the bed in the corner, there was an ugly, soiled chair with restraints, a table with various implements—some sharp—and a small refrigerator in the corner.

"These blood stains are old," Neil noted, pointing to multiple large stains on the floor. Others were visible on the chair.

The air was disgustingly stale.

I'd handled scenes much worse than this before, but this time I felt ill thinking how close Kelly had come to being the next victim abused and tortured down here.

"You're looking a little green, kid."

I probably looked better than I felt. "I'll be okay."

"Good, because we can't have you puking on the crime scene."

I needed to push through this, and it wasn't like we needed the evidence for a trial.

Neil stopped me as I ventured farther into the room. "Best to let the forensics guys get first crack at this."

"Yeah." I wanted to check the fridge, but getting to it without walking on the blood evidence would be tricky.

"He probably didn't clean up the blood on purpose, just to add to the horror factor."

I imagined how the girls would have felt upon first being dragged down here. Neil was right. The sight and smell would have instilled abject terror.

I turned my back on the scene. "Seems clear this is our guy." I pulled out my phone.

Neil followed me. "Sure looks like it." He'd been careful to say he wasn't certain, leaving that call to me.

I dialed the ASAC.

Dempsey picked up right away. "Well?"

"We have a DB at the house. It's the other Smithsonian employee, Evelyn Gossen. We also have personal items that look like trophies from our victims, as well as from one additional missing person who could be an even earlier victim. It'll take DNA matches from forensics to confirm it, but it looks like we found the kill site in the basement. A lot of blood has been spilled down there."

"Okay. I'll get the coroner on the way. Leave that site to forensics, and work up your shooting report tonight."

I wasn't leaving Kelly alone tonight under any circumstances. "It'll have to be the morning. I have to relieve Brolin watching Benson until forensics here tells us there wasn't an accomplice."

"Okay for tonight, but the protection is off first thing in the morning unless we have an indication there's an accomplice. I expect you in the office tomorrow."

"I'll let forensics know." The geeks wouldn't be happy to hear the news.

Kelly also deserved a call from me.

My finger hovered over the phone before I changed my mind. This news needed to be in person.

"I'm going into the office to write it up while it's still fresh," Neil said. "You should probably do the same."

He was echoing Dempsey, as always.

"Tomorrow. Drop me at my place. I need to relieve Rylie on protection."

He raised an eyebrow but didn't say anything.

I'd been right. The forensics guys weren't happy to hear my interpretation of Dempsey's demand that we confirm or rule out an accomplice *and* confirm the DNA downstairs, all by tomorrow.

"You know putting more samples in makes everything go slower not faster," the lead tech grumbled.

As we drove off, Neil spoke up again. "You know inspection won't be happy if you wait until tomorrow to write up the shooting."

The Bureau's Inspection Division conducted an internal investigation of every agent-involved shooting, and that was in my future now.

"Tomorrow will have to do." Tonight Kelly needed me, and I needed her.

"Your call." His tone conveyed his disapproval.

~

Kelly

I couldn't concentrate on the TV with the sour state of my stomach. The thought that my bad choices had led to the shooting ate at me. And Rylie's warning about how it would impact Adam hurt as much as knowing that because of me we might not find Evelyn.

When my phone rang, I couldn't get to it fast enough, hoping I could at least hear Adam's voice. The screen disappointed me when it showed Momma's name.

"Hi, Momma," I answered.

Rylie got up and wandered toward the kitchen, blowing on her steaming coffee cup.

"It's wonderful news that you met someone, but your father didn't tell me any more than his name is Adam. So, what does he do?"

"Momma, you'll meet him in due time." I wasn't sure when that would be.

"I could fly out, if that would make it easier."

"Momma, it's not that. We're not ready yet."

"At least tell me he's from a good family."

"Very good," I replied without thinking.

We hung up after I rebuffed several more attempts at details.

Rylie came back to the couch after I put down the phone. "She doesn't know about Adam?"

I shook my head. "No, and I'm not sure how to tell them. Our fathers hate each other with a capital H. I mean, putting them in the same room would likely lead to an explosion."

She sat down. "I wouldn't be so sure about that."

I cocked my head. "You don't know my father."

"My dad was the same way about Sam, my husband."

"But I can't make mine change."

She sipped her coffee. "Sure you can."

"No way."

"My dad and his dad ran—well, still run—competing restaurants in Pittsburgh. My dad hired away some of Sam's father's employees, and he retaliated by hiring my dad's chef and stealing some recipes."

I giggled. That sounded small scale compared to Daddy's feud with Adam's father.

"Don't laugh. This was serious shit. They were ready to kill each other, until we ended it."

"How?"

"I told my father he wasn't welcome in our house, and he wouldn't ever get to see his grandchildren, if he didn't bury the hatchet with Sam's dad."

"And that fixed it?"

"Only after Sam said the same thing to his father. I knew my dad loved me more than the fight. But I—we—had to force that choice."

She made it sound easy, too easy.

We settled in to watch the television.

Later, when Adam finally arrived, he looked terrible.

"Evelyn?" I needed to hear that I hadn't screwed up our chance to find her.

His downcast eyes told the story even before he spoke. "I'm so sorry."

I fell into his arms, crying for what seemed like an eternity.

What had Evelyn done to deserve what had happened to her? What had any of them done? None of it made any sense.

~

HOURS LATER, RYLIE HAD GONE HOME, AND I LAY IN BED NEXT TO ADAM, MY arm draped over him and my head in the crook of his shoulder.

His heartbeat was still rapid. All this time, and he hadn't calmed down yet. He'd discovered a dead body tonight, and shot the killer. How did you sleep after a day like that?

We'd gotten into bed to hold each other.

He embraced me silently, occasionally stroking my back.

I soothed him as best I could, trying not to be clingy.

Rylie had warned me that Adam might go into quiet mode, and she'd been right about that, but it didn't matter.

All that mattered was my man was next to me. He was here for me, and I was here for him.

The clock had said two AM last time I checked.

"You can't sleep either?" Adam asked softly.

"No. Do you want to talk about it?" I'd asked earlier and gotten the standard Adam change of subject.

He took in a deep breath. "I was scared."

I pulled myself closer.

"The training is supposed to prepare you, but it doesn't really. Everything happened so fast, but seemed so slow, if that makes any sense."

"Yeah."

He sighed. "He raised his gun slowly on purpose. When he looked at me, his eyes were lifeless. He wanted to get shot. Suicide by cop."

I kept my comments short now that he was opening up. "Why?"

His head shook slightly. "Why does anyone commit suicide? He didn't have anyone to live for anymore. His wife died sometime in the last year, and all I can guess is he just thought it was easier than going to prison."

I hadn't known Len hardly at all, except to know that losing his wife had left him angry at insurance companies because of a medicine they wouldn't cover. "You had to shoot."

"I know. All I could see was the barrel of his gun coming up toward me. I waited as long as I could before pulling the trigger."

I waited, but no more words came. "I'm here for you."

He stroked my hair. "I know."

CHAPTER 36

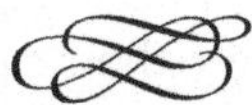

ADAM

I GOT UP BEFORE SUNRISE THE NEXT MORNING. I'D GOTTEN A LITTLE SLEEP AFTER my short talk with Kelly last night.

She'd still been asleep when I slipped out of bed.

Before leaving my place, I called the forensics lead I'd left at Sanderson's house.

"Nothing at all to indicate an accomplice yet," he told me. "Why don't you guys give us scenes that start in the morning instead of at night?" He sighed.

"I'll mention it to the next bad guy I arrest."

I wrote a note and left Kelly alone for the first time since this had started.

Instead of a shower at home that might have woken her, I decided to shower at the office, and I still made it to my desk before anyone else on the floor. Once I settled in, my report detailing yesterday's events began to come together slowly. When I closed my eyes, the shooting came back with such intensity that it made all my recollections of what had preceded it muddy.

The report ate up the morning, and I continued working through the lunch I didn't eat.

Early in the afternoon, Dempsey appeared in his doorway. "Cartwright, you done yet?"

"Yes, sir." He liked it when I called him *sir*, and right now I could use him on my side. I'd read over my report twice now, and I couldn't put my finger on it, but I sensed I'd left something out. I signed the report and walked it over to Dempsey.

He took it. "About time." Two agents I hadn't noticed before were in his office. "Come on in."

The agents stood and handed me their cards. *Inspection Division.*

"Agents Baker and Zalenski have a few questions," Dempsey said after handing Baker my report. He left the office and closed the door.

At least I wasn't in an interrogation room.

Zalenski started a recorder. "Why don't you describe the events for us."

"I just put it all in my report."

Baker tapped the pile of paper. "We'll get to that, but first you can run us through the timeline."

I started, and they listened without interrupting.

When I finished, Baker asked me to go through it again. They started down the endless-repetition road—the interview process we used on suspects to ferret out inconsistencies.

By about the tenth time through it, Zalenski was asking the endless what-happened-next questions.

Baker looked up from my report, which he'd started reading. "Why didn't you include that Agent Boxer disagreed with your decision to relocate to the east side?"

"Come again?" I asked. Exactly what I'd included in my report was fuzzy at this point.

"Agent Boxer stated clearly that he warned you not to relocate to the east side, and yet you did, which resulted in the west side going unmonitored, and you losing the opportunity to apprehend the suspect without gunfire."

I had to be careful. "Agent Boxer suggested we stay in place for a while after Miss Benson started moving, which we did."

Zalenski jumped in. "But when you did reposition, that left the west side uncovered and led to the running gun battle with the suspect in a crowded urban environment."

I tugged at my collar. It was getting hot in here. "A call needed to be made, and I made it," I said firmly. "The west side went unmonitored because the ASAC pulled the two agents necessary for full coverage less than an hour before we deployed."

Baker smiled. They'd just gotten me to react emotionally.

Zalenski leaned forward. "And your decision to move was purely tactical?"

"Protecting our asset was my top priority."

Baker smiled again, which meant I'd fucked something up.

"You said *my* priority, not *our* priority," he noted.

Now I understood where this was going, and it wasn't good. "As lead, our priority becomes my priority."

This time Zalenski asked the question. "Isn't it true that identifying and apprehending the SMK killer was the true priority of the op?"

"This op was part of an ongoing protection operation for Miss Benson."

Zalenski opened a folder while Baker kept up the attack. "And none of this had to do with your relationship with Miss Benson?"

"She's the protectee I was assigned. And that came down from the AD."

Zalenski started laying out photos. "It looks to me like this had become more than an assignment for you."

The pictures showed Kelly and me walking the Mall on Sunday. Warm memories of that day flooded over me.

Neil had been providing backup, and he had to be the source of the photos. Many of them showed the two of us holding hands, kissing, and acting goofy, but more importantly, looking completely smitten with one another.

I did my best to hold back the smile the pictures provoked. We were in a happy place—happy most of all to be with each other. To these guys, they were incriminating, but to me they only confirmed what I hadn't dared admit to myself. In a very short time, Kelly had snuck past the emotional armor I'd erected and into my heart.

"I'm undercover as her boyfriend," I said.

"And where did she spend the night last night?" Baker asked.

Standard protocol was to ask lots of questions you already knew the answers to, and his hint of a smirk said he knew the answer to this one.

The noose had tightened considerably.

"My place. Hers was trashed a few days ago by SMK, looking for the jewelry."

Zalenski gathered up the pictures. "It's pretty clear to me that you let your personal involvement with the protectee influence your judgment, and that's what precipitated a routine operation degenerating into a public shooting in downtown DC that makes us all look bad."

SMK's death looked bad on the evening news, and I'd become the sacrificial lamb.

Baker continued. "This looks like a repeat of your uncle's mistake, letting emotion alter your decisions and ending up with a tragic outcome. But, hell, why should we expect anything different from Jack Cartwright's nephew?"

My fists clenched, but I held back from responding angrily. "I think we're done here."

Zalenski put the photos away. "For today."

As I walked out, what bothered me most was that Baker had been right. This did look like I'd repeated Uncle Jack's mistake, only in reverse. He'd let his Benson hatred lead to a shootout that should have been avoided, and I'd let my love for Kelly lead to another shootout that could have been avoided.

Love? Had I really just used the word, even in my head? The thought rattled around. Did I know what the word meant?

My feelings for Kelly had grown into something I couldn't quantify, something I couldn't control.

Dempsey found me shortly after the Inspection Division creeps and I left his office. "To be clear, the Benson protection is off."

"Yes, sir. I got it."

He'd probably seen Neil's photos of Kelly and me.

Justice Department ethics rules didn't prohibit me from becoming friendly with Kelly, but Dempsey clearly had interpreted the images as me getting way too *friendly*.

When I got to my desk, I looked up a number for the Smithsonian.

Kelly

Adam had successfully snuck out this morning, and I'd woken to an empty bed.

I found a note on the nightstand.

Sugarbear

You are safe now. I've been pulled off of protection.

The back door at your house has been fixed if you want to start the cleanup. I wish I could help, but I'm needed at the office.

See you tonight,

Adam

The note brought a smile to my face and warmth to my heart. I was safe—and that was great news. But it was more than that.

I held the note to my chest—my first morning note from a guy ever. I could hear his voice as I read it, and feel the conviction. My safety had been his number-one concern. The forced togetherness had ended, but he still wanted to see me—not because he had to, but just because.

I'd watched hundreds of movies where the hero swept the heroine off her feet. In the fantasy world, he didn't leave after a quick romp in the hay, but stayed around, and you could see in their eyes they were committed to each other. The heroine got her happily ever after, something I'd wondered if I would ever feel. A first note didn't sound like much, but it was closer to the fantasy than I'd ever come before.

The decision to stay and face the Ghost had been the most difficult of my life, and now the most rewarding. At every turn, Adam's challenge to me to step out of my comfort zone had worked out pretty well, and I was ready for more—so long as it didn't involve converting to coffee.

Adam wasn't a math guy, but in a dozen ways, he was better.

Kirby had been right that I needed to broaden my horizons, and now that I could go out to lunch again, I'd have to tell her that—if I still had a job at the Smithsonian, that is, which was anything but certain with the way Krause felt about me.

I kissed the note. "I feel the same way, Adam."

I folded the paper. This was going with me.

I went out to his kitchen after showering and pulled eggs from the fridge, but then I stopped. If I was going to change things up, I might as well start first thing in the morning. I rooted around in the cupboards until I found something I definitely had never had for breakfast: one-minute oatmeal. Trying new things could start one spoonful at a time.

The message arrived while I was eating.

ADAM: Did you get the note?

I put down my spoon and typed a reply.

ME: Yes

I decided that wasn't enough and took another risk.

ME: Thank you and I feel the same way

The hot cereal became warm, then almost cold as I spooned out itsy bitsy swallows, waiting for a reply.

ADAM: What way?

Well, there it was. I'd leaped for the golden ring and missed. Life had just slapped my face to wake me up.

I took the bowl to the sink, washed it out, and typed out the most face-saving thing I could think of.

ME: See you tonight

My finger hovered over the send icon. The screen taunted me. I was such a wuss. I didn't send it.

The morning Adam had accused me of being a cyborg who never took a single risk came flooding back, and so did my determination to prove him wrong. I modified the message and sent it. A baby step.

ME: I look forward to seeing you tonight too

I didn't have to wait long for my answer.

ADAM: As soon as I can

The walk from Adam's place to mine was refreshing. The ability to walk outside alone, not needing someone—even if it was Adam—to watch over me was invigorating. Freedom of movement was underappreciated, I decided. I took the long way on purpose, just because I could.

Instead of major thoroughfares with buses going by, I chose the smaller side streets. I traded diesel exhaust for birds in the trees. The sunshine and bird songs brightened the trip considerably.

AROUND TWO IN THE AFTERNOON, I FINISHED CLEANING UP THE KITCHEN. Another cup of tea and a bowl of soup became my reward. My house was starting to look like itself again. Downstairs was cleaned up enough to be livable, and upstairs would be next.

My phone rang, and the Smithsonian central number came up.

"Hello?" I answered tentatively.

"Is this Kelly Benson?" the lady asked.

"Yes."

She'd called me, so the answer should have been obvious, but I held back the sarcastic answer.

"Adriana Stebbins, Smithsonian Institute HR. I need you to come in this afternoon."

Great. My termination paperwork had finally made its way to HR. "I'm busy this afternoon." *Take that, giant bureaucracy.*

"That won't do," she said matter-of-factly.

After another round of give and take, I agreed to come into the office. It was time to take my medicine and join the ranks of the unemployed.

On the Metro ride in, I contemplated how I would explain my termination when interviewing for the next job.

CHAPTER 37

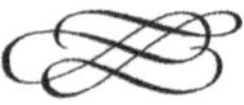

Kelly

Everything looked so normal as I entered work for the last time. I would miss this place.

Instead of going upstairs to my cubicle, I made my way directly to HR and located the door with the *Adriana Stebbins* nameplate.

The lady inside looked over her glasses at me. "Can I help you?"

"I'm Kelly Benson."

She rose from her chair. "That was quick."

I'd said I would leave right away, and I had. Perhaps that surprised her. Maybe she was used to people who didn't follow through.

She passed by me, making a beeline for the elevator bank I'd just left. "Let's get you upstairs."

I followed, hoping we weren't headed to the roof for a jumping-off ceremony.

Inside the elevator, I checked for a button labeled *roof*. There wasn't one.

She pressed the button for the top floor. "Mr. Krause will be so glad to see you."

"Glad?" I had to have heard her wrong.

"Yes, after what you did."

The door opened, and I followed her, even more confused than before.

Krause's office was in the corner, and he stood when we appeared in his doorway. "Come in, Miss Benson. Kelly, isn't it?"

I nodded and entered on weak legs. "That's right."

He thanked my escort.

She closed the door and left.

I took the seat closest to the desk, the better to hide the nervous jitter of my legs.

"We have two things to discuss today," he started. This was the way he started his Monday meetings, laying out an agenda. "I got a call from the FBI this morning." He sipped from his coffee cup, leaving me hanging.

I didn't offer any words to bridge the silence. Concentrating on stilling my leg didn't help.

"I was told you were instrumental in retrieving the lost items from the Hollywood movie jewelry exhibit."

A smile grew on my face. That could only have come from Adam. The nervous tick of my leg silenced itself.

"On behalf of the Institute, I want to thank you."

"Does this mean I'm no longer on suspension?"

"What suspension? My recollection is that we gave you time off to help with this matter. If we understand each other, I have a proposition for you."

I replayed his words in my head and nodded. The spin doctor was at work, and I was being instructed to keep the truth buried. My history had been rewritten.

In his alternate reality, he'd loaned me to the FBI to get the jewels back, which sounded a lot better than the truth. The media would have a field day if they learned he'd threatened to fire the very person the FBI credited with getting back his stolen items. It would be a public relations disaster for him, and at his level, PR trumped everything.

I chose a coy response. "I'm listening."

"Paul Heiden's mother has taken a turn for the worse."

My heart clenched. "I'm sorry to hear that."

"He's asked for some time off to be with her, and I need someone to fill in as acting manager while he's away. Temporarily, of course."

The prospect both thrilled and frightened me. What if my peers didn't like working for me?

Kirby had thought I should try for a supervisory job, but I was pretty sure she hadn't meant a whole department.

He stood. "Let's go down and tell your people."

I puffed up at the term *my people*. With the note from my man this morning, and now this, today was certainly looking up.

Downstairs, the announcement to the group went better than I would have guessed. Kirby was naturally the first, but not the last, to congratulate me.

After the discussion died down, Mark took the opportunity to suggest lunch tomorrow.

I responded with something I hadn't been able to say since arriving here. "I'll need to check with my boyfriend first."

His face dropped. "Sure. Uh... Congratulations again."

Kirby's voice sounded from my right. "Coffee time, Kell."

I turned. "Already?"

When I turned back to thank Mark for his thoughts, he was walking away.

She approached and leaned in. "You looked like you needed a lifeline."

"I don't think he'll be a problem anymore."

Krause had opened up the empty office next to Mr. Heiden's and instructed OPS to get me a key.

After the obligatory coffee run with Kirby, I settled in behind the desk. It might be temporary, but still, this was something else—unbelievable, actually.

I knew I wasn't supposed to call Adam during the day, so I typed my message.

ME: Thank you. I have news for tonight

No response came.

By the end of the day, I still hadn't heard from Adam. People I'd barely talked to in a month were coming into my new office nonstop, asking for advice or my opinion on one thing or another. It was so overwhelming that I bugged out earlier than normal.

Before heading down the escalator to board the Metro, I sent another text.

ME: You ok?

I only waited a minute before descending underground. The reception in the Metro system was good enough; I wouldn't miss his response when it came.

My phone rang almost as soon as I boarded the train going north.

But instead of Adam's name, Daddy's was on the screen.

Elation gave way to dread, but a good daughter would answer the phone, and I did.

"I'm calling to give you fair warning," he said.

"About what?"

"Your mother and I have a trip to Europe planned after next month, and..."

I didn't have to be a genius to figure out what was coming next.

He continued apologetically. "I tried to tell her you might not be ready yet, but she's hell bent on stopping in DC to meet you and Adam."

The inevitable was coming my way.

It sounded like an epic battle of wills, but the outcome had been preordained. Daddy might be a force to be reckoned with, but denying Momma something she really wanted was not his strong suit.

"He might have to travel," I ventured. "His schedule is always changing." A little lie was worth a try. Committing to a meeting before talking to Adam seemed somehow underhanded.

Daddy laughed. "Good try, baby girl, but you know that won't stop her."

I did. Momma would camp out on my doorstep for a month, or grab me and fly off to wherever Adam was. It could be Antarctica, and that wouldn't slow her down.

"I can't guarantee Adam will agree," I said.

Daddy ignored me. "I'll be in touch with the details, and your mother's not the only one looking forward to meeting the man impressive enough to catch your eye." Daddy was back to his normal self, sprinkling in compliments.

If Adam weren't a Cartwright, Daddy and he would get along great, but that was an *if* that couldn't be reversed.

"Tell him I'm looking forward to meeting him," Daddy added.

"I will."

After we hung up, I wasn't quite sure how to broach this with Adam, but I knew I wanted it on my turf, so I sent another message.

ME: Dinner at my place tonight

At the train change, I still hadn't gotten anything back from Adam so I tried again.

ME: You ok?

~

ADAM

IT WAS ALMOST EIGHT BY THE TIME I EXITED THE FIELD OFFICE AND FOUND MY car. My phone stayed in my jacket until I was four blocks away, well out of sight.

Scrolling down the dozen messages from Kelly, I regretted not making an effort to answer earlier. I hadn't been alone all day, not even in the bathroom. But I probably could have typed out a quick response in the privacy of one of the stalls, but it needed to be in person. I sent a single reply before pulling back into traffic.

ME: Sorry I couldn't answer. On the way now

When I opened the front door at her house, the aromas of tomato and herbs washed over me.

"I'm in the kitchen," Kelly called.

When I found her she was at the stove, facing away from me—the perfect picture of sex appeal. Her ass and legs were tightly wrapped in yoga pants, and she wore a top that hung off one shoulder. The distinct lack of a shoulder strap hinted at what would be poking through the fabric when she turned my way.

"Smells wonderful," I said as I entered the kitchen.

She turned to me, and the double-barreled salute of her nipples was as good as I'd imagined. "It's Momma's spaghetti and meatballs."

I opened the back door to check the work that had been done. A quick step outside to survey the scene showed everything in its place, and no intruders. I returned to the kitchen.

"What are you looking for?" she asked.

I closed the door. "Checking to see that the door was done properly."

"And what part of the door is in the backyard?"

"Sorry, force of habit. Just being careful."

Her mouth dropped open just a bit, and her head cocked to the side. "You think he's still out there?"

"No, of course not." I knew the forensic guys hadn't found a trace of anybody but Sanderson and the victims at his house, and that had to settle it, but the hairs on the back of my neck didn't agree.

I let go of the door handle I'd been leaning on, walked over, and wrapped her up in a bear hug. The feel of her soft breasts against my chest recharged me. It was something I'd been missing all day.

She wiggled to get loose. "You didn't text me back. I was worried."

"Busy day. Nonstop meetings." I'd kept my phone on silent and out of sight during the repeated interrogations by Baker and Zalenski.

She turned back to the stove and her meatballs. "Hungry?"

I was hungry, exhausted, and spent after today. I came up behind her, wrapped my arms around her waist, and nuzzled her neck. "For you."

She wiggled her ass against me. "Stop that. The stove's hot." My woman was being practical. "Dinner comes first."

Letting go, I let her cook in peace and went back to check the deadbolt on the door. The click as it slid into place felt reassuring.

Watching me at the door, her eyes narrowed. She turned back to the stove, added spaghetti to the pot of water, and set the timer.

I collapsed into a chair and breathed in the delicious smell. "What's your news?"

She didn't turn to look at me. "You didn't text me all day. I was worried. What kept you busy all day?"

"You said you had news."

"Not until you tell me the truth."

"Good news, I'll bet."

She put the spatula down and her eyes bored into me as she turned. "Stop it."

"Stop what? You said you had news."

She turned back to the stove. "Stop evading."

After a few minutes of silence, I went to the cabinet and selected a bottle of cabernet. "Cabernet okay?" When she didn't object, I took that as a yes.

The cork didn't cooperate, or maybe it was the corkscrew. "You need a better corkscrew."

She stayed silent.

I poured large glasses for each of us, and set hers on the counter next to her.

She left the stove to retrieve plates.

I settled back into the chair, leaned on the table, and started on my glass. After half had disappeared, I gave in. "I was in interrogation pretty much all day."

The timer sounded, and she poured the spaghetti water into a strainer. "Interrogating who?"

I waited while she split the noodles into two servings, added the meatballs and sauce, and brought over the steaming plates.

She sat across from me. "Can't tell me?"

"I was the one being interrogated."

The fork she'd speared a meatball with went still. "What for?"

I twirled a few noodles on my fork. "The shooting."

Her hand came to mine. "I'm sorry. That must be hard."

I sighed. "It's easier to be the one asking the questions. SMK is dead, and that's a good thing. End of story. Let's talk about your day instead."

"You know you can talk to me about it."

What I knew was that talking wouldn't change anything about the Inspection Division's telescope up my ass. "You heard me. Your day. What's the news you're keeping from me?"

As she twisted her fork in the noodles, a wicked grin consumed her face. "Krause made me acting manager of the department."

My eyes went wide. "That's terrific. Good for you."

"It's only temporary. Mr. Heiden's mother is terminally ill, so he's taking some time off." She hesitated. "And I know you called Krause."

I shrugged. All I'd done was tell him the truth. Without her, the jewels would be long gone, and the Great Smithsonian Heist would be in the papers. It could even have led to a congressional inquiry. That was all he needed to know.

"Thank you," she added before finally taking a bite of her meal.

"This is delicious."

She shrugged. "Momma's recipe." Slowly, she began to elaborate on her interactions with the rest of the department, and her pride showed through.

I kept her focused on the good outcome to her day with occasional follow-up questions.

We were finishing the meal, as well as our glasses of wine, when she looked toward her phone for the umpteenth time.

"What is it? Expecting a call?"

She held her glass out. "I could use some more."

I poured us both more wine.

"No. It's a call I already got today."

I didn't hazard a guess.

"Daddy. He and Momma are coming out. I'm going to have to tell them."

I swallowed. "Yeah, I understand."

"Will you come with me?"

I took her hand. "Of course. And we have my family to deal with too." My dad could be volatile, and I didn't see an easy way to have an encounter that was anything short of explosive.

We disagreed on which family would be harder for a few minutes before I stood and pulled her into the hug she deserved. "It'll be okay. They'll understand." I didn't really believe it would be easy, but where there was a will, there was a way.

"You think so?"

I hugged her tighter. "I know so, Sugarbear. We'll make it through this."

We had to make them understand. I wasn't giving her up.

CHAPTER 38

Kelly (Three weeks later)

It had been three weeks since that terrible day—the day I'd screwed up and forced Adam into a shooting situation, the day I'd learned the guard trying to chat me up for lunch was the Ghost, the man who'd killed women I worked with.

I'd settled into my temporary role as department manager. The hardest day had been when the details of Len's basement had hit the *Post*.

Adam hadn't wanted to tell me any of the particulars of what he'd found that night, but it had leaked to the paper. I'd puked that morning after reading the story, and I'd barely been able to go into work.

Adam had been my rock. He'd pointed out that the responsibility I'd taken on filling in for Mr. Heiden meant I had to be strong for everyone else. He'd been right. That day at the office, a half dozen people wandered into my office to talk about it. Each of those talks had been difficult, but necessary for the group to heal.

Work hadn't gone as well for Adam since the shooting. The investigation had dragged on, and every day he felt less certain of the outcome.

But we had my house all to ourselves now that Yolanda had decided to move in with Bogdan. The exercise of cooking dinner with Adam each night had helped me feel normal again after the terror of that day.

He'd turned our nightly ritual into another boundary-expanding test for me. We opened up one of the cookbooks Momma had bought me, and I had to pick a recipe I hadn't eaten before. Tonight it had been spinach and chicken lasagna.

After dinner, Adam checked the fridge. "You want another glass of wine?"

I looked over from loading the last of the dinner dishes in the dishwasher. "No. One's enough for me."

He closed the refrigerator and located a bottle of scotch instead. "Want something stronger?"

I shook my head and started the dishwasher. "No thanks." I came up behind and wrapped him up in a hug. "What's bothering you?"

He took a slug of his drink before turning to face me. "The shooting report is due tomorrow." He sighed.

I'd known this day would come, so I'd prepared. "Then come with me." I tugged him toward the door.

He didn't budge. "What?"

"Let's snuggle and veg out in front of the TV."

He patted the granite in front of him. "I don't think we've tried this counter yet."

"Not tonight." I pulled him harder toward the other room.

Adam grabbed the bottle before coming along.

I flicked on the TV and scrolled through the menu after settling into the couch.

Adam reached the bottom of his glass and poured again before he finally sat.

The special episode of *Bonanza* I'd found started on the big screen. It had taken me an hour of IMDB research to find the right episode.

"I thought you didn't like this," he said as his arm came around me.

"It's growing on me. I like seeing Adam Cartwright outwit the bad guy and win in the end."

He took another swallow. "I only wish it were as simple as they make it look."

Another two glasses of scotch went down Adam's hatch as he watched his namesake on the screen with me.

In this one, Adam Cartwright had been forced to shoot a man. The shooting had taken place away from the ranch, and the sheriff of the town had been the dead man's brother and quickly arrested Adam for murder. Without the support of his family, it had been touch and go for a while, but in the end, truth had won out and Adam was acquitted.

As the episode finished, Adam stroked my head. "You know it doesn't always work out like that."

I purred as I snuggled closer. "I have faith."

He lifted his glass to his lips. "We'll see." He finished it, and letting go of me, reached for the bottle to refill it.

I pulled at his arm. "That's enough for tonight. I have more planned, and I don't want you falling asleep on me."

"One more and I'm done."

I got up and pulled on his hand. "You, Mr. Special Agent Man, are over the legal limit."

"I'm not driving."

"Exactly. Tonight, I'm driving us." I pulled him to stand. "And the passenger has to obey the driver."

"Where to?"

We started toward the stairs. "Bed."

"That's a destination I don't mind."

Upstairs, I quickly worked his clothes off and pushed him back onto the bed. "Remember to obey the driver's instructions." The sight of his engorged cock laying heavily on his abdomen had me wet with anticipation.

After getting down to my panties, I climbed on the bed and leaned over to blow on the tip of his cock, giving it a quick lick. It bounced upward at the attention, so I licked the length of him, from his balls to the tip, which resulted in a moan of satisfaction.

Tonight was Adam's turn to be the center of attention.

I climbed atop him and ground down on him.

As I leaned forward, he lavished my breasts with the kind of attention he always did, fondling, licking, and sucking.

I straightened up, pulling away from his mouth and pulled my panties to the side, sliding my slick folds over his length. The back-and-forth friction increased my desire for what was to come. Settling farther down his legs, I grasped his shaft and pulled it to my mouth. Spreading the bead of precum around the tip with my tongue, I took my time before sucking on the salty crown.

"Oh, baby," he groaned.

More moans of pleasure greeted me as I stroked my tongue against his cock and moved farther down. I took what I could in my mouth, slurping, sucking, licking, and pulling with my hands.

"Oh, baby, keep it up."

He laced his fingers in my hair as he guided my head. His eyes burned with desire as he watched me.

I worked him with both hands, pulling and twisting with the rhythm.

When I cupped his balls and pulled lightly on the sac, his eyes widened.

Shifting back to two hands on my prize, I watched his eyes and listened to his moans to gauge my speed.

He began to tense as his hands encouraged me to go faster.

I stopped.

The look of alarm in his eyes was priceless.

I quickly pulled off my panties and moved back to straddle him. After sliding my wetness over him a few times, his moans coincided with the shocks that went through me every time my clit slid over his tip.

Soon it was time for the question, and I stopped again. "I'm on the pill."

His eyes widened. "I don't have anything, if that's what you're asking."

"Me neither." I reached down to guide him to my entrance.

He started to pull my hips, but I lifted up. "I'm in charge tonight," I reminded him.

Settling back into the bed, his hands moved to breast-massaging duty.

Slowly, tantalizingly, I slid down his length and tried to tense my core around him. My tightness had always been a turn on for him.

His eyes closed, and he took a breath through gritted teeth as I took him all the way to the root.

With me in charge tonight, he was at my mercy for a change. As I slowed down and sped up, I relished my power. It was my turn to control his pleasure while I gave myself mine. The tension built within me, but I was still the driver on this journey. He tensed up, and I slowed down to prolong it, then changed the tempo again.

I ground down on him, taking him fully, wiggling my ass and teasing him by lifting all the way up before thrusting down again. But I soon lost the ability to control myself. The sensations cascaded higher and higher as I rode him, and my pleasure couldn't be contained. Desire took over as I rode him faster and harder. Could I hold off long enough to give him his release before I lost my mind?

When I'd started this, I'd been sure I could. But it wasn't so clear anymore.

After a few more thrusts, he tensed underneath me, arched upward, and pulled my hips down hard. "Oh fuck, baby."

I felt the pulses of his climax deep inside me as he lost control. I'd won, but just barely. As his cock throbbed inside me, I ground forward against my clit.

Seeing what I wanted, he moved his thumb to rub me on the down strokes, and after a few more rapid movements, my blood sang.

I lost myself in the waves of pleasure and collapsed onto him with my core clamped down on his still-pulsing cock.

Neither of us moved for the longest time.

He scratched my back. "You can drive anytime, Sugarbear."

I rolled off, and he grabbed tissue from the nightstand and handed it to me to clean up.

Without the latex between us, the sensations had been better than I'd imagined. All I had to do now was make sure I didn't get stuck sleeping on the wet spot.

~

ADAM

WHEN I WOKE UP THE NEXT MORNING, KELLY WAS ALREADY OUT OF BED. MY cock still tingled from last night. But the clock said I didn't have time to indulge in another round of Kelly.

In the bathroom, the shower was wet from recent use as I searched for the Advil I'd need to function properly this morning.

I'd just finished brushing my teeth when Kelly surprised me, carrying in a tray with breakfast.

"I made you French toast."

I set the tray on the counter and gave her the kiss she deserved. "You're too good to me." After letting her go, I downed two pills with a gulp of the orange juice she'd brought.

"You know your head wouldn't hurt if you'd stopped drinking a little earlier."

"You're not my mother."

Her hands went to her hips. "No. I'm your girlfriend, and it's my job to tell you the truth even if you don't want to hear it."

I took another swig of juice.

"How many scotches did you have last night?"

I thought back and admitted the truth. "I don't remember."

"That makes it at least one too many."

Her logic was hard to dispute, and I didn't want to start the day arguing with my woman. I pulled her to me again. "How did you get so smart?"

She looked up and smiled. "It comes naturally to a Benson." She wiggled loose. "I have to leave early. I'm making a donut run on the way in."

That was my woman, going out of her way to make life a little bit better for her team.

"Thanks for breakfast, Sugarbear," I called as she left.

She poked her head back in. "Text me with your news?"

"Sure."

My stomach lurched. As I turned on the shower, I dreaded the prospect of what awaited me when I got into the office.

It was almost lunchtime when a somber Dempsey emerged from his office.

"Cartwright." He waved me over.

It was time to learn my fate.

Baker and Zalenski were already seated when I entered. Their faces were impassive, not giving me any clue as to the verdict.

I took a seat.

After Dempsey retook his chair behind the desk, Baker began.

"This investigation took longer than usual. The unusual urban nature of this encounter turns out to have given us late-arriving material to review in terms of civilian video input."

I'd heard we had cell phone footage of the shooting captured by two different bystanders, but I hadn't wanted to review either of them. Reliving the incident and second-guessing myself couldn't lead anywhere positive.

Baker handed me a folder. "We have determined that you acted within guidelines in the incident, and this inquiry is concluded."

I felt my eyes go wide. Just like that, it was over, and the weight on me lifted.

They left quickly, and I was alone with Dempsey.

He closed the door again. "They let you off the hook, but for my money, you screwed up just like your uncle did. There's no room in this job for personal feelings to interfere."

I held back any comment.

He tapped the folder on his desk. "All this says is you didn't do a bad job. That's not the same as doing a good job. Now get outta here."

"Yes, sir." I left the office, slumped into my chair, and typed out a text to Kelly.

ME: They cleared me

I took a deep breath. I still had my badge and a shot at the Organized Crime Task Force.

CHAPTER 39

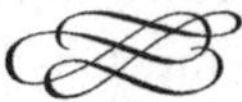

Adam

On Sunday afternoon, my phone rang on the kitchen counter.

Kelly walked the phone over to me. "It's your father."

I took the phone, declined the call, and went back to watching the game.

"Chicken." Kelly shook her head and walked away. "You have to talk to him sooner or later."

"Later, then." I'd settled into a very comfortable state with Kelly: Mom and Dad didn't know, and I was on the opposite end of the country.

"For a bad-ass FBI secret agent, you sure are a pussy."

I sucked in a breath. "Special agent, and I'm just waiting for the right time."

Her hands went to her hips. "I should have known. You're ashamed of me." She was goading me.

The phone rang again. Kelly turned off the TV.

"Hi, Dad," I said into the phone.

"We need to talk," my father announced.

"Okay. I was just watching the game. I've got time now."

"Your mother and I are here. We're staying at the usual place. She's got a dinner with her old college roommate, and you and I can get together at the restaurant here at the hotel."

As usual, my father told me what I was going to do rather than asking.

"I might be able to make that." I left it at *might*—my little rebellion at being treated like a child.

"Good. See you at six."

One big question remained. "What do you want to discuss?"

The online business news had run a story about Dad taking a run at Dennis Benson's company, and as much as I disliked Dennis, I wasn't interested in getting roped into anything further related to his takeover fight.

"See you at six." He hung up without answering my question.

That was one trait of his I was determined to not develop. Avoiding rudeness always paid dividends.

Kelly plopped down next to me, a little too cheerily. "What's the plan?"

"He wants to get together for dinner to talk."

"What time?"

"Six at his hotel on K Street." Dad was a creature of habit, and after he found a place he liked, a pattern set in.

She checked the time. "I'll be ready. Is this a fancy place?"

"Hold on, Sugarbear. It's just me and him."

She faced me, and her stare could have frozen the Potomac. "We talked about this. I was going to come along the next time he came out. That was the plan."

I reached a hand out. "Yeah, but not this time."

She pulled back. "We agreed on this." She got up and headed to the fridge.

We had agreed, and at the time, it had sounded like a reasonable fallback plan to the alternative of a trip to California.

"Sugarbear—"

"Don't you Sugarbear me. We have to face them, and putting it off only makes it worse. Hi, Dad, I'd like you to meet the girl I've been seeing for months, but was too ashamed to tell you about." She opened the fridge. "Sounds like a perfect way to start the conversation to me."

I got up to follow. "It's not like that, and you know it."

She pulled a Diet Coke from the refrigerator and grabbed her purse. "I'm going back to my place."

This was going downhill way too fast. "Kells, please don't go. He set this up to talk about something else. We just can't move too fast. The timing needs to be right."

She paused at the door. "You can tell me about it tomorrow."

She'd been gone five minutes before I knew what to do. I got online and ordered flowers to be delivered to her at work.

~

Kelly

When I got home, I searched the internet and found the hotel on K Street Adam had told me about—the one his father favored. The restaurant there was a standard hotel grill, nothing too fancy, so I picked out a nice, conservative dress from my work collection and paired it with the red heels Adam liked so much.

My doorbell rang.

Kirby marched in, bag in hand. "You said it was an emergency."

"It is. I'm surprising Adam and his dad."

"First time, huh?"

I nodded. "Yeah, and I want to make a good impression."

"Easy peasy," she said. "Take a seat."

I sat in the chair and draped a towel over my shoulders.

She moved a floor lamp closer and opened her cosmetic bag on the table.

Kirby had been a makeup artist before going to college to get into accounting. She was ten times better at this than I was.

"You're wearing black?" she asked.

I lifted the towel. "I think simple and elegant for tonight."

She nodded. "That works, but personally I'd go with something a little lower cut."

"I don't want to look like a tramp."

"No, but if you've got it, flaunt it, and you've definitely got it. You're gorgeous."

I blushed. "I think I'll stick with this."

A half hour later, we stood in front of my bathroom mirror.

"What do you think?" she asked.

"I think you're a true artist." Even though I'd tried, I could never get the hang of blending in different shades and making each eye look the same.

"It's just practice. Now go knock 'em dead."

She had no idea how relevant death could be when talking about a Benson-Cartwright meeting.

It was almost six when I left. My evil plan was to surprise Adam after he and his father had already settled in.

We had to tackle the family feud issue, and I meant to force it. Like Adam said, we were stronger together.

I was sure that after his father got over the initial shock, he'd see how right we were for each other. He'd surely want what would make his only son happy, and it was my job to convince him I was the answer to that—the right answer.

~

Adam

When I reached the restaurant, Dad was already there. He checked his watch.

The gesture bugged me, but I ignored it. "Hi, Dad."

I'd checked the time before reaching the door. I wasn't late.

It was just one of his annoying quirks, a constant reminder that I'd been late to meet him once or twice when I was younger.

He led the way to the hostess table. "You're looking good."

His greeting was another thing that never changed.

The hostess showed us to a window table.

Dad busied himself with the wine list and ended up picking the most expensive bottle, same as the last three times. Nothing but the best for a Cartwright, he'd told me more than once.

Growing up, I'd been proud that Dad thought we were worth the best. Our family name was an out-of-proportion source of pride for him. But knowing what Uncle Jack had done, I wasn't so thrilled with our name anymore.

By the time our wine arrived and Dad had gone through the show of taste-testing the bottle, I'd learned that Mom had tagged along on this trip just to interrogate me about my dating life.

"Surprise her and answer the questions for a change," Dad said.

I sipped some of the dark wine, and *damn* if it wasn't smooth. "The ones I can," I told him. Last year I hadn't had anything to hide, and Mom still hadn't believed me.

"I'm still working on that Benson transaction," Dad said, changing the subject. "Pretty soon I'll have him right where I want him. And you'll have your revenge."

"What do you mean?" I had no illusions that Dad was doing this on my behalf. He attacked anything and everything Benson for his own benefit.

"Benson's oldest won't just lose his company, I'll have him in prison with any luck, thanks to that package you forwarded to the SEC."

"You mean it's criminal?"

"Sure. Didn't you read it?"

"No. I didn't have time." I hadn't even opened the files he'd sent me. I'd passed them along, assuming they were run-of-the-mill financial discrepancies Dad was exploiting to gain leverage as they had been the last time.

I put down my glass. The wine didn't taste as good anymore.

"Was it all true?"

His look turned quizzical. "Who cares? He'll be getting what he deserves. That's all that matters."

I didn't recognize the man across from me anymore.

He'd so much as admitted to using me to pass along false information to frame Dennis Benson for something.

The motto that went with my badge was *Fidelity, Bravery, and Integrity.* He'd asked me to sully that without so much as batting an eye. Tonight, the brotherly resemblance to Uncle Jack became too clear to ignore. Right and wrong mattered not a whit when it came to dealing with anything or anyone Benson.

I disliked Dennis Benson, all right, but Kelly had taught me that a family's last name didn't preordain them all to be either bad or good.

"You're wrong about DNA being destiny," I told him.

He put down his glass and huffed. "Bullshit. What's gotten into you?"

"My girlfriend is Kelly Benson." *There, I said it.* "She's a Benson, and she's a good person." Good was only the beginning; Kelly was much more than that.

Anger clouded his face. "There's no such thing as a good Benson. Now that you've fucked her, you can dump her." He poured himself another glass of wine.

I shook my head. "You're wrong."

The vein on his temple throbbed. "You dump her, and I mean now, or I'll—"

"Or you'll what, Dad?"

He'd threatened to disown me more than once, but I didn't care anymore.

"You continue to see her, and I'll ruin you. I'll see that the SEC learns you falsified that last affidavit. You'll be done at the FBI."

I couldn't believe I'd heard him right. He was threatening me, his own son.

The waiter arrived, interrupting our exchange.

Dad opened his menu. "Just a second."

"I can give you more time, if you like," the waiter offered.

"No need," Dad told him.

I turned to the entrées. The words on the page swam in circles as I tried to calm myself enough to read.

Dad ordered the salmon.

"I'll need another minute to decide," I told the waiter.

He left.

I pulled out the box I had in my pocket.

"What's that?" Dad asked.

I opened it to show him the ring. "I'm going to marry her."

"No, you're not."

I pocketed the box and excused myself to use the restroom.

Dad ignored me.

Once behind the door, I splashed water on my face, dried off, and did my best to calm down and get my head around what had just happened.

Walking back to the table, I pulled out my phone and waved it when I reached my father. "I have to go. Work."

He put down the wine glass. "Don't forget we have dinner with your mother tomorrow."

"I have to go." I didn't plan on making that engagement, but the argument could wait until tomorrow. Standing Mom up wasn't my first choice, but replaying this argument in front of her would be worse.

While I waited for the valet to bring my car, I dialed Kelly.

It went to voicemail, so I left a message. "Hi, Sugarbear. Dad bailed on dinner, so why don't we go out tonight? Give me a call."

The wait for my car was interminable, and all I could do was keep checking my phone for something from Kelly.

Nothing came.

The valet returned and handed me my keys.

Before getting in the car, I took the time to remove the large silver C from the keyring and dropped it in the trash by the door. This evening it disgusted me.

CHAPTER 40

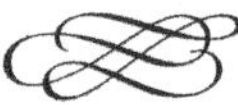

Kelly

I'd arrived at the hotel late enough that I could be confident Adam and his father weren't in the lobby.

As expected, the lobby didn't contain my boyfriend.

"I'm meeting a party who's already here," I told the hostess.

She nodded, and I passed her by.

It didn't take long to catch sight of Adam and his father at a table by the window, beyond the bar.

Adam had his back to me.

"Bullshit. What's gotten into you?" I heard his father almost yell.

A couple at a nearby table looked over, clearly not happy about the disturbance.

I pulled up short and took a seat at the bar, close enough to hear.

Showing up in the middle of a family argument was not a good strategy. And, maybe the whole showing up unannounced thing wasn't such a good idea. As I listened a bit longer, I couldn't believe my ears. Adam had told his father about me after all.

"What'll you have?" the bartender asked, interrupting my listening session.

I waved him off. "In a minute."

"You continue to see her, and I'll ruin you," I heard his father continue. The group at the next table laughed before he added, "You'll be done at the FBI."

As their waiter approached the table, I turned for the door. I pulled a tissue from my purse before reaching the street. I grabbed the first taxi and gave the driver my address as the tears began to flow.

She shot me a concerned look in the rearview mirror. "You okay, dear?"

Okay was not a part of my world right now, but I nodded to her anyway. "I will be."

"He's not worth it. Don't let him ruin your life."

She had it all wrong—he was the one in danger of me ruining his life.

There was only one thing to do. "Change of plans," I told the driver with a sniffle. I gave her Adam's address.

My tissue was soaked, and it came away from my face with smudges of the makeup Kirby had so carefully applied. Leaving my house, my future had looked sunny, just like my makeup. Now it was as messed up as my face.

My phone rang. It was Adam.

"If that's him, let him stew," the driver said.

I declined the call.

We stopped at a light, and a couple passed in front of us on the crosswalk. They held hands and walked in lock-step. The woman looked his way and smiled.

Yesterday, I'd been in her shoes: happy to be walking with my boyfriend toward a bright future. Today, his father was determined to rip that possibility away from us.

The light turned green, and my driver looked back at me again. "You have a sister?"

I nodded.

"When I have problems, I talk to my sister."

I considered it for only a millisecond before discarding the idea. I'd been a fool to think it could work between Adam and me. What never could have worked didn't need to be fixed; it needed to be ended.

She pulled to a stop in front of Adam's.

"Can you wait for me to get a few things? I'll just be a minute."

"His place?" she asked.

"Yeah."

"Take all the time you need."

I let myself in, threw the things I'd brought over into my suitcase, and wrote a note.

My key went under the mat after I locked his door for the last time.

When we arrived at my house, I handed her two twenties.

"The advice was free, dear."

"Keep the change," I said as I opened the door.

The advice might not have been worth it, but the compassion had been.

Adam

I PARKED AT HOME AND CHECKED MY PHONE. STILL NO RESPONSE FROM KELLY.

Once inside, I shucked off my suit and climbed into more comfortable clothes.

On my way to the fridge, I saw the piece of paper on the counter. What had been a miserable evening with Dad turned even worse as I read the note.

> Adam
> You're a great guy, and I can't thank you enough.
> But I've been doing a lot of thinking, and I need to move on.
> I wish you all the best in your career.
> Goodbye,
> Kelly
> My key is under the mat. You can mail me your key.

My fist came down hard on the counter. "Move on? What the fuck?" I yelled.

Send her the key?

Like, not even talk to her?

No fucking way in hell.

I looked at my phone for a second before pocketing it. This wasn't a phone conversation.

The drive over was too short for me to formulate any kind of speech.

Reaching her door, I didn't use the key. I knocked—a polite knock, two raps.

Maybe this was a joke, and I'd played right into her hand by flying off the handle?

She had looked hurt when I'd told her she couldn't come to dinner with Dad—and good thing she hadn't come along. Dad had been his own brand of asshole tonight.

Was this a sick test of my feelings to get back at me for not bringing her along?

I banished that idea instantly.

Kelly wasn't sadistic, and this note tore my heart out. Joke made more sense—mean joke, but she probably hadn't realized how strongly I'd react. She wouldn't be intentionally mean.

With no answer, I knocked again, and harder. "Kelly, we have to talk."

One of her neighbors walked by.

I pounded harder on the door. "Kelly, let me in. We have to talk." A few seconds later, I heard sounds from inside.

"Please go away. There's nothing to talk about."

My hope that this was a joke, or even a test, evaporated.

Nothing to talk about? Fuck that. There was a ton to talk about, starting with whatever had brought this on.

"I don't understand." My brain went into overdrive, analyzing everything I'd said to her today and coming up empty.

It wasn't her birthday, was it? No, that was six months away.

It took a while for her to say anything. "It was fun, Adam. We're done. We both need to move on. That's all I have to say."

What the hell did *it was fun* mean? Yesterday we'd been talking about the future and tonight she wanted to end it?

"I'm not leaving until you talk to me."

Only silence came back from inside.

"Kelly?"

When she didn't answer, I leaned my head against the door to listen.

An MPD cruiser pulled up with its lights flashing. The pair of officers climbed out and started toward me. The short one had his hand on the butt of his gun. "Sir," he called out. "Move away from the door."

I left the entry and pulled out my credentials. "FBI," I said as I reached them.

"We need you to step away from the house," the tall one said.

His nametag read Jones, the other was Walker.

"I'm just here to see my girlfriend."

Walker made his way toward Kelly's door.

Jones pointed to the street. "The sidewalk, sir." He followed me there.

"Did she call you?" I asked.

"No. A concerned neighbor."

Kelly opened the door for Officer Walker.

"We need to talk," I called.

Jones stood between me and the open door.

I watched Kelly talk to the cop a few seconds before the door closed again.

Walker returned. "She doesn't want to talk to you."

"But—"

"You need to leave, sir," Officer Walker said.

I watched the door. It stayed closed.

"If you refuse to leave, or if you come back uninvited, I'll be forced to write you up," Jones said. His face had lost its friendly demeanor. "I don't think you want that."

I sure as shit didn't want any paperwork on this to reach Dempsey. I was just trying to talk to her, and these assholes were overreacting. But I was on their turf, and they knew it. My badge didn't do me any good in this situation.

Still, I stayed put.

"Do you?" Jones asked.

"Fine." I walked toward my car.

My phone vibrated in my pocket. The text almost doubled me over.

KELLY: We both have to move on

The uniforms were still watching me when I looked back before climbing into my car.

~

Kelly

Tears streamed down my face as I peeked out the blinds and watched Adam walk away.

He had to go to save himself. I wouldn't let his father ruin his career.

Breathing became difficult. This had been even harder than I'd thought. I hadn't expected him to come over.

If I'd lapsed and opened the door, he would have seen right through me.

The cops at the door made it especially difficult. He probably thought I'd called them, but I couldn't be that mean. I *wouldn't* be that mean.

I collapsed on the floor, unable to watch him drive away and out of my life forever. The best thing that had happened to me was walking away, and I was letting him—I was making him.

I wiped my cheek with my sleeve and typed out the text. This was one experience I couldn't bear to repeat. I wouldn't survive a next time. I hit send.

ME: We both have to move on

It was the kindest thing I could do for him, for both of us.

I jerked at the sound of another knock on my door. *It couldn't be.* The text was meant to keep him from coming back, not bring him here again.

"Miss Benson, it's Officer Walker."

Struggling to my feet, I wiped the tears away with my sleeve and opened the door.

"He's gone now. We warned him to not come back. If he does, you need to call 9-1-1 right away."

I nodded. "Thank you." Not that I would ever call the cops on Adam.

Once I closed the door again and locked it, I was alone with my despair, and my guilt. But it was the right thing to do for him—the only thing.

Yolanda was taking a week in the Bahamas with Bogdan and wouldn't be around to talk to.

I considered calling Kirby, or even taking my cabbie's advice and calling my sister, but Serena wouldn't understand.

She hadn't heard the vitriol in his father's voice. She couldn't understand how certain I was that he'd follow through on his threat to ruin Adam.

Serena wasn't the person to talk to. She was too kind, too trusting. It would be too easy in her world to think his father was just blowing off steam. She'd try to talk me into ruining Adam's future.

That was one thing I wouldn't do.

In the end, I walked to the liquor cabinet.

A full bottle of tequila looked like the best memory-erasing medicine, but then I remembered my last encounter with too much tequila. The bottle of scotch wasn't as full, but it would do.

There was nothing about this evening I wanted to remember, not a single fucking thing.

My phone vibrated.

I turned it off.

The glass of scotch went down with a burn, which turned into warmth when it hit my stomach—a warmth I needed to offset the chill in my heart.

I was doing the right thing. To sacrifice for someone was the true measure of love, and I'd come to love Adam without realizing how strongly the word applied.

He'd joined the FBI on a mission, and it had become his calling, his reason for being—it defined him. Special Agent had become more a part of his name than Cartwright.

They could do a movie about him, Special Agent Adam Cartwright. Instead of the man with the golden gun, he was the man with the golden heart—defender of the weak, punisher of the evil, and the epitome of the Bureau's motto *Fidelity, Bravery, and Integrity.*

I couldn't give him the chance to sacrifice his career and ruin his relationship with his family over me. That would be selfish, and we wouldn't end up in a happy place. It would eat away at him, and in the end it would destroy us. There wasn't a happy place left for us after his father's threat.

It should have been obvious from the start. But the heart wants what the heart wants, and I hadn't been able to resist the allure of the prize I couldn't have. Now he'd be some other woman's prize.

Daddy had always emphasized that family came first, and I had to allow Adam to put his first. Anything less would be sacrilege, and I wouldn't be able to live with myself knowing what I'd cost him.

It would destroy him to give up his dreams, it would torture me, and in the end, it would tear us apart.

Like ripping off a Band-Aid, the only right way to minimize his pain, my pain, our pain, was to get it over with quickly. It hurt like hell to put him through this, but it was kinder than drawing it out.

If this was the less painful way, I was sure as hell not subjecting either of us to the harder way of talking ourselves in circles before coming to the same conclusion. That would be self-flagellation in the extreme.

I poured and guzzled another glass of the amber liquid and downed it. It wouldn't be the last this evening.

CHAPTER 41

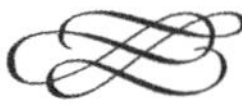

ADAM (TWO WEEKS LATER)

I COULDN'T MAKE OUT THE TIME ON THE CLOCK AT THE FAR END OF THE BAR, BUT I knew it wasn't late enough to shuffle home yet. Fuck, the place was still open. I'd taken to not wearing my watch after work, so I couldn't focus on how slowly the time went by as I tried to forget Kelly—my Kelly. It had been two weeks, and it felt like two years.

"I'll have another," I told Tommy behind the bar.

"You ought to slow down, you know."

Tommy's was his place, and the best place for me to tie one on, because it was within walking distance of my apartment.

"I pay. You serve. That's the way it works."

It had to be after midnight, because that's when he'd been hassling me to stop since I'd started coming here a week ago. It was a nightly ritual: he bitched, and I told him to shove it.

He didn't actually cut me off. He knew I wasn't driving, and I'd stopped an armed robbery attempt here a year ago, so I'd earned the right to give him shit.

He refilled my glass. "I'll call you a cab after this one."

I knocked back half the glass. "Fuck that shit." I could still make it under my own power.

"Your funeral," he muttered before moving down the bar to take another order. This wasn't the worst part of town, but none of DC's darker streets were a picnic after midnight. Enough congressmen had been mugged here over the years to make that point.

I pondered how many more I'd need tonight as I swirled the drink in my glass. When I looked to my right, I got a shock I wasn't expecting.

My new partner, Rylie, had parked her pretty butt on the stool next to mine. "Hey, Adam. Neil thought I might find you here."

Neil had been temporarily assigned to Baltimore, and Dempsey had teamed me with Rylie in the meantime. She'd been an improvement so far—smart and easygoing.

I had no idea why she was here, but she was certainly better company than Tommy, or smelly Pete who'd vacated that stool a while ago. "Hey, Tommy, the lady here would like…" I tried to remember what she drank, but couldn't. "An appletini."

She waved him off. "Nothing for me, thanks. How many has my friend had?"

Tommy slid down the bar and leaned toward Rylie. "He doesn't need a date. This isn't that kind of place."

Rylie was looking good tonight. She'd changed out of her conservative work clothes. I'd only seen her in a skirt a few times before, and she was one hot number in a dress—nice legs.

I stifled my laugh at Tommy's implication that she was a hooker and sat back to watch the fireworks. It would be a shame if she shot him. I liked this bar.

Of course she might just fly over the bar and put him in a choke hold for insulting her. The gentlest response I expected was for her to wave her weapon in his face and give the poor guy a heart attack. She didn't take that kind of shit from anybody.

She surprised me by laying her creds on the bar instead of her weapon. "How many?" she asked Tommy firmly.

He backed away. "More than enough."

"And I'm not done yet," I added as I lifted my glass, a little surprised that she'd toned down her response. For a second I wondered if I was supposed to punch Tommy for disrespecting my partner.

Rylie grabbed my raised hand. "You're done."

"Fuck that."

Her other hand jabbed my ribs, hard, as she yanked the glass away. She slid it down the bar.

"I paid for that," I complained. Technically, I hadn't yet, but Tommy had my credit card for the tab.

"You can finish it tomorrow," he told me as he poured the contents down the sink.

I grabbed Rylie's hand. "What is your problem?"

"You. We're going to your place."

"I told you, I'm not done yet."

She yanked her hand free. "As your partner, I'm asking you nicely." Making a point like that wasn't like her, and when I got sober, I'd have to reevaluate whether she really was an improvement over Neil.

A few of the other patrons had started watching the commotion, and I decided to deescalate the argument so as to avoid their stares when I came back tomorrow. I really did like this place. I stood and steadied myself against the bar for a second. "Lead the way."

"I'll drive," she said when we reached the street.

"I walked."

She pulled me to the right, toward the hovel that I called my home in this stupid city. "First good decision you've made this week."

What the hell had I done to deserve a comment like that? "Fuck you."

"No. That's my husband's job."

I laughed. "Sorry. I didn't mean…" I wasn't sure how to finish the sentence. She'd taken her turn to deescalate the argument, and shame me at the same time. I'd always treated her like one of the guys, and here she was giving it back to me like in one of our sexual harassment lectures.

She punched my shoulder, guy style. "I know. I'm messing with you."

I blew out a relieved breath. Being shitfaced was no excuse for fucking up —no, make that *screwing* up our partnership.

She walked with me, and we made the turn down my street.

"Why the escort?" I asked.

"You need to level with me and tell me what's wrong."

"Says who?"

She grabbed my arm and jerked me to a stop. "Your fucking partner is who."

"I thought we agreed I wasn't fucking you."

Even in the dim light, her glare was unmistakable. "Quit the word games and talk."

I didn't see any other way to get rid of her. "Kelly called it quits." I started walking again.

"Why?"

"Fuck if I know."

"Sorry, I didn't know." She was quiet for a block. "So what's the plan? When do you go talk to her and figure out what you fucked up?"

"Who says I fucked up?"

"It's obvious you're not upset at something she did, so it had to be you."

We reached my place, and I stopped. "No plan."

"It's up to you to fix it."

I moved to my door and turned the key. "Thanks for the pep talk."

She backed up. "Maybe Dempsey's right about you after all. You can't handle anything tough."

I went in and closed the door behind me.

CHAPTER 42

Adam

On Tuesday morning, my head pounded as I trudged up the stairs to our lookout across the street from the human trafficking house. Three knocks before opening the door were meant to make sure I didn't get shot for startling the agent I was replacing. "Hey, Doug. Anything new?"

He rose from the chair he'd pulled to the window. "Not a damned thing. I think it's way past time somebody double-checked the intel on this place."

"Take it up with Dempsey."

He shook his head as he stretched. "Right."

We both knew that wouldn't go anywhere.

"Want me to get you anything?" Doug asked from the door.

I held up my thermos of coffee. "I'm good."

I downed a few more Advil after the door closed and settled into the chair. The world needed a better hangover cure than these fucking pills.

Watching the street, my eyelids became heavy, and I chugged some more coffee. All I could think about was the look on Kelly's face as she'd talked with MPD Officer Walker.

She'd told him she didn't want to talk to me, and she couldn't even tell me herself.

What the fuck was with that?

Getting almost fall-down drunk had become the only way to get any sleep, even shitty, restless sleep. Kelly had energized me, then wrecked me, and right now, letting myself fall for her had been both the best and worst experience of my pathetic existence.

One Benson had ruined my future in the NFL, and now Kelly had finished the job of ruining my life. First she'd introduced me to the hope of a better future, then yanked it away, just like that.

I had another four hours of this monotony to endure before Harper showed up to relieve me—assuming he was on time for a change. I blinked back the fatigue and slurped some more coffee. The pain in my chest would get better with time. At least that's what conventional wisdom said.

~

Kelly

Last night, just as every night, Adam's face had appeared when I closed my eyes. There was no escaping him, whether I was trying and failing to fall asleep or trying to concentrate at work. It was as if he was the screensaver in my brain. He showed up on the blank screen of my computer, on my phone, and in the window when I looked outside.

If only my name weren't Benson. Then I could be waking up in his arms every morning and looking forward to a bright future, instead of the dull, gray haze that now enveloped me. The Metro jerked to a halt, and I disembarked for the escalator and short walk to our building.

As tired as I was from lack of sleep, I hadn't felt safe driving since the day I'd cut it off with Adam. Still, I knew I'd done the right thing, the humane thing, the only thing. Adam couldn't be Adam without the FBI.

I'd only just set my heavy purse down when Helmut Krause arrived in my office doorway. "Paul called."

I waited for more. We knew Mr. Heiden's mother had passed away last week, and he'd planned to bury her over the weekend in Colorado, but none of us had heard anything more.

"He said he'd be in by lunchtime today."

I stood. "I'll get back to my cube right away."

"Take your time. You've done well in his absence."

Krause wasn't a people person—he didn't get it.

I had no intention of being anywhere but back in my old cubicle when Mr. Heiden walked in. It would be best if things looked and felt just as they had when he'd left. I owed it to him to make him as comfortable as possible.

He didn't need me making it look like he'd been replaced while taking time off to care for his mother in her final days.

Krause had only been gone a minute when Kirby showed up. "Coffee run."

I filled her in on Krause's news while making my tea.

"Why's he in such a hurry to get back?"

I shrugged. "If I had that kind of turmoil in my life, I'd probably bury myself in work for a while to get it out of my head."

She added sweetener to her cup. "Me, I'd go to the Caribbean, lay on a beach, and bake it out of my brain."

I laughed—it was so Kirby to say something like that. I kept dunking my teabag and realized I'd stopped counting dunks, another small impact Adam had made on me.

She nodded toward my cup. "Still not sleeping well?"

I'd switched from English Breakfast to these Zest teabags with triple the caffeine, more even than her coffee. "It's hard."

"I don't see why you don't—"

I cut her off with a raised hand. "I don't want to debate it. I did the right thing."

She shook her head, but thankfully didn't keep after me. She meant well, but she didn't understand the consequences the way I did. I couldn't very well tell her what Adam's father had threatened.

Back in my temporary office, I cleaned everything out and had myself relocated to my comfy cube before lunch.

Adam

"Wake the fuck up, jerkoff," Sal Harper bellowed.

My eyes yanked themselves open, and my feet fell to the floor as the stool

Sal had kicked skittered across the floor. I blinked up at the howling madman.

"How long have you been asleep?" he demanded.

I shoved myself up out of the chair. "I was just resting my eyes for a second." The soreness in my back said I probably hadn't moved in hours.

"Bullshit, you were fucking snoring. Get the hell back to the office. Now."

I stretched my shoulders, grabbed my bag, and lit out of there before we got into it physically. The door slammed behind me, and I checked the time again. No memory of anything after the first half hour of my four-hour stint came back to me. I'd fucked up royally, and Harper would be letting the ASAC know.

On the drive back to the field office, the irony struck me. Dad had threatened to derail my career if I didn't break it off with Kelly, which hadn't turned out to be a choice I got to make anyway. And here I was destroying it myself because Kelly had broken it off with me. I was screwed all the way around.

No Kelly, and no career. How the hell was that fair?

When life threw me a curve, it was a damned wicked one.

I slowed down and drove carefully, knowing what awaited me upstairs when I reached the office.

As soon as the elevator doors parted, Dempsey was at his door. "Cartwright, my office. Now."

The other agents on the floor kept their eyes down. Nobody wanted to be noticed when the boss was in this kind of mood.

I closed the door behind me and didn't have to wait even a second for the assault to begin.

"This isn't a fucking country club with naptime whenever you feel like it."

I nodded rather than say anything.

"Do you have any idea how important this trafficking ring is?"

"Yes, sir."

"And if you just missed the next drop off of girls, and they pick up stakes and leave town, what am I supposed to tell HQ? Fuck, what the hell am I supposed to tell the families whose daughters we lost because you fucked up? Huh?"

I knew better than to attempt to answer.

"We have over a month on this op, and you have to… I don't know what your problem is. And frankly, I don't fucking care. You come in hungover every morning."

I lifted my head and opened my mouth to object, but stopped myself. He was right. I'd been hungover every day since Kelly told me to take a hike.

"Don't think I can't tell when you've been drinking. And don't start about how it's only off-duty. What do you have to say for yourself?"

This wasn't really an offer to let me defend myself. I'd learned that lesson.

Contrition was the best policy with him. "You're right. I'll do better."

"First you screw up that SMK drop and shoot a suspect that should be in custody, and then you go and jeopardize a huge operation by falling fucking asleep."

When he put it that way, it sounded bad even to me.

"You're suspended."

I wasn't sure I'd heard him correctly. "What?"

"Deaf as well as stupid?"

I didn't attempt an answer.

"You're suspended for the rest of the week. We'll talk on Friday and see where to go after that."

I tried to swallow, but my throat was too dry.

"Now get out of my sight."

I stood and retreated from his office.

None of the other agents on my team met my gaze as I looked around, except for Rylie.

When the elevator arrived, I punched the button for the garage level, and the doors closed.

Would this be my last view of the inside of this building?

I'd failed utterly, and had nobody to blame but myself.

CHAPTER 43

KELLY

MR. HEIDEN ARRIVED IN THE EARLY AFTERNOON. AFTER WE ALL WELCOMED HIM back and expressed sorrow at his loss, he shooed us away and locked himself in his office. He didn't come out for almost two hours, and when he did, I was his first stop.

"Benson, I want to see you."

I followed him to his office.

"Shut the door."

I did and took a seat.

His eyes were dark and cold, but how should they be after losing his mother?

"While I was out, you…" He seemed to search for what to say next.

"Mr. Krause asked me to handle things while you were gone."

"You took over," he said. "You, of all people, should have known better."

I blinked and searched for the underlying meaning in his words without luck. The office was colder than I remembered. I folded my arms. It wasn't right that I get blamed for helping out while he was gone. "But Mr. Krause—"

"Doesn't know his ass from a hole in the ground." The anger in his tone was uncharacteristic for Heiden. The loss clearly still hung over him.

I nodded, agreeing in general with his assessment of Krause, and hoping that would calm him. His opinion on the big boss wasn't one he'd shared before.

"It wasn't right," he hissed. His finger tapped an angry staccato on the desk. He'd suddenly become the rhino you didn't want to piss off. "Let's get started."

Task by task, we reviewed the notes I'd left for him.

"You should have known better," he said for the fourth or fifth time when he disagreed with a decision I'd made in his absence.

After the next one, I'd had enough. "Krause put me in charge while you were gone. I didn't ask for it, and I didn't want it."

He looked back at me blankly, apparently not registering my words. "Let's go on to the next."

We did, and after two more minor items, we reached the end of my notes for him.

I stood. "Is there anything else you want to yell at me about?"

He rubbed his temples. "You should leave."

As I closed the door behind me, I decided to take him literally and go home.

Kirby walked toward me as I closed Heiden's office door.

"You don't want to go in there," I warned her.

"That bad, huh?"

"Enter at your own risk."

She held up a sheet of paper. "I have to get him to sign this."

While I packed up my purse to head home, I could hear Heiden rip into Kirby, even with the door closed. With my desk locked for the night, I left the ogre behind.

Adam

I sat in my car in the garage and leaned my head on the wheel for a moment. Closing my eyes, I took several deep breaths.

My funk over Kelly had now fucked up my career. No… *I'd* fucked up my career. The Bureau didn't have much tolerance for the kind of screw-up I'd been the last two weeks.

Banging on the passenger window startled me, and my hand went to the butt of my gun.

Rylie rapped on the window again. "Open up."

I rolled down the window. "What?"

"Are you going to make me stand out here?"

I hit the unlock button.

She slid into the passenger seat.

"What?" I asked.

"Well, I'm fine, thank you. How are you?"

I sighed. "I have to get going."

"Somewhere important to rush off to?"

I didn't answer her smart-ass question.

"Like Tommy's?"

"Yeah. At least there I don't have to put up with mouthy busybodies."

"You're a chicken shit. When are you going to man up and go talk to her?"

"Maybe you didn't hear me last time. She made it pretty damned clear she's not interested in talking. And I've moved on."

"You want to know what I think?"

"No."

"You're both scared shitless. Her I understand, but you I don't get. You'd face down a crackhead with a shotgun in a second, but a little woman and you're shittin' your pants."

"Are you done?"

"I think you don't have the balls. The big man with the big gun can't face a poor, defenseless woman. She's in love with you, man, and you have to go fix whatever it is you fucked up, and get her back before it's too late."

I tried to wrap my head around what she'd just said. She thought Kelly cared, when I'd been sure she'd changed her mind.

She poked and angry finger at me. "Are you going to admit it or what?"

"Admit what?"

"That you love her so much you can't live without her. Why else would you be drinking yourself to death and fucking up your career?"

"Are you done?"

"Are you so scared you need me to go with you?"

I waited for a second while another agent walked behind the car. "Fuck that. I don't need her."

"If you don't have the balls to go talk to her, don't bother coming back here. I sure don't want you as my partner if you can't manage something that simple."

She opened the door and got out. "Your choice." She slammed the door and walked back toward the elevator.

I started the car and headed for the ramp to street level.

Arriving in front of Tommy's bar, I stopped out front and turned off the ignition.

The one thing Rylie had right was that all the drinking I'd done hadn't achieved anything. It hadn't eliminated the pain, only postponed it a few hours at a time. I'd been taking the coward's way out.

I started the car again, turned around, and drove to where it had all begun.

Inside Angelica's, they were just opening, and the dining room was empty. The hostess checked the time.

"Off work early," I explained.

She led me toward a booth.

I ignored her. "I'd prefer this one." I stopped beside the table where I'd met Kelly when this all began.

The hostess threw me a flirty smile. "That works too."

I sat and ordered the same meal I'd eaten that first evening.

The food arrived, piping hot, looking and smelling as good as ever, but the first bite wasn't the same. The next bite told the same story. It wouldn't ever be the same.

I stared at my plate and played that night back in my head. I'd demanded complete honesty from her, and here I was not being honest with anybody.

I'd told Tommy at the bar I didn't care anymore: lie. I'd told Rylie I didn't need Kelly: lie. I'd told myself I could forget her and move on: the biggest lie of all.

Kelly dominated my thoughts, my dreams when I looked back at my time with her, and my nightmares when I looked forward to see a future without her.

The next bite I tried tasted awful—my punishment for self-deceit.

After peeling a Benjamin out of my wallet, I stood, left the bill on the table, and walked back to my car.

Kelly's house was fifteen minutes away in this traffic, and I tried formulating the words as I drove. It didn't go well. We needed to talk, but everything I came up with sounded juvenile.

I reached her address and parked across the street and down two houses.

She probably isn't home yet, I told myself. That gave me time to work on my speech: the most fucking important speech of my life, the words that would win her back.

I banged my head against the wheel when inspiration wouldn't come. Opening my eyes again, I looked up.

A dumpy, older, balding guy walked down the sidewalk carrying flowers—a nice gesture for his wife.

I rubbed my eyes for a second, trying for the words to start with. When I looked up again, he'd stopped at Kelly's house.

He walked to the door and rang the bell. Obviously the guy was senile and couldn't even find his own house.

The door opened.

Kelly smiled and let him in.

The door closed.

What the fucking hell?

~

KELLY

I'D GOTTEN HOME AND FINISHED MY FIRST GLASS OF WINE WHEN THE DOORBELL rang. Putting my glass down, I went to the peephole and was surprised to find Mr. Heiden outside, with a bouquet of flowers.

I unlatched the deadbolt and opened the door.

He spoke first. "I'm sorry I was short with you this afternoon." He held out the flowers. "May I come in?"

I opened the door farther and took the flowers as he passed. "You didn't need to."

"I thought it appropriate." He wore the face of sadness, of loss.

I closed the door, latched the deadbolt, and carried the flowers to the kitchen to locate a vase. "I'll just put these in water. Can I get you something to drink?"

It was a standard offer, but so lacking. A glass of water or cup of coffee wouldn't heal the wound he carried. Nothing I could offer would provide an escape from the pain of his loss.

He followed me into the kitchen. "No, thank you. I remember you have a roommate who also works with us, isn't that right?"

I pulled a vase down from the cabinet and settled the flowers inside. "I did. Yolanda is a curator in Natural History."

He moved to the back door and checked outside.

I went to the sink and started adding water. "But she moved out."

He sighed impatiently. "It's all your fault."

I turned off the water and set the vase on the counter. "Pardon?" When I looked back, he had turned away and leaned on the table.

"She's dead because of you," he snarled.

My eyes went wide, my heart raced, and I screamed louder than I ever had before.

He had a gun pointed at me. "Scream again, and I'll shoot," he yelled.

Pee dribbled down my leg. I couldn't breathe.

He waved the gun, motioning me toward the refrigerator. "Move or die."

I stumbled toward the fridge and fell before I reached it. *Adam.* I needed Adam.

"Get up."

As I lifted myself to my feet again, all I could think of was Adam. I'd made him think I hated him, and he'd never know how much I cared. *Adam.* I concentrated on his name. If ever there were a time for ESP to work, now was that time.

"Get up, I said."

Adam. Adam. Adam. I pulled myself up with the fridge handle. *Adam. Adam. Adam.*

"No more tricks. Phone on the counter." He waved me to the side with the gun. Gone was the face of sorrow. A mask of hatred replaced it.

I put my phone on the granite.

I love you Adam. I love you. I love you so much.

CHAPTER 44

Adam

The old guy had to be a flower-delivery service.

I waited for the door to open again, and the guy to walk back to his truck, wherever it was.

My blood began to boil as the seconds ticked by and the door didn't open.

Flower delivery guy didn't compute anymore.

No fucking way is some douchebag like him taking my woman away from me. She deserves better.

I threw open the car door and stormed to Kelly's house. I'd pound on the damned door until she opened it—until she talked to me. I didn't care if she called the cops. Getting Kelly away from this loser was the priority.

If Baldy wasn't flower delivery, who the hell was he? I approached, ready to pound on the door until she talked to me. My fist hovered, nervous that I still didn't have a speech prepared.

Kelly screamed from inside.

I dug the house key out of my pocket, but before I could insert it in the lock, the words froze me.

"Scream again, and I'll shoot," the man yelled.

Barging into a situation I couldn't see against an armed suspect was not the way to go. Against a guy with a hostage, it was stupid, and with Kelly as the hostage, it was absolutely insane.

I ducked down and scurried around the side of the house. Through a window, I caught a glimpse of Baldy waving a Beretta, urging Kelly to the front of the house.

He'd made the choice for me.

I had to hope the key Kelly had given me also worked on the back kitchen door. I'd sneak in through there and come up behind Baldy.

I pulled out my phone to dial 9-1-1, but decided against it.

MPD only arrived on scene one way: with sirens blaring, and that could turn this situation ugly in a hurry.

Instead I dialed the person I trusted most right now—Rylie.

"I'm busy talking to—"

I cut her off. "Shut up and listen. Hostage situation. Armed suspect in Kelly's house. I'm going to try entry through the back. Make it a silent approach. No MPD." I hung up and flicked the phone to silent. The last thing I needed was Dempsey calling me back to tell me to hold off.

As soon as I returned the phone to my pocket, it vibrated with Dempsey's name on the screen. The phone was off by the time I made my way to the back porch steps.

The yelling had started again inside. Baldy was a maniac, claiming something was all Kelly's fault, and she should have left well enough alone.

I concentrated on making it up the stairs silently. Outside the back door, luck was still on my side: the key slipped in and gentle pressure turned the lock. As I cracked open the door, it was clear they wouldn't be able to see me if I opened it enough to enter.

I drew my weapon.

I could only hope the door didn't squeak.

Kelly

Heiden slid around to the other side of the room, keeping his distance, apparently worried I might pounce and disarm him somehow.

"Why are you doing this?" I asked when I got my breath back.

"Shut up. All you had to do was follow instructions."

He made no sense at all. He hadn't asked me to do anything.

He waved the gun toward the door leading to the front this time. "Move."

I slid sideways slowly on shaky legs. "What did I not do?"

"She's dead because of you." When he reached my phone, he smashed it twice with the butt of the ugly gun.

I left the kitchen and started toward the front. "Who?" I asked as softly as I could.

"Mom," he yelled. "You killed my mom." He'd slipped into serious delusions.

I'd never even met his mother.

He followed me. "Evelyn did what she was told. She grabbed the rocks and hid them in your purse. All you had to do was carry them out and bring them to the office Monday. Why couldn't you get that right?"

I didn't attempt an answer.

His eyes bulged. He waved the gun wildly.

I never got to tell Adam how much I loved him—or why I'd broken both our hearts. I closed my eyes and recalled the night we shared dessert at the restaurant. If I was going to die, it would be while thinking about Adam.

Adam

I slowly opened the door, far enough to scoot through it. It hadn't squeaked. Gently, I closed it.

After I got it shut, a leaf blower started in the neighbor's yard. If that had started up a few seconds earlier, it could have been bad.

Sliding to the left, I stopped by the fridge.

"Stop right there," Baldy said loudly from the other room.

I ducked lower.

"If you'd just done what you were supposed to, I'd have had the money for the new treatments, and she'd still be with us."

None of it made any sense, but a man waving a gun often didn't.

I moved to the door and peeked around. The man had his back mostly to me, but Kelly was behind him.

I pulled back and moved my finger from the ready position alongside the trigger guard to the trigger itself. Whatever I did, this was going to go down quickly. If he kept talking and I moved quietly, I could get closer. From here, it was too dangerous with Kelly right behind him.

I wiped the sweat off my brow.

"Why Evelyn?" Kelly asked.

"Len picked her," Baldy responded.

Len?

My breath caught. He meant Len Sanderson. This guy was in league with SMK.

When I peeked again, Kelly was fully behind him. I cleared the corner and stepped into the hallway to get closer.

The damned floor squeaked.

I yelled the standard call out. "FBI, drop the weapon." My heart raced.

He grabbed Kelly and turned to face me with his arm around her neck. "Back off."

His gun was at her temple. He had the advantage here.

I sighted at his head, but he wasn't tall, and he was mostly blocked by Kelly.

"FBI," I said again. "Drop the weapon, and we can all walk out of here."

"Adam," Kelly cried.

I took a step closer.

Baldy's gun hand shook, and his voice cracked. "Get back or she dies."

I stopped moving forward. "Kelly, it's going to be okay." My heart raced into overdrive. I'd practiced hostage situations, but nothing had prepared me for this, with Kelly in the line of fire.

She nodded as much as his grasp would allow.

Baldy was melting down. His gun waved between pointing at me and pointing at Kelly. "You drop it. Or else."

I pointed my weapon off to the side. "Okay. Take it easy."

"Drop it," he yelled.

"Kelly, it'll be okay. Just remember what I'd never ask you to do."

I could only hope she remembered.

Recognition flashed in her eyes as she nodded again, and her heel came down hard on Baldy's foot.

He yowled, "Fuck!"

Kelly slipped down a few inches as his grasp loosened.

I raised my gun.

One shot.

One scream.

CHAPTER 45

Kelly

I SCREAMED AND FELL TO THE FLOOR, SHAKING.

Adam rushed to me. He knelt and took me in his arms. "I've got you."

I held on for dear life. "He…"

"Shhh. I know. I've got you."

I shook so hard I could barely force out the words. "He…he was working with Len."

He pulled me tighter and rocked me in his arms. "I know. You'll be okay."

I buried my head in his chest. "I called, and you came."

"Sugarbear, I've got you."

With all I put him through, I'm still his Sugarbear? "I was afraid."

"That's okay. It's over now."

"No." I sobbed and pulled back to look into his eyes. "I was afraid I'd never get to tell you how much I love you."

"Metropolitan Police. Open up." The yell came from outside the door.

"FBI," Adam yelled. "Suspect down. Use the back door."

With a crash, my front door splintered and flew open.

"Hands up," the cop yelled.

"No," Adam said. "FBI. ID back right pocket. I'm not letting go of her."

The cop kicked Adam's gun away. "I said, hands up."

"Stand down. He's one of us." Rylie's voice came from outside. She rushed in and got the cop to back down.

Adam held me tight. "I've got you, Sugarbear, and I love you too."

It took Rylie several minutes to get the DC cops out of my house. "FBI jurisdiction," she kept telling them.

I rocked in Adam's arms the whole time, finally safe in my man's embrace. The man I loved. The man I now realized loved me. The blood on the floor, the smell of the gunpowder in the room, the arguing of the cops in the background—none of it mattered while he held me. My shivers slowly subsided.

Rylie came back in. "Cartwright, you have got to stop shooting everybody."

"He's the second SMK. The accomplice," Adam told her.

"Accomplice?"

"You heard me," Adam said. "He admitted he was working with Sanderson."

She knelt down next to us. "Adam, you have to let go of her. I have to take her statement. You know how this works."

He continued to rock me. "Not yet. Give us a little time."

"I need to—" she began.

"I said not yet," he growled.

She stood and backed off.

"I love you," I repeated several times.

"I love you too, Sugarbear. It'll be okay," he said each time.

Rylie returned. "Adam."

"I'll be okay," I assured him, and he finally released me.

In the next hour, they took Heiden's body away, and Rylie and another agent asked me over and over what happened.

They'd taken Adam into another room.

I recounted how Mr. Heiden had only just gotten back to town, and how he'd been strange at the office and then brought flowers to my door before turning a gun on me. I explained as best I could how the loss of his mother had driven him to blame me, and what he'd said about the theft, and Evelyn and Len. Then, I detailed how he'd threatened to kill me and how Adam had saved me by clueing me to step on Heiden's foot.

When the agents were finally done with me, the others were still questioning Adam.

All I could think of were Rylie's words after the first shooting. Adam would need me, and his father could shove it. There was no way I wouldn't be there for my man now.

~

ADAM

NEIL AND DOUG TOOK ME INTO A DIFFERENT ROOM FOR THE DEBRIEF.

"Who the hell called MPD?" I asked. "If they'd gotten here two minutes earlier, this would have gone sideways."

Neil shrugged. "Dempsey made the call."

"It was a bad one," I shot back.

For over an hour, they kept after me about the timeline and the details of my arrival at the house, breaking into the back, and shooting the suspect. And I confirmed that I'd never met Paul Heiden before today.

When they finally released me, it was another half hour before the EMTs and forensics guys finished checking out me and Kelly.

"You have a broken door again, so you're coming with me," I told her as she changed into fresh clothes to replace the ones now in the evidence bags.

A half hour after that, we'd driven to my place, and I turned on the shower.

I ushered her in and joined her. "Here we are again." I pulled the strawberry shampoo she'd left here from the ledge. "Turn around. I need to wash your hair."

She ran her hair under the water and faced away without asking why, which was good. She might not have reacted well if I'd told her she had blood spatter in her hair from the bullet that took down Heiden.

"Why'd he do it?"

"It's too soon to know."

"But why me?"

I didn't have any witty response to lighten the mood. "The man clearly wasn't rational."

She went quiet for a while. "Please keep that up," she murmured as I massaged her scalp.

I kept at it.

"Adam, I was so scared."

I pulled her back into me. "I know."

"It was like a miracle. I said your name over and over in my head, willing you to hear me. And you came."

"I said I'd never let anything happen to you." I moved back and pulled her into the water to rinse her hair.

She sobbed. "What's going to happen when your father finds out?"

I moved around to face her.

She wouldn't look at me.

We were naked, and yet she'd put up a wall.

I pulled her chin up. "He doesn't matter."

"But he said—"

My anger boiled up. "Did he call you?"

She looked away.

"Did he?"

She looked down. "No."

"What are you not telling me?"

She moved and pushed me toward the water. "You're getting cold."

"No, I'm frustrated that you still refuse to be honest with me."

She sighed and hugged me. "I heard him threaten to kill your career if you kept seeing me." She sobbed. "That's why I ended things."

I rubbed her back and rotated us to put her under the hot water. "You're nuts, you know that? And even if he'd tried, I'd happily give it up to keep you."

"You're just saying that. I know how much the Bureau means to you."

Her recalcitrance was becoming annoying.

I pushed her back enough to fix her eyes with mine. "Listen to me, Sugarbear. I love you. Nothing else matters. Nothing."

At first, I couldn't tell if the words registered with her.

She plastered herself against me and cried. "I love you too. But what if he follows through? I don't want you to resent me."

"That was an empty threat."

~

Kelly

I couldn't get his father's words out of my mind. "Are you sure your father can't hurt your career?"

He slapped my ass. "Stop that. Negative thinking is bad for you. I was thinking about moving to ATF anyway."

I couldn't help but worry that his father would find a way to smear Adam's reputation at the Bureau. "But what if—"

He put his finger to my lips. "Stop right there, and don't move."

I watched him leave the shower and pull something from the pocket of his pants before rejoining me.

"Do you want to know why I was at your house today?"

"ESP?"

"Close your eyes, Sugarbear."

I did as he asked. It still got to me every time he uttered that ridiculously sweet nickname.

"I brought you this, because I had an important question for you."

I opened my eyes. My heart stopped. The water streamed over a small, turquoise leather box—a Tiffany blue box—a fucking jewelry box. "My God."

He pressed the tiny silver button on the front, and the lid popped open. A gorgeous diamond ring sat in the black velvet—wet black velvet now.

"Kelly, will you do me the honor of taking my name? And, no I'm not going to kneel in here."

I couldn't believe it. The ring every little girl dreamed of stared up at me. All I had to do was say yes. I schooled my face into as impassive a look as I could manage. "What if I want to keep my name?"

He shook his head. "Non-negotiable. And we're not doing hyphenated either."

I couldn't contain my smile any longer. "Okay, okay, okay. Yes." I jumped up into his arms to kiss him.

Bad idea.

The box fell from his hand and ended up on the floor of the shower.

Adam slipped as he caught me, and we almost ended up in a heap on the tile, before he steadied himself and held me up by the ass. "Careful there.

Telling your family about this is going to be hard enough without having to explain you getting injured hopping onto my dick."

I laughed so hard I almost couldn't hold on. "I may have to leave some parts out when the kids ask how you proposed." My insides heated at the thought we'd be making babies together.

"Good idea."

The water on my back was running colder now. "You need a bigger water heater."

"Yeah, it's only going to get worse." He put me down.

I leaned down to retrieve the little leather box. It was empty. "The ring. It's gone."

"Do you see it?"

"Don't move." I knelt and scanned the floor. A chill ran through me when I saw it.

The gold band had slipped into the slotted drain, and caught on the stone. A smaller diamond would have been a goner now. With my fingernails, I grabbed the stone setting and gently lifted.

It came up through the slot in one piece, and I could finally breathe again. "I got it."

He laughed. "That would have complicated the story."

I palmed the ring and stood.

Adam took the ring and slid it on my finger. "It's official now. You're mine."

"You mean, you're mine."

He turned off the water. "That too."

As we dried off, I couldn't help but look over at my man and wonder how I'd gotten so lucky.

Two months ago, I'd been stuck in a rut of my own making. Every day the same as the last, and every man I met as boring as the last. A future of endless gray.

Today, he'd said he loved me and wanted me forever—the words every little girl wanted to hear from the man of her dreams. My special agent had saved me in more ways than one.

I'd just have to learn to live with the last name.

CHAPTER 46

Adam

The next morning, I took Kelly back to her house and met the guy I'd called to fix her door.

It was after lunch and the contractor was still hard at work when the call from Rylie came. "Adam, how are you doing?"

"Okay, considering."

"Yeah, I know it's rough."

"What's up?" I asked.

"I wanted to let you know that Heiden's house turned out to have all the answers."

"Like what?"

"The tech guys located the laptop he used to communicate with your girl, as well as the other victims. We even got a banking transaction for the sale of a stolen moon rock from the Smithsonian last year."

"Anything else?"

"Found his communications with Sanderson. Looks like they bonded through a cancer support group. Anyway, the bigger news is that we have four more bodies in his backyard from before he recruited Sanderson."

"Four?"

"Yeah, Heiden was SMK, and Sanderson was the helper—not the other way around. We're IDing the victims now, and HQ is going nuts over this. I wanted to let you know before it hit the news tonight."

"Thanks for the heads up."

We finished up the call, and Kelly looked over. "Work?" she asked.

"Yeah. Nothing important." The details could wait. She didn't need any more trauma today.

Kelly wanted to order pizza and watch *Bonanza* all day, so that was the plan.

We were interrupted in the late afternoon by another call, this time from Dempsey.

Kelly paused the TV.

"Cartwright," I answered.

"We have an appointment at HQ at five."

"I'm off today. You suspended me, remember?"

"Not when HQ calls, you're not."

"Send Rylie to relieve me, or I'm not budging."

Dempsey fumed, but then agreed.

"What is that about?" Kelly asked.

"I have to go in for a meeting at HQ."

"The shooting?"

"Probably. Two shootings in a career is bad. Two in a year is worse, and two in a month has to be about the worst there is." I squeezed her tight as I restarted the show. I had Kelly back, and nothing else mattered.

A LITTLE WHILE LATER, RYLIE SHOWED UP TO KEEP KELLY COMPANY, AND I LEFT to be at the entrance to the J. Edgar Hoover Building at five as ordered.

I was in time to cool my heels for a few minutes before anyone else arrived.

"What's this about?" I asked Dempsey when he walked up.

"Yesterday's shooting is all I know. Your ass is grass this time, Cartwright. The AD wants to talk to us."

I blew out a breath and followed him in. So long and goodbye, career.

Upstairs we were escorted directly to AD Donnelly's office.

He met us at the door.

Dempsey offered his hand.

The AD ignored him. Instead, Donnelly offered to shake my hand. "Cartwright, welcome. Gentlemen, have a seat."

"If this is about yesterday—" Dempsey started.

Donnelly waved him off. "Just hold it, Jarvis." He got situated behind his desk. "I'm recommending Cartwright for the Medal of Valor."

Dempsey's face fell.

Words failed me. This was the same guy who'd reamed me a month ago for asking about Uncle Jack.

Dempsey held up a hand. "But the shooting investigation is still open."

Donnelly ignored him and turned to me. "I hear you want to be posted to the New York Organized Crime Task Force. Is that right?"

"No, sir." I shook my head. "Not any longer."

Donnelly's brows raised. "No?"

"I don't want to leave DC." No way was I leaving my Kelly. "I still have a lot to learn from the ASAC," I added.

Dempsey straightened in his chair with a smile.

"DC it is, then," Donnelly said. "I wanted to personally thank you for taking down the SMK killers." He paused and the hint of a tear came to his eye. "She's been missing four years now, but I just learned my daughter was one of the bodies found in that backyard." He took a long breath. "I always thought it was those damned traffickers." He wiped his eye. "At least now we know she didn't suffer for a long time. I appreciate you bringing us closure."

"Yes, sir," was all I could think to say. Words couldn't help the AD's pain. The focus he had us placing on human trafficking cases now made sense.

He sniffed, blinked back the tear, and straightened up. "That'll be all."

I got another handshake on the way out, as did the ASAC.

Dempsey turned to me as soon as the elevator closed. "Just because you're today's golden boy, don't think I'm going to go easy on you, Cartwright."

I nodded. "Yes, boss." And I didn't smile until he looked away.

~

Kelly

. . .

ADAM HAD BEEN GONE ABOUT AN HOUR, AND RYLIE AND I WERE CHATTING IN the kitchen when a loud series of knocks sounded on the front door.

"Stay here," she said as she got up.

The knocks stopped, and I heard the door open.

"Can I help you?" Rylie said.

"Is Kelly here?" It was Daddy's voice.

I jumped up, but stopped short of the hallway. I tugged at the diamond ring on my finger.

"Who's asking?" Rylie asked in a less-than-civil tone.

I pocketed the ring before rounding the corner to the hallway. "Daddy." I started to run.

Rylie lifted the hand she'd rested on her gun and stepped aside.

Daddy came in, and we collided.

I hugged him with all my might. "What are you doing here?"

"I called and called, but you didn't answer."

"My phone died."

He let me go after another squeeze. "You think I wouldn't find out my baby girl got attacked?"

I straightened up. "I'm fine."

Daddy turned to Rylie and offered his hand. "Lloyd Benson."

Rylie shook with him. "Special Agent Rylie Brolin, FBI."

Daddy added a second hand to his vigorous shake. "I can't thank you enough for saving my baby girl."

Rylie retrieved her hand. "That would be Adam you should thank."

Daddy's brows raised as he turned to me. "The same Adam?"

I nodded. "Yeah."

"I definitely need to meet this Adam now." He extended his hand toward the kitchen. "It was a long flight. Could I trouble you for a cup of Earl Grey?"

I led the way, and Rylie followed.

I wasn't prepared for this meeting now. *We* weren't prepared. Adam and I had planned to work out a script, but we hadn't yet.

"He can join us for dinner tomorrow," I offered, "if you're still in town."

"Nonsense. We can have dinner tonight." Daddy wasn't going for it. "I'll visit with you until he gets back from work or whatever."

There was no avoiding the meeting now. "Daddy, I have coffee, if you'd prefer."

"What does Adam drink?" The question wasn't really about coffee, but confirming that Adam and I were shacking up.

"No idea. Some fancy coffee."

"Sure. I'll have some."

"Rylie?" I asked.

"Nothing for me, thanks."

I started tea for myself and coffee for Daddy.

"Rylie, you work with Adam?"

She glanced toward me.

I nodded. There was no sense trying to hide the obvious.

"Yes. We're both in the local field office," she said.

"Quite an exciting job being an FBI agent, I suppose."

"It has its days," she answered shyly.

Daddy had shifted into interrogator mode. "And are you here because my daughter is still in danger?"

"No, sir. I'm here because Adam wanted me here."

"Is he your boss?"

"Daddy, stop it," I complained.

She snorted. "It's okay. No, he's not my boss; he's my partner."

I handed Daddy his coffee. "You can stop with the questions now."

"I'm just trying to learn why you've been hiding him from me."

Rylie came to my rescue. "Adam is a man I respect, and one you should be proud your daughter has found."

Daddy nodded and smiled at me. "Can't wait to meet him." He sipped his coffee. "This is quite good. You really should try it." He lifted his cup to me.

"You know better than that," I responded.

The sound of the front door deadbolt being opened said Daddy wasn't going to have to wait any longer.

"Sugarbear?" Adam called.

"In the kitchen," I said. "We have company."

"Really?" Adam appeared at the entrance to the kitchen.

Daddy approached and extended his hand. "Lloyd Benson."

I was right in assuming Daddy wouldn't recognize Adam as his arch-enemy's son.

Adam shook with him and managed a nervous smile. "Mr. Benson, you surprised us."

"I couldn't stay away when I heard what had happened." Daddy continued shaking Adam's hand. "I want to thank you for keeping my baby girl safe. Anything I can ever do for you, all you have to do is ask. Anything at all."

They broke the handshake.

"All in the line of duty," Adam responded.

Rylie snorted. "Bullshit," she mumbled.

"Impressive," Daddy answered.

I pointed at Adam. "He stopped a pair of men that killed eight women in this town, including women I worked with."

Daddy cocked his head. "I get it already." His gaze settled on me. "And why are you putting on the hard sell, young lady?"

I glanced at Adam.

He fingered his left hand. "Aren't you underdressed, Sugarbear?"

"Now?" I asked.

Adam nodded, and Daddy looked perplexed by our exchange.

I pulled the ring from my pocket.

"Because," Adam started. "I asked her to become Kelly Cartwright."

"Adam..." Daddy's jaw dropped halfway to the floor. "You're Carson's son?"

Adam nodded. "Not that it should matter, but yes."

I slipped the ring on my finger and held it out. "And I said yes."

Daddy regained his composure as he turned back to Adam. "I take it you're not asking my permission?"

Adam slid sideways to put his arm around me. "No, sir. But your blessing would be appreciated."

"Daddy you said anything he asked," I reminded him.

Daddy looked between the two of us for a moment. "For twenty years, I've blamed your uncle for what happened to my young niece." Daddy rubbed his goatee. "But it wouldn't be right for me to hold that against you." A smile grew slowly on Daddy's face, and he nodded. "Kelly, I like this one. He has backbone."

I waited for his answer.

"Of course you have my blessing." He held up a warning finger. "But if you hurt her..." He didn't finish the threat.

"You don't need to worry about that," Adam answered.

I giggled. A bruise from doing it up against the wall tonight wouldn't count.

Daddy sipped more of his brown sludge. "Who's up for dinner, then?"

"I have to get home," Rylie said as she backed toward the door. "See you next week?" she asked Adam.

"First thing tomorrow," he responded.

As we headed for the door, Daddy put his hand on Adam's shoulder. "What kind of coffee is this? I like it quite a lot."

"St. Helena beans."

THAT NIGHT, AFTER DADDY HAD GONE BACK TO HIS HOTEL, WE RETURNED TO THE house—our house.

Dead tired after the last two days, I climbed under the covers and snuggled up to my man, my fiancé, my everything. "I thought tonight went well."

"A lot easier than I expected. Your old man is not half bad."

I jabbed him. "Not half bad?"

"Okay," he chuckled. "I admit it. I like him. He's a nice guy."

I pulled his chin my direction. "You didn't tell me why you got called into work."

"Just a meeting about the case."

"Are you in trouble?"

His chest expanded with a deep breath. "I don't think so. They're talking about giving me a stupid medal or something. I think it's a joke."

"I'm sure it's well deserved." Relieved that his career didn't seem to be in jeopardy, I kissed his ear. "Do you notice anything?"

He looked left and right in the dim light provided by the star stickers on my ceiling. "No." He turned toward me and kissed my nose. "But then all I ever notice when I'm with you is how beautiful you are."

"Listen."

"You changed the sound machine to ocean waves," he said after a moment. "See? I told you it wouldn't hurt you to experiment a little."

He was right about that. And in the morning I intended to add breakfast table sex to my experimenting.

EPILOGUE

IF I HAD A FLOWER FOR EVERY TIME I THOUGHT OF YOU... I COULD WALK THROUGH MY GARDEN FOREVER. - ALFRED TENNYSON

Kelly

The tingle between my legs from this morning's love-making distracted me. My throw missed the paper Adam had placed on the dartboard in the kitchen. It was a picture of Mr. Heiden.

He handed me another dart. "Try again."

"You know, there are easier ways to pick a meal."

He shook his head. "Have a little fun." This was his way of getting me to experiment and deal with my anger at what had happened to my friends at the same time. It wouldn't bring Melinda or Evelyn back, but it did let me take my feelings out on their killers, one dart at a time.

I threw again. This time the dart found its mark and hit Mr. Heiden in the eye.

"Good one." Adam pulled the paper down and turned it over to show me the recipes he'd written on the back.

I whooped. Yesterday's dart had selected pineapple pancakes, but today I'd finally hit egg and soldiers. I'd insisted he include it in the possibilities. Even though I'd learned to appreciate the variety he enforced, I still wanted one of my old favorites every now and again.

He opened the fridge to start cooking while I went back upstairs to finish my makeup.

This morning's breakfast ended up being just as delicious as that very first meal he'd fixed me. I'd lucked into a man who cooked me breakfast on a regular basis. How many women could say that?

"Did anybody chicken out?" he asked after a sip of orange juice.

I finished chewing before answering. "Not that I know of. They should land around three. What about your mom and dad?"

"No idea. Radio silence."

Daddy was flying the family out for our engagement party, and Adam's parents had been invited as well. We hoped that doing it in the neutral territory of DC instead of California would lessen the conflict between the families.

After eating, I helped Adam clean up.

On the way toward the door, I patted the top of the dining room table. "Tonight?"

"Or tomorrow at sunrise," Adam replied with a devilish grin.

"No way. Let's try nighttime first." Sex on the table with a window facing the street and the sun up was a little further than I wanted to venture just yet.

"Your call."

Today we were out of the house earlier than I used to leave, and some days we were a little later. Today Mr. Dark Suit was nowhere to be seen. It didn't matter. I had my fiancé next to me. That was all the reassurance I needed that all was right with the world.

Of course, being named acting department manager while a replacement for Mr. Heiden was recruited allowed me to have a more flexible schedule—except for Mondays. As a department head, Krause now expected me to sit up front for his boring meetings.

Back at the house that afternoon, my leg was jittery. My nerves had been fried running up to today.

"Don't worry, it's probably traffic," my brother Vincent said as he came up behind me.

I'd been pacing in front of the window, watching the street.

"Yeah," his wife, Ashley, added. "Because he flew the corporate jet, they have to land at Dulles."

I hadn't considered that.

Moments later, a black town car pulled up and deposited my parents.

I checked the street again. "Where's everybody else?" I asked Daddy after he and Momma came in.

"We took separate cars from the airport. I guess our driver knew a better shortcut."

Adam appeared from the kitchen, and I introduced him to Momma. Daddy gave him a quick handshake.

Momma, however, engulfed him in a hug. "It's so nice to meet you, Adam. Kelly's told us such wonderful things about you."

"Hopefully only half of them are lies," Adam said.

After a few more pleasantries, he escorted them back to the kitchen for drinks.

I didn't have to wait long for Josh to arrive.

This time his plus one was a pretty girl named Nicole.

Serena arrived shortly after.

Her boyfriend, Duke, had even more ink than I remembered from when I'd last been out to California.

Another half hour had passed when Adam came out and found me still at the window.

"This isn't where the guest of honor should be hanging out," he said.

"A polite hostess greets her guests at the door."

He pulled me toward the kitchen. "It's your family. You should mingle."

From the sound of it, the group was having a jolly time without me. Dennis still hadn't arrived, and I was worried now that he wouldn't show.

I'd relied on Serena's assurance that Dennis would be okay here with Adam after what had happened between them. For my part, I thought it would be a tough meeting, but I expected Adam to be classy about it. That's what he'd promised me.

With Adam constantly refilling the champagne glasses, my family was getting rowdy. I'd worried that Daddy's years of ranting about the Cartwrights would lead to a chilly reception, but Adam moved seamlessly from one group to another around the room without a hint of animosity from my family.

The women all took turns admiring my ring, which was flattering.

At one point Duke lifted his shirt to show off and explain his latest tats. Serena, Nicole, and Momma listened intently. In Momma's case it was probably the champagne, because she had never liked tattoos. She'd even objected to me getting my cousin's initials on my ankle.

I overheard Daddy off to the side, once more trying to convince Vincent to come back to California.

My brother was being polite about it, but between the lines, the message was *no way in hell* was he leaving Boston.

Ashley and Adam were talking shop with FBI acronyms and case names none of the rest of us could relate to when I walked by.

"We just closed out our big trafficking case with thirty-two arrests," Adam told her.

Ashley sighed. "We're still working ours."

I moved on, passing out appetizers. The tiny wieners with barbecue sauce and the Swedish meatballs were the biggest hits. Every time I checked the clock on the oven, another minute had passed without my oldest brother.

When I joined Ashley and Adam, their hushed conversation stopped.

"Did I interrupt something?"

Ashley leaned closer. "You didn't tell me Adam was getting the Medal of Valor."

Adam shook his head. "It's not official yet."

I remembered now that he'd mentioned something about a medal the night after the shooting. "I didn't really know, myself." I raised an eyebrow.

"That's a really big deal," she said. "You should be enormously proud of him."

I wrapped my arm around my fiancé. "I am. But he hasn't told me much about it."

Serena joined us. "What's the big deal?"

"Nothing," Adam said quickly.

Serena gave him a stern look, but Adam didn't relent.

His phone rang, and he answered—"Yeah, Rylie, what's up?"—as he moved to the other room to take it.

Ashley nodded toward Adam. "I mean it. They don't give those out easily."

Slowly, I was getting the drift. Adam had been hiding the importance of this award.

A moment later, Adam was back with a concerned look on his face. "Ashley, you and I need a moment with Lloyd."

I tagged along as Adam pulled Daddy away from Vincent and Duke.

"What is it?" Daddy asked.

Adam didn't open up until we reached the corner. "It's about Debbie."

"What? Have you located her?" Daddy asked.

"Does Josh know?" Adam asked. "We need him for this conversation."

I looked between them. "What conversation?"

"Trust me," Adam replied.

Daddy shook his head and waved Josh over to join us. When he arrived, Daddy put an arm on his shoulder. "I need to tell you something about your cousin Debbie."

Josh nodded. "I already know she was spotted. Dennis told me and Serena."

Daddy shook his head. "Can't any of you keep a secret around here?"

"I just got a call," Adam said. "Debbie called into the tip line. She wants to talk to Josh."

Josh pointed at his chest. "Me?"

Adam nodded. "She's going to call back tomorrow, and all I know is she'll only talk to you."

"And that's it?" Daddy asked.

"That's it until tomorrow."

"Okay," Daddy said. "I guess we'll hear tomorrow. Now, not a word of this to the others."

The group disbanded, and I knew the secret wouldn't last a day with this family.

"Big development?" I asked Adam after we were alone again.

"No telling. She might not even call back."

I freshened my champagne glass.

The doorbell rang.

Serena followed me to the front. "That better be the big lug."

Adam wasn't far behind.

When I opened the door, it was Dennis, finally—with a green-eyed beauty in tow.

"Jennifer, you've met Serena, and this is my youngest sister, Kelly," he said.

Serena and I each hugged Jennifer briefly.

Adam moved forward to offer his hand. "Adam Cartwright."

She took it with a gracious smile.

I felt Adam brace himself as the two adversaries appraised each other.

Dennis made the first move and produced a bottle from behind his back. He offered it to Adam. "A peace offering."

Adam accepted it, and the two shook. "Welcome to our home."

Dennis had visited me before, and he lifted a brow at Adam's calling this *our* house now. "Glad you invited us."

Adam examined the bottle. "Macallan 1926?" A hint of a smile crept across his face. Adam did enjoy his scotch.

"Dennis thought you'd like it," Jennifer interjected.

I urged them to move from the entryway to the living room.

Serena grabbed Jennifer. "Let me introduce you to Vincent and his wife. They're down from Boston." After they left, it was just me and the two silent bulls eyeing one another.

"I have something to say," Dennis started.

Adam crossed his arms over his chest.

"I wanted to…" The words seemed to catch in his throat. "Apologize."

Adam's only reaction was to shift his weight.

"Celeste told me it was you who'd forced yourself on her, and she didn't admit it was actually Alex until after our fight."

Adam scoffed. "You mean ambush, you asshole. You didn't have the guts to take me on man to man."

I reached an arm over to Adam. "He's trying to apologize."

"A lot of good that does me now."

Dennis moved forward. "Look, she told me it was you, and her story didn't change until after we broke up."

Adam's head jerked. "What the fuck did you say?"

Serena wandered back into the room.

Dennis looked down. "I'm sorry you got hurt, but I honestly thought you'd assaulted my girlfriend."

Adam huffed. "You got shit for memory. Celeste was my girl, not yours."

Dennis's brow creased. "Your girl?"

Serena stepped forward. "Did you two idiots really not know that this whole time?"

Dennis looked at her incredulously, followed by Adam.

Serena laughed. "I thought everybody knew. She was two-timing Alex—

make that three-timing him—with both of you to make him jealous. Why do you think she left school right after he did?"

Adam's shoulders slumped. "Seriously?"

Dennis shook his head. "I had no idea."

"She told me it was Alex," Adam said.

Serena laughed. "And she probably told Alex it was Dennis."

Knowing what the episode had cost Adam, I didn't think it was funny.

"So?" Dennis asked, extending his hand.

Adam took a long breath. "She was one crazy bitch." He accepted Dennis's hand and shook. "Apology accepted."

Dennis grimaced.

It took a few seconds to register, but I realized Adam was attempting to crush my brother's hand.

I forced my way between them, breaking up the test of strength. "Let's go into the other room and open that bottle."

They followed, with Dennis shaking out his hand.

Before long, everybody had a glass of expensive scotch in hand, and they were all commenting on it.

I couldn't tell the difference between this and Adam's regular stuff.

"A toast to the couple," Dennis said loudly.

The group quieted.

Dennis held up his glass. "To a long, happy, and fruitful—"

"That means lots of babies," Serena added.

The giggles took a second to subside.

Dennis continued, "Marriage. To the future Mr. Cartwright and Mrs. Benson-Cartwright."

"Mr. and Mrs. Cartwright," I corrected him.

The laughs continued—well-meaning laughs.

Adam disappeared a few minutes later.

I found him in the front, looking out toward the street.

"Do you think they'll come?" I asked.

He shook his head and looked up the street again. "I thought so, but now I don't know."

"Your father is a prideful man," my mother said from behind us. She joined us at the window.

Adam sucked in a breath. "My father? I guess."

Momma nodded and placed a hand on Adam's shoulder. "He took it very hard when I chose to marry Lloyd instead of him."

This was a bombshell I'd never heard before.

Adam's brow creased. "I didn't know that."

"Give him time," Momma said. "We should join the others."

Later, after the bottle of scotch had been drained, I found Adam looking through the pantry. "You're not going to find another bottle like that," I teased.

He smiled. "I'm looking for olive oil."

I pulled it from the lower shelf and handed it to him. "What for?"

He tugged on his finger. "I hope this works." He opened the bottle, took it to the sink and poured a little over his finger—the one with the Dallas Cowboys ring. "Today is about looking forward, not back, right?"

"Do you want some help?" I offered.

"No. This is something I have to do myself."

Warmth filled me as I looked over at Dennis and back to my fiancé. If Adam was removing the reminder of the dream he'd lost, the grudge was finally behind us. I didn't know how I could have gone forward with hatred simmering between the two men.

Serena's boyfriend, Duke, came over, and it took a minute, but Adam eventually let him help.

The ring finally came off.

"I'm proud of you," I whispered into Adam's ear.

He was still rubbing his sore finger when he handed me the ring. "Toss this for me."

"You sure?"

He pulled up my left hand and kissed the ring he'd given me. "I'm sure. This is the only ring that matters to me today. The one that says you're mine."

"And you're mine too," I reminded him.

The ring really did say it all.

THE END

THE FOLLOWING PAGES CONTAIN AN EXCERPT OF **TRAPPED WITH THE BILLIONAIRE** (Josh & Nicole's story)

SNEAK PEEK: TRAPPED WITH THE BILLIONAIRE

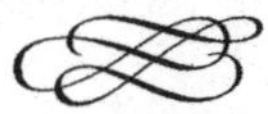

CHAPTER 1

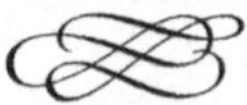

Nicole

Sandi removed her sunglasses and scanned the crowd to the left. "The guy in blue you were checking out earlier is watching you."

"Pass." The man in the blue polo was more than cute, but by the time I looked, Mr. Studious had his head down in his iPad, same as he had for most of this afternoon on the beach. He didn't seem *that* interested in me, or any of the women here, for that matter.

I forked another bite of my apple slaw salad and checked my phone. My text this morning checking on my cousin, Lara, had gone unanswered, as had the two follow-ups this afternoon. Uncle Ernst hadn't answered my question about how his meeting with the bank had gone either. What was with my family?

"Last night here." Sandi sucked on the straw in her mango margarita. "You don't want to let it go to waste."

My best friend's idea of a night in Barbados going to waste was not finding a man's room to spend it in. So far she'd wasted only three nights of our week down here, but she didn't want to make it four.

"I saw you checking him out again this afternoon," she added.

Now that the glow of the sunset was fading, I removed my shades as well and looked for our waiter, Diego. I caught his attention with a wave.

"Don't try to deny it."

Diego hurried over, saving me from having to answer her.

I lifted my glass. "Could I get some more water, please?"

"Certainly," he replied.

"One more thing." Sandi pointed past the family with the rambunctious kids toward Mr. Studious. "Can you tell me what the gentleman in blue over there is drinking?"

Diego peered over. "He's drinking tonight's special, a green monkey. Would you like one?"

I scooped a large bite of pasta into my mouth.

Sandi pointed to me. "No. My friend here would like to order him another."

Diego smiled and backed away before I could complain.

I almost choked getting my food down. "What are you doing?"

The evil Sandi grin appeared. "Just helping. Did you know he's glanced at you seven times now?"

"Bull, and you're paying for the drink." That wouldn't slow her down, Sandi wasn't as tight on money as I was.

I brought my water to my mouth. "I came down here to bake the worries out of my system." Condensation from the icy glass dripped on my shorts.

"You came down here to forget about your dickhead ex."

"Well, that too." Maurice Dickman had seemed okay at first—a lesson about first impressions. In the end, Sandi had been right. *Dickhead, dickless*, or *dickwad* suited him better than Dickman.

While I savored another mouthful of my penne marinara, I caught Mr. Studious actually looking our direction.

Sandi winked. "That makes eight."

My phone vibrated with a text message.

ERNST: We'll talk when you get back

I laid the phone down. Pursuing it tonight wouldn't get me anywhere.

Diego returned to top off my water glass.

I ignored her and scooped up more of my dinner. "What time's our flight?"

"Late enough in the afternoon that you two can sleep in."

Diego delivered the green cocktail to Mr. Studious with a quick point in our direction.

A smile grew on the man's face as he looked over and lifted his glass to me. The smile was a definite improvement.

Sandi kicked me under the table. "Wave back."

I returned his smile and offered a quick wave before returning to my dinner.

"Now that wasn't so hard, was it?"

"No," I admitted. Glancing up again, I couldn't avert my gaze when I caught him looking our way.

Mr. Studious took a sip of his drink and nodded at me with a pucker of his lips. Had he just thrown me a kiss? His lips moved a little more. He seemed to be asking a silent question, but what?

Lip reading was Sandi's thing, but she hadn't been looking over.

What was I supposed to do now? I could tell when some idiot driver honked at me and mouthed *fuck you* through his window, but that was about as far as my talent went. I settled for a pinky wave before averting my gaze and forking the last of my salad.

"That's a good start. Just a little flirty. Keep him on the line."

"I'm not fishing, just being polite."

"It's time to get back in the saddle, girl. The longer you put it off, the more power you're giving Mo."

"It's not the right time yet," I countered.

"Sure it is. One last night here in paradise. Loosen up. Allow yourself to have a little fun. Get crazy, for God's sake. You'll never see the guy again. What could be simpler?"

I moved the last of my pasta around on my plate. "It's a little soon."

"Six days is soon. It's been six months since you caught him."

My fork dropped, and my hand went to my mouth, holding back the urge to upchuck.

Sandi grimaced. "Sorry. I shouldn't have said that."

As the spasms in my gut lessened, I took another sip of water. The image of Mo with his pants around his ankles, balls deep into Jane Evans was one I wished I could forget.

"Will you be okay?" she asked, rubbing my shoulder.

Another sip of water helped. "Sure."

"I still say the best way to forget your bad memories is to create new good ones, starting with tonight."

"If you think he's so hot, why don't you walk over and pick him up or whatever?"

"I would, but you saw him first, and I'm a better friend than that."

She truly was a good friend. And she was right on the other count. I'd made the mistake of pointing him out the first day. It was supposed to be a fun game for us, rating the guys hot or not.

That first day, he'd risen out of the ocean and walked up the sand to his lounge chair, looking like Daniel Craig in that Bond film, only taller and more muscular. Dripping with saltwater, the man had pegged the hotness meter. He'd even made toweling off look sexy. I'd averted my eyes when he laid back down and picked up his iPad, but only for a few seconds. Watching him made me forget what I'd just read in my book, and I'd had to back up a few pages.

After that afternoon, I'd made sure we waited until he'd already gone to the beach. We could then pick a chair under one of the green umbrellas nearby, just one row back. Like they said in real estate: location was everything.

Sandi pulled me back to the present. "You better now?"

I took another sip of my water and pushed my plate away. "Yeah."

Diego arrived with that same green drink on his tray. "From the gentleman in blue." He placed it in front of me.

I avoided looking over and turned the straw toward me. "What's in it?"

"Rum, passion fruit juice, sweet and sour, and blue curacao." The curacao clinched it for me: the secret ingredient of my favorite blue Hawaii drink. The waiter lingered, watching me. "He wants to know if you like it."

I took a sip. "Tell him yes." Looking past the family between us, I gave Mr. Studious a thumbs up.

He lifted his glass and nodded.

I'd spent the afternoons wondering what he did for a living. He was here alone, and constantly reading, but not likely a student, given his age and what they charged for rooms at this place. Not a lawyer either, with the plastic watch he wore. I'd given up and decided on man of mystery. I'd never know.

"Now you're making progress," Sandi said.

After another dainty sip, I offered it to Sandi. "Try it."

She did. "Not bad, but I think I'll stick to tequila tonight."

Diego came back after a bit to clear our plates.

Settling in my chair, I sipped on my drink and took in the relaxing vibe of this place. Warm weather, a light breeze, waves lapping at the beach in the post-sunset dimness, and soft music in the background: our last dinner in paradise before returning to the work-a-day world.

"I needed this," I told Sandi. "Thanks for insisting I come along."

"What else is a friend for?"

Diego returned with dessert menus. His smile grew as he handed me mine.

Sandi looked down at the selections, taking her time, even though they'd been the same all week. "I'm going to change it up and try the cheesecake tonight."

He took down her order.

I set the menu aside without opening it. "I'm good."

Diego cocked an eyebrow. "I really think you should check tonight's special."

Relenting, I opened the menu. A note slipped out.

Care to join me for dessert?

It wasn't signed.

Diego nodded his head toward Mr. Studious.

Looking over, I found him watching me.

"Your answer?" Diego asked.

Sandi grabbed the note and read it. "Tell him yes," she instructed Diego.

I waited until Diego had left to argue. "Don't I get a vote?"

"It's just dessert. I'll drag you over there if I have to." And she meant it too. "I'll watch from here."

I sipped down the last of my green liquid courage before hefting my purse and grabbing my phone off the table. "Here goes nothing." *It's only dessert.*

His smile mesmerized me even from this distance.

I decided on the poolside long way around the family with loud kids—more time to chicken out.

My phone rang with a number I knew too well: the county jail.

I slowed my walk and answered the call. "Hello?"

My cousin Lara's slurred voice came over the line. "I need you to bail me out."

Not again…

The big kid shoved his smaller sibling right at me.

I dodged left. "I'm still in—"

Bad idea. I moved too far and tumbled into the water. I never got to tell Lara I was in Barbados.

I came up sputtering. "Hey," was the only thing I thought to yell.

The little kid had also landed in the pool, but at least not *on* me. His big brother laughed his head off.

I set my drowned phone up on the cement.

"Jimmy, what the hell did you do?" yelled the dad of the out-of-control family. He started toward us.

Looking behind me, I located my purse on the bottom of the pool. Seeing no other options, I dove down to retrieve it.

Moving toward the edge of the pool, I heard a crunch as Bad Dad stepped on my phone when he extended his hand to me. "Sorry about Jimmy," he said.

I grasped the side of the pool. "You should control your kids." I picked up the poor carcass of my phone—cracked all right.

"You should be careful where you walk," he shot back.

Mr. Studious appeared next to him. "Back off." He pushed Bad Dad to the side, leaned over, and offered me his hand.

I took it.

"Both hands," Studious said.

I put the phone down and added my other hand, only to be yanked up out of the water by Hercules.

Sandi arrived and took my soaked purse from me. "It was your damned fault," she yelled at Bad Dad.

I leaned over to get the carcass of my ruined phone.

"You owe the lady a phone," Studious told Bad Dad in a commanding tone.

"Says who?" the dad asked.

Mr. Studious was in his face. "Says me." With more than six inches on Bad Dad and a scowl that wasn't to be messed with, he grabbed the other man by the collar and backed him to the edge of the pool.

It took the smaller man all of three seconds to whip out his wallet and offer a stack of bills.

Mr. Studious sneered. "Another hundred should do it."

Bad Dad mumbled and came up with more before my benefactor let him go.

Still dripping wet, I accepted the money from Mr. Studious. "Thank you."

"Perhaps dessert another time, Nicole," he offered.

I nodded. "Another time."

He was gone before it registered that he knew my name.

Sandi helped me back toward the room. "Well, that didn't go the way I expected."

~

Josh

The kids had been loud and roughhousing all evening. The parents made no effort to control them.

Making the asshole who'd allowed his family to ruin everyone else's quiet evening pay for her phone had been the right thing to do.

I should have also pushed him in for a swim.

When I lifted her out of the pool, the white fabric of her shirt and shorts turned translucent. The red of her bra and thong showed through enticingly, and it had taken all the will power I had to let her escape to her room to change.

"Another time," she'd said without a hint of surprise that I'd extracted her name from our waiter.

Back at my room, I plugged my tablet in to recharge. Going over the financials of another potential target all day had drained it into the red. Settling back onto the bed, I stared up at the ceiling. I had to get this one right.

Dad's words were etched into my memory: *"A business is like a machine. It works best when all the parts operate in well-oiled unison, pulling together in the same direction."* Obvious, but profound at the same time.

On this break, I'd consumed four different management books, looking for the concept those words came from. Success had eluded me so far.

Clearly I'd have to expand my search. Once I found the teacher Dad had learned from, I'd be able to incorporate the concept well enough to impress even the great Lloyd Benson.

I got up, moved the chair closer to the charger tethering my tablet, and started the next book. Four more days in the sun and still five books to go through. If I got ahead, I'd have some time to spare for actual relaxation, and I now knew just who to relax with.

I closed my eyes, and her words came back to me: "*another time.*" Dessert with her tomorrow was now on the calendar, and I had a few more days to get to know her.

CHAPTER 2

Nicole

The next morning, Sandi slept in while I lay awake in bed wondering what kind of trouble Lara had gotten into. There wasn't anything I could do about it until I got back. The jail didn't take messages. But that knowledge didn't keep me from worrying just the same.

I'd taken in my only cousin, Lara Martini, and given her refuge after she'd had a big fight with her stepdad, Uncle Ernst. She was Aunt Rossella's only child from her first marriage and had always been a wild one.

I'd never had any particular problem with Uncle Ernst, but Lara called him *creepy*, without getting any more specific than that.

The bad blood ran so deep that the second time Lara had gotten into trouble, my aunt and uncle had refused to help, and it had fallen to me to bail her out.

Since then, Lara hadn't even bothered to call them.

When Sandi finally got up, she and I spent our last morning down by the beach.

"Maybe he'll show up for lunch by the pool," Sandi said after my umpteenth scan of the beach.

"Who?"

"Don't give me that."

I rolled my eyes. "Am I that obvious?"

"You're transparent as Saran Wrap. Let's stake out the restaurant so you can at least get his number."

We abandoned the beach chairs to stroll by the restaurant. Last night I'd agreed to dessert another night before remembering I didn't *have* another night. It seemed fitting that after visually stalking him for several days, I'd lose the chance to meet him because I'd hadn't gotten up the courage earlier. Now he'd be relegated to a memory of what might have been, if I'd been bolder.

Eventually the time came, and without a Studious sighting, we headed off to the airport.

"WHAT'D SHE GET ARRESTED FOR THIS TIME?" SANDI ASKED AS WE WAITED OUR turn at the gate to board the plane.

"No idea. We got cut off before I found out."

"I say leave her in jail for a while this time. It'll do her good." Sandi knew better than to suggest getting my aunt and uncle involved.

I understood her perspective, and this *was* getting old. "Well, she's there until I get back, I guess, but I can't abandon her. She's my cousin, and I'm responsible. You want me to let her end up like the Kings' son?"

The Kings from down the street had left their son, Jeremy, in jail a week as punishment for his DUI, and he'd ended up beaten and raped. He'd come home with a broken arm, three missing teeth, and terrible psychological scars. His parents now had to live with the knowledge that they could have prevented it.

The women's jail was certainly safer, but I wasn't willing to take a chance. I'd get her out as soon as I got back.

"I guess not," Sandi admitted. "But she needs to learn a lesson sooner or later. How many times have you bailed her out now? Three?"

I didn't answer. This would be the fifth.

"She needs some tough love."

"That's easy for you to say," I shot back.

What Lara had needed was parental guidance before she'd gotten herself as screwed up as she had.

Our disagreement was cut short when they called our group to board.

Rain had been threatening for the past hour or so, and we got up the stairs and into the plane's cabin just before the drops began to fall. Once settled into my aisle seat, I closed my eyes and blotted out the sounds of the other passengers. Last night's scene played itself back on my eyelids. The falling-in-the-pool part hadn't been great, but what had led up to it had been, and Mr. Studious' lesson to the dad had etched itself into my permanent highlight reel.

"*Says me,*" he'd growled as he'd coerced him into paying for my phone.

It had been abject fear on the dad's face, and the money I'd received was way more than my two-year-old phone was worth. It was enough to get me the latest new one when I got home.

~

Josh

I WAS IN THE SHOWER THE NEXT MORNING WHEN THE ROOM PHONE RANG.

I ignored it.

After having run three fast laps to the end of the boardwalk and back, I relished the shower. It was an indulgence I wasn't willing to cut short.

Whatever the desk clerk wanted could wait.

Between the temperature and the humidity, even a morning run in the tropics produced a gallon of sweat to rinse off.

After toweling dry, the blinking red light on the phone begged for attention, but I pulled on cargo shorts and a shirt before I gave in. After punching in the numbers to retrieve my message, Dad's voice boomed in my ear: "Change of plans, Josh. Need you back here pronto. You're coming home today. Hope you had a relaxing week." *Click.*

Short and to the point, even if not accurate. Leaving today meant I didn't get the whole week I'd planned. And as usual, my dad had *told* me the way things would be instead of asking.

I'd turned off my phone when I arrived last week, as I'd planned this to be unplugged time. The phone took a minute to power up, and when it did, it showed the success of my strategy. Being powered off had prevented my phone from delivering eighty-two voicemail messages to interrupt my down time.

I punched up dad's contact.

"What's the emergency?" I asked when he answered.

"We closed the latest deal early. I need you to go over and get involved right away."

I sighed as quietly as I could manage. "Why not have Tony handle it?"

"This one needs your talents."

Saying I had talents was more of a compliment than I usually got, and it was welcome, but it didn't make up for cutting my vacation short.

Giving in, I took a breath. "When's the plane arrive?"

"Our plane is in the shop, so Libby booked you commercial. See you first thing tomorrow. Gotta go. Now hold on the line and Libby will give you the details." Silence. He was gone

Love you too, Dad.

"Sorry about this, Josh," Libby said after a moment. "But he said to get you back as soon as possible."

"Yeah. Go ahead."

She read the details of my flight, leaving this afternoon with a connection through JFK. I started to gather my things. Three days here was better than nothing, but not the week I'd planned on.

Since I was the only remaining Benson son in the company, I'd expected to catch a break at some point, but I'd been wrong so far. Maybe my oldest brother Dennis's idea of splitting off a piece of the company and leaving everybody else to deal with Dad had been the right one. And maybe not. He was having a hell of a time recently as a public company, even dealing with a takeover attempt. At least at Benson Corp. I didn't have to deal with that level of shit.

I spent the morning reading in my room, away from the distraction of bikinis on the beach, and I skipped lunch at the restaurant as well. So much for the enticing Nicole…

On the way to the airport that afternoon, I looked out the window of the taxi and the dichotomy between the housing in the countryside and the resort I'd been staying at struck me. The houses weren't mud huts or anything, but lots of them weren't complete, with rebar sticking up out of the roofs as if they hadn't been able to afford the upper floor.

My head pivoted as we passed the third coconut stand on the side of the road. "What's the deal with the coconut vendors?"

"Selling fresh coconut water. Good for the health," my driver responded. "You want me to stop at the next one?"

Another bullshit marketing ploy, as far as I was concerned. "No thanks."

"I drink one almost every day." He laughed.

After reaching the airport and enduring a long line, I handed my passport to the pretty agent behind the counter.

She held up the document, comparing it to my face. "Did you have a pleasant stay with us, Mr. Benson?"

"Yes, just shorter than I wanted."

She typed on her keyboard. "It always seems that way, doesn't it?" She hit a few more keystrokes. "How many bags will you be checking?"

"Just the one." I hefted my bag onto the scale.

A minute later, she handed me my boarding pass in a folder. "Gate ten. Boarding will begin at three-oh-five."

Only after she handed me the envelope did I notice the error. The seat assignment said 31B. I handed it back. "There must be some mistake. This should be first class."

She took it back and clacked the keys again. "I'm sorry, Mr. Benson, the flight is completely full, and it was booked as coach."

I'd never flown economy. Hell, I'd only flown commercial once as a kid, and I would definitely be having a chat with Libby when I got back.

"At the gate, you can put yourself on the wait list for an upgrade," she offered.

I took the envelope back and headed for security. Damned Libby. What had I done to deserve this?

At the gate, the agent took my name, but the look on his face was clear: fat chance getting into first.

Since the flight was connecting at JFK instead of Miami, it would be more than five hours of torture, and a middle seat no less.

Dad should have waited until the company plane was ready.

I hung out at the gate 'till the last minute, hoping one of the first-class passengers would be a no-show. No luck.

It was raining when I walked to the plane. The airport was old-school, with stairs to board instead of a jetway. By the time I reached the door, I was soaked.

"I'm sorry, sir. All the overhead bins are full. Your bag will need to be checked."

I relinquished my roller bag to her, bound for the belly of the plane. When I reached my row, things got even better.

I wasn't a small guy, but I was a shrimp compared to the man in the window seat. The middle seat was going to be a tight fit.

Granny seated on the aisle got up to let me in.

Just as I buckled myself in, the window guy let out one stinker of a fart.

With the narrow seats, I was forced up against Granny's side, and my knees hit the seat in front of me as well.

Libby was definitely going to pay for this.

Granny pulled out a bag of Cheetos and started munching. "Like some?"

I declined.

Fart guy let loose another one.

All I could do was breathe through my mouth and concentrate on reading my iPad. After we took off, the cabin cooled down considerably, and my shivering made it difficult to hold the device steady enough to read. Shutting down the overhead vent helped, but the real problem was my wet clothes, and without my bag, I had nothing dry to put on.

Fart guy detonated again, and I had to decide between the cold and being able to breathe. I chose fresh air and opened the overhead vent again. My clothes would dry out sooner or later.

Granny seemed oblivious to the smell, and after a consuming a second bag of Cheetos, she fell asleep against me.

It wasn't until later that I noticed the orange drool adorning my shirt sleeve.

I checked my watch for the bad news: another four hours to go. I was *so* going to get Libby back for this.

CHAPTER 3

Nicole

He took the middle seat one row ahead of us. Mr. Studious was on the same plane to JFK, but hadn't noticed me or Sandi when he boarded.

Sandi cocked her head and pointed.

"I know," I whispered.

"Say hi," she mouthed.

I shook my head.

She shrugged. "Your loss." She tapped the screen on the seatback in front of her, scrolling through the movie choices.

Before long we were airborne, without another word about him.

Every once in a while, Mr. Studious shifted in his seat, and the smell of a fart traveled back to us.

"Somebody should lay off the beans," Sandi said more than once.

During the flight, I tried watching the movie, but kept glancing through the gap in the seats at Mr. Studious.

He read on his tablet the whole time—a real bookworm. I couldn't see much, but his jawline and the stubble were seriously hot.

When we finally landed, his row exited before ours, and he rushed off without even a glance back in our direction. The man was itching to get off this plane.

Sandi went ahead. "See you on the jetway."

I had to wait to get my bag from the overhead two rows back. "Sure."

"He's up ahead somewhere," Sandi said when I reached her in the terminal. "If you want to find him and say hi, that is."

"Nah. He farts too much."

She laughed. "That was the guy in the window seat, not your guy."

"Oh." I still had more self-respect than to chase a guy whose name I didn't even know—one I'd said a grand total of two words to. That didn't make him *my guy*.

After immigration and getting our bags through customs and back into the airline system, we located the gate for the next leg of our flight.

"I vote for Hawaii next year," Sandi said after plopping down in a seat. "This immigration and connecting-flight shit sucks."

"Pick an island. I'm with you."

"Maui, Kauai, the big island, I don't care. Anything that doesn't mean all day in airplanes."

Eventually our boarding time neared, and they asked for volunteers to be bumped to a later flight in return for a two-hundred-dollar travel voucher.

One of the two gate agents started calling names over the PA. "Nicole Rossi, please come to the counter."

"What's that about?" I asked Sandi.

She shrugged. "I doubt you got an upgrade."

In line at the counter, I could see it definitely wasn't an upgrade. The person in front of me threw a monster fit, and the agent called her supervisor, who I heard call security.

I stepped back until they got the situation resolved.

"Next," the agent said a moment later.

I presented my boarding pass. "Nicole Rossi."

The agent pasted on a phony smile and handed me a slip of paper. "Here's your five-hundred-dollar travel voucher, and you've been confirmed on flight seventy-three. It leaves in two hours from gate eight." She pointed to the right.

"But I didn't volunteer," I objected.

Her smile brightened. "I know. That's why you're getting the larger voucher."

"But I really need to get back."

"You'll still arrive tonight, just a little later than planned." She moved to the side and pasted on that same fake smile again. "Next."

I shuffled back to Sandi. "I got bumped."

"That sucks. Till when?"

I blew out a breath. "Two hours—if it's not late."

"Well, that's the beauty of big companies like these airlines. They're so cheap they won't feed you anymore, and then they overbook to maximize their revenue, and at the same time ruin the customer experience. I don't think they'll ever learn."

We commiserated about the evils of airline consolidation until it was time for her to board.

I gave her a sendoff hug. "I'll be in touch as soon as I replace my phone."

"I still think you should think about how quickly you come to Lara's rescue this time."

"Sure." I turned and trudged off in search of a bite to eat while I waited. Though Sandi wasn't wrong, Lara was family, and I couldn't turn my back on her like that.

Josh

After escaping the plane, I had to wait to be admitted back into the States before heading to the ticket counters.

There, I was told, "I'm sorry, Mr. Benson," after inquiring about first-class seats available to LAX on my next flight.

"I'm sorry, sir," said the next airline ticket agent, followed by the same answer from the third.

Getting back through security to the gates was a uniquely unpleasant experience. I had to take my shoes and belt off, got yelled at for not taking my tablet out of my bag, was electronically frisked, and then chosen for a random pat-down. How did people put up with this shit every time they flew?

Dad would occasionally wonder if his corporate plane was worth all we paid to keep it and the crew. Today, I knew my answer was an unqualified *yes*.

Once again, I put my name in for an upgrade as soon as the agent arrived at the gate counter. Now it was just a matter of waiting for a no-show. I located a seat with an outlet and began reading on my tablet again.

Hours later, the last few passengers were having their boarding passes scanned when I went back to the counter.

"Sorry, Mr. Benson," the gate agent said.

I got in line behind the last person and readied my boarding pass: seat 34A. At least it wasn't a middle seat.

The lady in front of me turned to hand over her sheet of paper. It was Cheetos Granny from my last flight.

At the bottom of the jetway, I pulled a sweatshirt from my carry-on and handed the bag over to the agent to check. I knew now that as the last one to board, I had no hope of finding a space for it. I kept my small backpack and my plastic bag of dinner.

No wonder airlines had a greater proportion of unhappy customers than any other business. When dentists beat you out for the bottom of the list, you were definitely doing things wrong.

When I reached row 29, I figured out the bad news. With five more to go, I'd gotten the very last row on the airplane.

Granny also reached the last row and put her purse down on the aisle seat on my side of the plane. "Hello, dear," she said.

The woman in the middle seat rose. "Are you in here?"

My heart sped up. It was my almost-dessert date from last night. Nicole.

CHAPTER 4

Nicole

"No, dear, I'm on the aisle," the gray-haired lady said.

"I'm the window seat," the man behind her said. His lips tipped up in a smile as my eyes met his. It was my rescuer from last night, Mr. Studious.

The older lady moved to allow me out so Studious could slide in.

I followed him back in, and my hand brushed his as we both searched for our seatbelt. The gentle shock was like a spark of static electricity.

"I think that one's mine," he said, looking at the two buckle ends in my hands.

The spark of his touch must have short-circuited my brain. "Oh, yeah, sorry." I traded the buckle for the tab end he held.

When my eyes rose to meet his, he smiled again. "Recover okay from your swim?"

Heat rose in my cheeks. "Yes…and thank you. That was embarrassing."

He offered his hand. "Josh." His pale blue eyes held me captive.

I shook with him. "Nicole, but you already know that."

The spark from our previous touch returned in force. His grip was warm and strong, reminding me of the ease with which he'd hauled me out of the pool last night. I was no featherweight, but he'd lifted me like I was nothing.

The jet lurched slightly as we started to move back from the gate.

I pulled my hand away and forced myself to look forward, lest I be paralyzed by the strength of his gaze. His eyes had peered deep into me, almost hypnotic in their pull. At a distance on the beach, I'd taken in the breadth of his shoulders, his washboard abs, those massive arms. I hadn't been close enough to notice the eyes, or the slight scar on his chin that only made his face more interesting.

The overhead speakers began the safety announcements, but the whir of the engines starting soon made the words hard to understand.

"And the lavatories for the main cabin are located at the rear of the plane," she said at the end—a reminder that we'd have the pleasure of people hovering in the aisle waiting to use the facilities later in the flight. Ah, the joys of sitting in the last row of the airplane.

The aisle-seat lady tapped my shoulder. "Would you like some Cheetos?" She offered an open bag.

"No, but thank you."

She pulled out a few with orange-crusted fingers and popped them in her mouth, mumbling something about them being better than Twinkies.

Josh leaned over. "Granny has an endless supply of those things."

Every time I looked out the window as we taxied, I caught sight of his chin, and that profile. I needed to keep myself focused. I pulled out the safety card in front of me and pretended to check it. The man in person was even better than from afar.

"How are people supposed to fit in this space?" he asked after a moment. "I've never been in a seat this small." His knees banged against the seatback in front of him, but these seats were just like every other airline: crappy.

"First time?" He looked like a first-class-only guy.

"Second. How'd you guess?"

"After a while, you get used to being treated like crap instead of a paying customer."

"I guess. But I don't know how I'd ever get used to this." He opened his iPad with a huff and started scrolling, just as he had at the beach each day I'd seen him—okay, more like watched him, or spied on him. A shiver shot through me as I realized that was akin to being a stalker.

He finger-swiped to the next page, and I looked over again.

Bad girl.

I took his concentration on his tablet as a signal that he didn't want to talk

—so much for the friendly guy who'd wanted to have dessert last night. I checked the movie selections on the screen in front of me. In the end, though, I left the screen set on the map of our progress. I pulled out the romance paperback I'd finished on the beach. The story was still a good one, even if I knew the ending, and worth reading again—anything to make this trip go by faster.

The turbulence as we climbed through the clouds was probably only moderate for a seasoned flier, but it rated as severe on my anxiety scale. I closed my book in my lap. The bumps kept forcing me up against Josh's solid arm. The warm contact provided an oddly calming effect.

He kept reading, ignoring the bumps that forced the tablet back and forth enough that it would have had me air sick.

At altitude, the ride smoothed out, and the seatbelt sign went off.

Josh stowed his iPad and leaned forward to reach something at his feet. "Excuse me."

"Sure," I said, pulling my book out of the way.

With the seatbacks in our faces, and as tall as he was, he had to contort himself over toward my lap to reach, which only gave me a view of rippling back muscles straining against his shirt. He came up with two bags, the first a plastic bag labeled *Papa's Pastaria.*

"You brought dinner?"

"Sure." He showed me the second bag, from Dunkin' Donuts. "Sorry. They didn't have any tiramisu."

I laughed. "So when you said another time, you meant on this flight?"

He shook his head. "No. I got called back to work early. My stay was supposed to last another four days."

"That sucks. It's terrible that your boss would do that to you."

"Yeah, I guess."

"You should have refused."

"You wouldn't say that if you knew my dad."

He wasn't the international man of mystery I'd presumed, but in business working for his dad.

"I get it. I work in a family-run company too," I told him.

Now I understood his predicament. People had the misconception that working for family members made it easy, but the opposite was true. Uncle Ernst wouldn't hesitate to ask me to do something he'd never in a million years expect a non-family-member employee to do.

Josh nodded with raised brows, but didn't pursue the question. The bag of Italian food he opened had well-sealed plastic containers instead of those leaky Styrofoam boxes.

The delicious aroma hit me as soon as he popped the lid. Fettuccine with marinara and small meatballs, all topped with a sprinkling of parmesan.

He held up the container. "Want some? I've got plenty."

"No thanks. I ate." I said no, but my salivary glands disagreed. I swallowed to keep from drooling. The cardboard sandwich I'd gotten at the airport had lasted only a single bite, and my survey of the surroundings had found all the decent restaurants closed up for the night. Apparently I hadn't gone far enough to find real food.

"You sure?"

I nodded, afraid my voice would betray me if I tried to verbally decline.

He shrugged. "Your loss."

I opened my book and started reading, hoping to keep my growling stomach at bay.

He'd forked about half of his pasta down before long, interspersed with mouthfuls of Caesar salad from the second container. At one point, he held up his fork for a second. "Hold on."

I looked over and couldn't help but stare at that beautifully imperfect chin. I wondered how he'd gotten the scar.

He brought a lone noodle to his lips. "So, you had to leave early too?" He sucked in the noodle.

I sighed. "No. I'd only planned a week, and my time is up. Now I wish I'd made it ten days instead."

He waved the fork. "So, let me understand. Last night when you agreed to join me for dessert another time, you planned on standing me up?"

I could almost feel the blood draining from my face. "No. Oh, no. I'm sorry. I was just so flustered after making a fool of myself, I answered without thinking."

"So you *did* want to join me?"

"Of course. I was walking over, wasn't I?"

He ate another bite of salad before speaking again. "In that case, the offer to split dessert tonight is still open."

"Donuts for dessert?"

"Only one. But I'm still offering to share. You like chocolate?"

An easy question. "Who doesn't? It's one of my main food groups."

After closing his dinner containers, he spread his legs to drop them to the floor. The warmth of his thigh against mine was more noticeable than it should have been. He kicked the plastic under the seat in front of him and opened the Dunkin' Donuts bag. He split the donut in half. "Pick one."

I chose the piece that looked smaller, as Mamma had taught me. "Thank you." I decided she would have declared Josh a gentleman. I held a hand under my mouth to catch the sprinkles that fell when I bit into the delicious morsel. I'd learned the hard way how sitting on sprinkles could result in stains. "This is good," I mumbled after a mouthful.

"Only the best for a beautiful lady."

I felt my blush rising to a low-grade fever.

He wiped his fingers with a napkin after the last bite and pulled out his iPad again.

"You sure read a lot."

"Work," he replied. "I'm behind. I expected to have all week, and like I said, it got cut short." He pointed at the book in the seat pocket in front of me. "You've been reading too."

"True. But I'm reading to relax."

"I'm envious." He lifted his tablet. "This book is on business strategy."

"Sounds pretty dry." I was happy to be done with books like that.

"It is," he said tilting the tablet my way.

I made out the title and author. It was one I'd been assigned in school, and *dry* only began to describe it. *Sleep-inducing* was more like it. "You might try one by Porter instead. At least it would be easier to stay awake."

His brows lifted, and his eyes narrowed. "Porter, huh? The Harvard prof?"

I shrugged. "Dunno." I'd already said too much.

He shifted to look more directly at me, and his eyes held me in their tractor beam. "You've read this one?"

"It sounds familiar," I admitted.

A smile followed his nod like he'd hooked a fish. "Tell me more, Nicole."

"Nothing to tell." I was already on a slippery slope. This is where it always went south with me and guys.

"Did you go to Harvard?"

I shook my head and took in a breath to admit the truth. "Stanford." That was always enough to have my dates change the subject.

"Impressive." He almost sounded like he meant it. "Undergrad?"

I nodded with a sigh.

He pointed a finger at me. "And that's not all, I bet." He rubbed his chin. "MBA as well. Nobody else would willingly read a book like this." He lifted his iPad.

Busted.

I nodded. "Yeah. How about you?" It was time to turn the tables.

"USC. Sort of a family expectation kind of thing."

"And now you work for your father?"

"Yeah, my older brothers got away before I did, so I'm stuck with it."

"You don't want to be in the family business?"

"You wouldn't understand. It's not an option."

He was right. I didn't understand that at all. Being part of the business my family had built was a natural fit for me, and I couldn't imagine being anywhere else. "I sort of like it, the family aspect," I said, soft-pedaling it.

"You're lucky," he said as he turned back to the tablet. "Let me work my way through more of this and I'll probably have some questions for you."

That was my cue to let him read in peace, so I picked up my novel, opened it to the dog-eared page, and started reading.

Granny was downing more Cheetos.

"Careful, she drools," Josh whispered, pointing to an orange stain on his shirt sleeve.

Yuck.

I compensated by leaning into him. He didn't complain.

Slowly, I got used to the warm contact, and it went from provocative to comforting. It had been a long time since I'd leaned on a man—either figuratively or literally. Maybe Sandi was right, and it *had* been too long.

An hour later, Josh and I were still reading. A line for the bathroom had formed, and I self-consciously avoided eye contact with the constant stream of strangers.

The PA came on again. "We're diverting north to avoid some weather ahead," the captain's voice said. "It will add some time to our trip, but I hope it will be a better ride." The seatbelt light came on again. *Better ride* and *hope* likely didn't mean smooth air, and I prepared for being on a bucking bronco.

The flight attendants shooed all the people in the restroom line back to their seats, and the jostling began in earnest. The airplane became the puppet, as the weather gods yanked the strings.

Granny woke with a start after the second or third big bump.

A big air pocket that felt like going over the top of a roller coaster had my heart racing. How strong did they build these airliners, anyway?

I put my book away to keep from needing the airsick bag. "What was that?" I asked Josh, hoping a conversation would keep my mind from wondering how much it took to break an airplane.

"Nervous?" he asked.

"What gave it away?"

He pointed. "Your death grip."

I missed that I had a white-knuckle grip on the armrest with one hand and my thigh with the other. It took a concerted effort to loosen up.

He offered his hand. "Squeeze this."

"I'm fine."

"You're white as a ghost." He loosened my hand from the armrest and took it in his.

I gripped his hand.

"It's a medical fact that physical touch lessens anxiety."

Several even bigger bumps hit the plane. "Really?"

"I wouldn't lie to you." His voice carried a conviction I didn't doubt. "Let your nervousness flow through your hand to me."

As I held onto him, my heart slowed. I closed my eyes and concentrated on the feel of my hand with his.

"Does that help?"

I opened my eyes and nodded.

"Flying's safer than driving," he said spouting a statistic that had never made me feel better.

"Tell that to the crash victims. I'd rather be driving."

"Why?"

That was an easy one. "Because then I'm in control, and I can avoid the potholes."

"They're downdrafts, updrafts, wind gusts, and all invisible. It doesn't mean we have a bad pilot. If you were up there, you couldn't avoid them either."

I squeezed his hand harder after the next air pocket, or downdraft or whatever.

He was remarkably calm for a first-time flier.

Bang!

The plane lurched left and then right.

I grabbed Josh's arm.

People screamed in the rows ahead of us.

A popping sound came from the left.

Long strings of fire streamed from the engine, visible out our window in sync with the noise.

I buried my head in Josh's shoulder and gripped his arm with all my strength.

Made in United States
North Haven, CT
09 July 2024